NEW RELIGIOUS MOVEMENTS
AND RAPID SOCIAL CHANGE

NEW RELIGIOUS MOVEMENTS AND RAPID SOCIAL CHANGE

Edited by

James A. Beckford
on behalf of
Research Committee 22
of the International Sociological Association

Ⓢ Sage Publications / Unesco

First published 1986
by the United Nations Educational,
Scientific and Cultural Organization,
7 Place de Fontenoy, 75700 Paris, France

and

SAGE Publications Ltd
28 Banner Street
London EC1Y 8QE

 SAGE Publications Inc
275 South Beverly Drive
Beverly Hills, California 90212
2111 West Hillcrest Drive
Newbury Park, California 91320

SAGE Publications India Pvt Ltd
C–236 Defence Colony
New Delhi 110 024

British Library Cataloguing in Publication Data

New religious movements and rapid social change.
  1. Religions
  I. Beckford, James A. II. International
  Sociological Association. *Research
  Committee 22*
  291.9   BL80.2

Unesco ISBN 92-3-102402-7
Sage Publications ISBN 0-8039-8003-5

Library of Congress Catalog Card Number 86-060924

Phototypeset by Sunrise Setting, Torquay, Devon
Printed in Great Britain by
Antony Rowe Ltd, Chippenham, Wiltshire

Reprinted 1988

Contents

* Asian names are presented in the English-language convention of personal name(s)
first and family name second.

Preface

Towards the mid-1970s, social scientists became aware of the effects of the rapid social changes that had affected from the early sixties not only those societies called 'traditional', but also highly-industrialized societies. These changes, more clearly seen at the political level, were present also at the level of social and economic structures and affected the content and the utilization of culture.

Many concepts have been forged and hypotheses elaborated in order, on the one hand, to analyse the social conflicts which accompanied the rapid social change of those years and, on the other, to adequately understand the new forms of relations which emerged.

Unesco, concerned both with the development of social sciences and with the impact of change on certain social categories, found it necessary to encourage the international social science community to study the manifestations of change in our time and the new complex relations which emerged. This book is therefore the fruit of a close co-operation between Unesco and the International Sociological Association.

Good reasons exist for the choice of this field of study. It has been well-known among sociologists and anthropologists that periods of rapid social change have been marked in many societies by the rise of Messianic movements. These have often been seen as confined to a pre-industrial past in Europe, or to formerly colonized countries under the twin impact of colonial rule and of technological change. In the 1970s, however, it became obvious that the emergence and the spread of new movements were in no way confined to pre-industrial societies. Sects often accompanied by a form of Messianism recruited within highly technologically advanced societies put into question some of the former social science paradigms.

Again, the rise of new religious movements called for sustained social analysis. Their emergence put into question accepted ideas of historic continuity, of the relationship between culture and religion, provoking sometimes a certain bewilderment within some segments of society. At the same time 'new religious movements' illustrated the profound social changes in ritual practices, economic production, the social organization of work as well as in family structures and relationships, community structures and the significance of life and death. Indeed the effects of those changes went beyond new religious movements to include the rise of a new religiosity within established religions.

Unesco, in sponsoring this book, has tried to avoid entering the realm of the complex debate as to the symbolic significance of what has sometimes been called the return to religion. Neither does Unesco pretend to examine or to pronounce on religion as such or on the finalities of religious belief. This is left to the theologian.

The aim of this book is more modest. It attempts to throw light on social factors without in any way minimizing the place of individual belief and action. The sociology of religion which has been a constant preoccupation since sociology as a discipline begins, sets itself the task of better understanding the social context within which religions emerge or spread and the social strata from which they recruit. Beliefs however are always respected and indeed as such are outside and beyond the domain of sociological analysis. Yet, if a new religious movement cannot be reduced to a social phenomenon easily carved into analytical elements, neither can it be denied that institutional influences, financial support and other factors such as conflicts between ethnic groups, can play a preponderant role in the formation and expansion (or diminution) of these new religious movements. In this connection it will be noted that we have only sparingly used the word 'sect', preferring at this point to avoid the debate concerning the criteria which separate 'sect' from 'religion'.

While Unesco has sponsored this book, the points of view expressed are those of the authors and do not necessarily commit the Secretariat.

Introduction

James A. Beckford

The basic assumption of this collection is that religion is intensely personal *and* unavoidably social. There is no contradiction here; for religious ideas and sentiments, which are often inseparable from people's innermost sense of selfhood, identity and destiny, tend to be socially patterned. In other words, the practice of religion displays broad patterns which, in turn, reflect people's patterned social experiences. But the social patterning of religion is far from being a passive or one-way process. On the contrary, patterns of religion tend to reproduce themselves over time, although the outcome is never entirely predictable. So many social and personal factors are involved in the reproduction of religion that there is no question of inevitability or necessity. The sociology of religion therefore studies the processes whereby religion, in all its variety and complexity, is interwoven with other social phenomena. All the chapters in this book are centrally concerned with the ways in which new patterns of religious activity have emerged from the interplay of social forces in various parts of the world since the mid-nineteenth century.

The question of how to conceptualize religion for present purposes must be tackled at this point, although this is not the place to discuss the voluminous literature on the topic. What needs to be emphasized is simply that, in a study of widely differing religious movements occurring within diverse religious and cultural traditions, it would be unwise to impose an excessively restrictive definition on the concept. Consequently, the main requirement is for a lowest common denominator which will adequately mark off religion from other phenomena and draw attention to its common sociological characteristics. For this purpose, the best strategy is to emphasize the shared capacity of all the movements under consideration in this book to evoke and cultivate concerns with the ultimate significance of human life. They each produce distinct and distinctive ways of interpreting life *sub specie aeternitatis*.

The fact that concern with the ultimate significance of human life may also be shared by groups which reject the label 'religion' does not necessarily detract from the usefulness of my conceptualization. The most important consideration is the degree to which such groups share sociological characteristics with religious groups. Only when this has been decided can an informed judgement be made about whether my inclusive conceptualization is adequate. But adequate for what? The answer is simple: adequate to the task of showing that religious movements operate in society in ways which are sufficiently distinctive to warrant their designation as a separate and important thread in the intricate weave of social life. In fact, of course, religious movements are inextricably woven into the social fabric, although the actual manner of their interweaving varies greatly across movements, time and place. For this reason, each chapter in this book deals with specific religious movements in certain societies at various times in recent history. All the authors come from the parts of the world about which they have written; and all are specialists in the study of religion as a social phenomenon.

The idea of a religious *movement* implies an organized attempt to introduce change in religion. This is normally accompanied by strain and conflict between religious movements and their competitors or opponents. Indeed, several chapters of this book place particular emphasis on the tendency for agencies of the nation state and more firmly established religious organizations to put obstacles in the path of some new religious movements. The chapters by Susumu Shimazono, Syn-Duk Choi, Friday Mbon and James Beckford and Martine Levasseur on the development of new religions in, respectively, Japan, the Republic of Korea, Nigeria and Western Europe offer instructive illustrations of the opposition mounted against religious movements. These illustrations recapitulate the pattern of struggles surrounding many of the sects which have typically arisen within the protestant wing of Christianity, but Laënnec Hurbon's chapter on the Caribbean region throws lights on the less common process whereby groups such as the Apostles of Love and Palma Sola have separated themselves from the Roman Catholic Church. Although Catholicism is widely believed to be capable of containing sectarian impulses within itself by means of various societies, fraternities and religious orders, the relatively recent proliferation of 'Catholic sects' in parts of Africa, Latin America and the Caribbean is beginning to call the received wisdom into question.

But the term 'movement' also suggests that *broad* shifts in people's religious ideas and sensibilities may occur independently of organized religious movements — at least, initially. Examples from the present era include the growing sympathy of Christians of many persuasions for the cultivation of charismatic Gifts of the Spirit; the resurgence of Islam, often in a puritanical spirit, in many parts of the Islamic world; and the veritable craze for spiritist activities in Brazil. Such broad shifts of religious sensibility are doubtless aided by the operations of specific movement-organizations, but there is a real danger of failing to see the wood for the trees if attention is too narrowly focused on only the organized components of religious movements.

The search for social factors to account for these broader changes is therefore another important task for sociologists. Thus, Robert Wuthnow's chapter interprets both new religious movements and movements of transformation within longer-established churches in the USA as, in part, responses to social changes which affect the whole of society but have special significance for young people. Gananath Obeyesekere's chapter also explains precisely why the increasingly urban, nucleated families of Sinhala Buddhists give credence to beliefs in sorcery which, in turn, calls for new cults of protective gods or spirits. And Laënnec Hurbon's chapter on the Caribbean region emphasizes the connection between the experience of colonialism and the elaboration of religious symbols which are not confined to organized movements. Paradoxically, the symbols are often borrowed from the Roman Catholic Church. A similar point about the continuity between ancient cultural traditions and new religious movements in the Republic of Korea is made by Syn-Duk Choi.

The contributors to this book have tried to keep both senses of 'movement' firmly in mind; that is, they offer explanations of *general* shifts in religious sensibilities as well as of the more *specific* and deliberate innovations in religion produced by movement-organizations. The retention of this dual focus on both the diffuse and the specific aspects of movements in religion is uncommon in the sociology of religion but essential to a full appreciation of their social significance.

If religious movements, by definition, denote attempts to introduce new forms of religion, what is the point of calling them 'new'? Isn't the term 'new' redundant? The answer to these questions is bound up with the reason for including the phrase 'rapid social change' in the book's title. To begin with, the point must be made that religion, as a social phenomenon, is never entirely static: change is endemic. The history of religion could be written as an unceasing struggle between the forces of institutionalization and disruption. Religious movements have always existed, despite the fact that there is a tendency in most academic studies of religion to deny their importance in favour of emphasizing the continuity, if not dominion, of large and stable complexes of teachings, sentiments and rituals in the major world religious traditions. But it is mainly in the context of sociological studies of religion, where concern with orthodoxy and religious truth is weaker, that proper attention has been given to the constant interplay of competing forces in religion. Consequently, what had formerly appeared to be fairly unitary religious traditions or institutions are now, under the sociological gaze, beginning to appear as complex and shifting patterns of power relationships. This point is amply demonstrated in Arvind Sharma's chapter on new religious movements in Hinduism and in Saïd Arjomand's chapter on the build-up to the Islamic revolution in Iran.

Nevertheless, the *rate* at which challenges to institutionalized religion occur is not constant. There have been periods of convulsive unrest at certain times; and at other times the dominant religious authorities have met with little opposition or competition. This is why it is important to investigate the connection between the rise or decline of innovative movements in religion and the rate of social change. The underlying assumption of this book is, in fact, that religious movements tend to proliferate in conditions of rapid social change. As it stands, however, this sociological generalization lacks specificity. What it requires is careful specification of (a) the kinds of movement which proliferate, (b) the aspects of rapid social change which account for their proliferation, and (c) the mechanisms by which rapid social change actually affects the pattern of religious change. In their different ways the contributions to this collection are all designed to meet these requirements and thereby to refine the often taken-for-granted, but rarely examined, linkages between change in religion and change in wider social conditions. Incidentally, the social conditions in which religious movements decline are no less interesting than those in which they arise, but sociologists have tended to ignore the former. It should be an important item on the agenda for future research.

It is not surprising that the Caribbean, India, Iran and Sri Lanka have spawned large numbers of religious movements in areas where social change in the twentieth century has been rapid. For the most part, however, they are modifications of existing religious practices. This was also found to be true of the new religions of Japan, which began to emerge in the mid-nineteenth century. The situation in urban centres of Nigeria and the Republic of Korea, however, is different, in the sense that a more thoroughgoing disruption of premodern forms of social and cultural life has created the conditions in which religious movements of a Christian and less traditional form have flourished. The cases of North America and Western Europe are characterized, above all, by variety: religious movements of many kinds have proliferated since the second world war. Some are modifications of Christian and Jewish practices, but others are either syncretistic or radically novel. This variety is to be expected in segments of societies and cultures which are markedly differentiated and fragmented in complex ways.

To return to the matter of definition, the term 'new' has a double reference in the book's title. On the one hand, it refers commonsensically to the fact that the religious movements which are analysed below convey novel forms of religion. In this sense the term is virtually redundant in conjunction with 'movement'. On the other hand, there is a reference to the fact that, in periods of rapid social change, *many* religious movements may emerge. This sense of 'new' therefore strengthens the idea that their quantitative proliferation represents a qualitatively new situation. It is the more or less simultaneous development of an unusually large number of religious movements which makes the situation new. The novelty lies as much in their aggregate presence as in their separate character. This is as true for North America, Western Europe, the Caribbean and Nigeria nowadays as it has been at other times in India, Japan and Korea.

Although the new religious movements that are discussed in this book, taken separately or together, represent unique responses and contributions to rapid social change, it is nevertheless possible to make three generalizations about their shared tendencies. The following remarks are offered tentatively and with the aim of stimulating further research — not as formulations of a general theory or explanation.

First, new religious movements tend to attract public attention for propagating ideas or practices which are said to be more *specialized* or esoteric than those of longer-established religious groups. The emphasis on healing in Japanese, Korean and Nigerian movements; the focus on the realm of spirits in Caribbean movements; the preoccupation with authentic selfhood in many movements in North America and Western Europe; and the exclusive devotion to particular deities in Indian and Sri Lankan movements — are all examples of the alleged specificity or narrowness of new movements in religion. Yet, the degree of specificity should not be exaggerated. It is pronounced in some cases for the simple reason that, as Gananath Obeyesekere explains with regard to the Hūniyan cult in Sri Lanka, the new practice is only one expression of a much richer and more diffuse religious tradition from which it has arisen. Susumu Shimazono makes a similar point about the Honmichi movement in Japan which accentuates millennial themes without abandoning all other aspects of Japanese religion. And Laënnec Hurbon stresses the ubiquity in the Caribbean region of a powerful nucleus of shared symbols derived from various cultures, which is refracted differently in each apparently distinctive new movement.

It is ironic that some movements inadvertently reproduce, in the conversion experiences of their own members, some of the most strongly abhorred features of the traditional religious systems. In other words, the tendency for new religious movements to appear to be abnormally specialized or narrow in their teachings or practices is the result of a re-ordering of priorities rooted in older and broader religious traditions. Saïd Arjomand's chapter on the revitalization of Islam in Iran is particularly instructive for showing that the potential for revitalization had long been present, but largely dormant, in many sectors of Iranian society before the 'revolution' actually erupted in 1979.

Syn-Duk Choi's chapter on two powerful new religious movements in the Republic of Korea, and Friday Mbon's chapter on a well-established movement in Nigeria, raise the allied point that judgements about the relative specificity or diffuseness of movements must take account of the length of time for which they have been in operation. The Unification Church, the Full Gospel Central Church and the Brotherhood of the Cross and the Star have all survived for a few decades. Consequently, their outreach to members and prospective recruits is now based on a much wider range of facilities and services than they were able to offer in their formative years.

Second, and closely related to the question of specificity, is the tendency for new religious movements to allow *lay people* to participate more fully in their activities than is common in many older religious organizations. Again, this may change over time as movements, such as the Brotherhood of the Cross and the Star or the Full Gospel Central Church in Korea, acquire a degree of political influence and achieve a modest division of labour among their own officials. Thus, the growing popularity of the relatively new cult of Hūniyan among lay Sinhala Buddhists has put pressure on the leaders of Buddhist temples to accommodate it. Similarly, Christian Churches and denominations in North America and Western Europe have been obliged to revise their liturgy and government in order to provide for greater involvement by lay members. Divisions between clerical and lay functions in Caribbean spiritist movements are either non-existent or extremely flexible. Even the clerically inspired revitalization of Islam in Iran is distinctive for the newly important role accorded to the laity in furthering the movement's aims.

Third, virtually all the movements considered in this book offer to their participants various encouragements to translate their spirituality into *practical, everyday action*. This is, of course, possible in older forms of religious organization as well, but an emphasis on the value of practical applications of faith is much more evident in new movements. It includes the Rastafarians' broadly political programmes in Jamaica; the involvement of the Brotherhood of the Cross and the Star in diverse economic and welfare projects in Nigeria; the highly instrumental reasons given by devotees of the deity Skanda in Sri Lanka for participation in its worship; the emergence of a missionary orientation in such Indian movements as Sai Baba and ISKCON (The International Society of Krishna Consciousness); the reported improvements in the material conditions of life sought by members of the Full Gospel Central Church in the Republic of Korea; the socio-psychological benefits claimed by participants in such movements as Scientology and the Rajneesh Foundation in North America and Western Europe; and the preoccupation with physical well-being in a number of Japanese new religions and Caribbean movements. It is definitely *not* being suggested here, however, that new religious movements are any less spiritual for emphasizing the practical applications or results of their activities. What seems to be happening is that conceptual boundaries between the spiritual and the material are being rethought or redrawn in many new religious movements.

In sum, rapid social change in the twentieth century is associated with the rise of a large number of new religious movements. They are both a response to change and a means of contributing to it. They are pro-active as well as reactive, as the innovative strategies of the longer established movements in Japan, Korea and Nigeria clearly demonstrate. Yet, a note of caution must be sounded: the lives of *non-members* have not yet been greatly affected by the activities of the new religious movements under consideration here. And their impact on general patterns of culture and social relations is not impressive. But this is no reason to ignore them. The point is, rather, that new religious movements are important indicators of stressful changes in culture and society. They are also interesting attempts to come to terms with rapid social change by imposing new interpretations on it and by experimenting with practical responses. They therefore amount to social and cultural laboratories where experiments in ideas, feelings and social relations are carried out. They are a normal aspect of social life and a critical guide to societal problems and prospects.

1

Religious movements and counter-movements in North America

Robert Wuthnow

In the first three decades following the second world war, the United States and Canada witnessed the founding of more religious movements than at any other time in these nations' histories. By the end of this period as many as 5 percent of their adult populations had participated in some of the more esoteric of these movements; the number of local groups established as part of the new religions ranged in the thousands; virtually the entire public had become aware of the presence of new religious activity; vigorous anti-cult sentiment had appeared; and counter-movements were founded, both with the specific intent of combating the growth of cults and for the more general purpose of restoring traditional morality to the society. Moreover, all this took place against the backdrop of broader changes in US and Canadian religion, including the formation of interdenominational alliances, a growing cleavage between liberal and evangelical denominations, an unprecedented series of denominational mergers and schisms, a decline in denominationalism as a mode of religious organization, growing disaffiliation from established religious practices and the appearance of a sharp generational and educational gap in religious orientations. The details of many of these developments have been documented in case histories and in ethnographic studies; it remains, however, to chart the main contours of these developments in relation to one another and in relation to the broader social and cultural changes that conditioned them. (For literature reviews, see Zaretsky and Leone, 1973; Glock and Bellah, 1976; Robbins et al., 1978; Robbins and Anthony, 1981.)

Religious movements of the 1950s
At the close of the second world war the religious landscape of North America was by no means devoid of religious movements or of the effects of previous religious movements. In addition to mainstream denominations like Methodists, Baptists and Disciples of Christ (which had evolved from sectarian movements of the eighteenth and nineteenth centuries), there were scattered movements that remained very much on the fringes of established religion. The largest of these was the Latter-Day Saints (Mormons), a movement

more than a century old with a membership of 1.1 million in 1950. Christ Unity Science Church claimed almost 700,000 members, followed by Seventh-Day Adventists with 246,000 and Spiritualists with 163,000 (*Yearbook of American Churches*, 1952). Others included Baha'i, Vedanta, Theosophy and the American Ethical Union, all with fewer than 5,000 members.

The 1950s were to be a time of growth for several of these movements, particularly Seventh-Day Adventists and Latter-Day Saints, just as it was for most of the mainline denominations, largely because of natural increases from the 'baby boom' following the war. The most far-reaching religious movements of the 1950s, however, were not the fringe groups, but movements involving reorganization and expansion at the centre of North American Christianity, many of which were simply extensions of efforts that had begun in the 1930s and had been left unfinished when the war began. Of these, the so-called 'ecumenical movement', which prompted mergers and co-operative programmes among Protestant denominations, was one of the most prominent. Its actual accomplishments were relatively few until some time later, but during the 1950s it was an active force in many denominations. As in the past, these movements towards a more unified Christianity were accompanied by counter-movements representing persons with conservative theological views who chose to leave their denominations rather than merge.

Alongside the ecumenical efforts within denominations was the movement to promote denominational co-operation through inter-denominational agencies. As the United States shouldered the responsibility of leadership in rebuilding the 'free world', promoting the United Nations (1945), the International Monetary Fund (1945) and the Organization of American States (1951), US churches sought to create a broad co-operative platform for the promotion of world Christianity. The most notable of these efforts was the National Council of Churches (NCC), founded in 1950 (the Canadian Council of Churches had been formed in 1944), representing an estimated 40 million Christians in the United States alone, and oriented towards the promotion of world peace, worldwide medical and relief services, a global literacy programme and greater co-operation among all denominations and faiths (Barstow, 1951). Its counterpart, the World Council of Churches, sought similar aims through the participation of representatives from religious bodies throughout the world. These agencies were paralleled by similar movements on a smaller scale or within single denominations. The World Council of Christians emerged in 1948 to promote, among other goals, international trade among Christian businessmen. In the same year, ultra-fundamentalist preacher Carl McIntire founded the International

Council of Christian Churches as an alternative to the World Council of Churches with the intent of awakening Christians to 'the insidious dangers of modernism'.

Among evangelical groups, there were also major new movements to promote missionary activities on a global scale. By 1952, the United States and Canada had 18,536 missionaries overseas, of which 8,160 were supported by evangelical (non-NCC) organizations; by 1960 the total number had grown to 29,380, of which 19,056 were under evangelical sponsorship (Hogg, 1977).

The major religious movements of the 1950s can be understood as efforts to *accommodate* to the new opportunities created by the role of the United States in world affairs and by new social conditions which permitted greater co-operation among denominations, and as *sectarian reactions* to these efforts on the part of groups who felt their theological orientations and life-styles threatened by the changes taking place (cf. Wuthnow, 1980). On a smaller scale, these responses can be seen in many of the other movements of the 1950s as well. For example, efforts to accommodate to the expanding influences of science and higher education can be seen in a number of movements, such as the United Secularists of America (1946), a California movement oriented towards science and humanism as alternatives to conventional religion; the Institute of Religion in an Age of Science (1954), a professional organization concerned with promoting greater communication between religion and science; and the Rationalist Association (1955), oriented towards reason and science as a worldview. Movements reacting against the emerging social patterns, in addition to the ones already mentioned, included Christian Crusade (1950), founded by Billy James Hargis; the Christian Citizens' Crusade (1952); and the Christian Anti-Communist Crusade (1953).

The 1950s also presaged some of the important religious developments which were to emerge full-blown by the end of the 1960s. Esoteric movements inspired by beliefs outside the Judaeo-Christian tradition were to become a significant phenomenon in the 1960s, but it was in the 1950s that many of these movements quietly laid their foundations. The Church of Scientology, an amalgam of popular psychology and spiritualism, was founded in 1952 (Malko, 1970). In 1955 a charismatic pastor in Indianapolis started an inner-city mission which was to evolve into the infamous People's Temple of Jonestown, Guyana. In 1959 the Zen Center of San Francisco was established, the same year in which the Unification Church began work in North America (Lofland, 1978). All of these groups, like their successors in the 1960s, represented clear departures from conventional religion, but by comparison they attracted scarcely any mass followings and functioned chiefly at a single location, disseminating their ideas through reading rooms and correspondence courses.

The decade of religious turbulence

The period of most vigorous new religious movement activity was the 1960s and the first three years of the 1970s, since the Vietnam War which brought the religious and cultural unrest to a climax did not end until 1973. During this period movements and counter-movements within established denominations intensified. Parallel with the civil rights movement in the larger society, black caucuses and civil rights pressure groups sprang up in the churches. At the same time, more movements appeared with secularity as their goal: the Confraternity of Deists, begun in Florida by a former Roman Catholic to advance science and the arts within religion; the Church of the Humanitarian God (1969), oriented chiefly towards promoting non-violence; and American Atheists, Inc. (officially founded in 1970), Madeline Murray O'Hair's group which had succeeded in 1963 in getting the US Supreme Court to outlaw prayer in the schools. Mergers and liberal reforms also intensified within the denominations, including the formation of the United Methodist Church, adoption of a new confession by the United Presbyterian Church emphasizing social concern and liberal theology (1967); the Second Vatican Council (1962–65) (henceforth, 'Vatican II'); and the Consultation on Church Union, constituted in 1962 to explore co-operation and possible mergers among ten major denominations.

These and other reforms resulted in a veritable avalanche of counter-movements. In anticipation of the Presbyterians' confessional innovation, two nationwide organizations (the Presbyterian Lay Committee and Presbyterians United for Biblical Concerns) were organized in 1965 to reassert spiritual discipline, the Bible and Reformation doctrines. Talks of merger between the Lutheran Church–Missouri Synod and the American Lutheran Church resulted in two separatist denominations, Lutheran Churches of the Reformation (1964) and the Federation for Authentic Lutheranism (1971). In 1972 the Presbyterian Church in America split from the Presbyterian Church in the US (southern) because of its support of the National Council of Churches, the latter's involvement in social action and talks of merger with the United Presbyterian Church USA. At least four new denominations formed in response to the 1968 creation of the United Methodist Church. Roman Catholics responded to the Vatican II reforms by forming the Catholic Traditionalist Movement (1964), and many observers have linked the Catholic charismatic movement — originated at Notre Dame

University in 1967 and claiming a membership of 350,000 by 1974 — with the Vatican II reforms (Lane, 1976; McGuire, 1982). Other movements sprang up against the secularizing and liberalizing tendencies perceived in the culture at large.

The big story of the 1960s, however, was the rise of the 'new religions' among young people. Movements inspired by Asian religious traditions played a prominent role here. Zen Buddhism has already been mentioned. Although there had been localized interest in Zen since the early part of the century, it was not until the 1960s that it began to attract sizeable followings in cities like New York, Chicago, Los Angeles and San Francisco (Needleman, 1970). By 1970 the Zen Center of San Francisco, with 300 regular students and affiliates in five locations, had become a focal point for the movement. A survey conducted in the San Francisco area in 1973 showed that an estimated 3 percent of the population had taken part in Zen at one time or another; that 30 percent of the public claimed some knowledge of it; and that about 12 percent said it was attractive to them (Wuthnow, 1976a: 33). A replication of the question two years later among a national sample in Canada showed that more than half the public had heard of Zen and about 8 percent were attracted to it (Bibby, 1979). Transcendental Meditation (TM) attracted an even larger following. Some 5 percent of the San Francisco Bay Area sample had taken part in it, 32 percent were knowledgeable about it, and around 10 percent were attracted by its teachings. The Canadian study in 1975 showed that fully 71 percent had heard of TM, with 21 percent expressing attraction. In the United States a Gallup survey the following year found that 4 percent of the adult public claimed to be practising TM (Gallup, 1980: 34). Yoga groups also became a popular religious alternative, although not all who participated in them viewed yoga as a religion and some who did continued to practise conventional faiths.

These movements, especially TM and yoga, were widely publicized and were easily accessible to the general public because of introductory classes, short courses, soft pedalling of esoteric doctrine, co-operative ventures with schools and YMCAs and non-demanding life-styles. Many of the other Eastern religions, by comparison, imposed greater demands and, accordingly, attracted fewer devotees. The International Society of Krishna Consciousness (ISKCON), better known as Hare Krishna, was one example (Judah, 1974; Daner, 1976). Although the distinctive garb and public appearances of its members made it widely known, as evidenced by the fact that 39 percent of the Bay Area residents in 1973 and 64 percent of the Canadians in 1975 were familiar with it, it nevertheless had established only 22 local centres by 1970 and involved fewer than 2 percent of the population in places like the Bay Area. The Healthy–Happy–Holy Organization (3HO), a blend of Sikh doctrine and vigorous kundalini yoga techniques, founded in 1968 in Los Angeles, was another example; by 1973 it had ashrams in 80 locations, but most of these were sparsely attended, and even at its peak in the mid-1970s only about 5,000 persons were listed as members (Tobey, 1976).

A second variety of new religion that began to flourish during the 1960s consisted of the various groups, techniques and spiritual disciplines which came to be known collectively as the 'human potential movement'. In some ways, the human potential movement was an offshoot of the encounter group movement which flourished on college campuses during the 1960s (Back, 1972) and of popular psychology which had blossomed in a good many minds since the heyday of Fulton Sheen and Norman Vincent Peale in the 1950s. But the 1960s witnessed an intensification of these activities, a secularization of them with respect to conventional religion, and a noticeable syncretism when it came to influences from mysticism, science, the occult and Asian religions.

One of the first of the human potential groups was the Inner Peace Movement (1964), dedicated to self-realization, personal growth and the exploitation of psychic energy. By 1972 it had established 590 centres in the United States and Canada. Scientology experienced most of its growth in North America towards the end of the 1960s, resulting in the establishment of centres in 28 locations by the early 1970s, with members totalling around 2,000. Erhard Seminars Training ('*est*') was not founded until 1971, but as time progressed it gained one of the more devoted followings of the human potential groups (Tipton, 1982). Blending a brash, pragmatic self-help ideology with a mixture of psychic experience, self-awareness techniques and social concern, it 'trained' some 20,000 people during the first three years of its existence. Dozens of other, more localized, less publicized or more informally organized personal growth groups and techniques also came into being during the late 1960s: Arica, bioenergetics, psychosynthesis, Rolfing and Silva Mind Control, to name a few.

A third category of new religions was 'new' only in organization, in that its ideas resembled established religion rather closely. This was the Jesus movement, consisting of an inestimable variety of groups, ranging from The Way, which gained national followings around 1968 even though it had been in existence since 1953, and the Children of God, a highly authoritarian sect which emerged in 1969 as part of a Los Angeles skid row mission, to the highly intellectual, ex-hippie, Berkeley-based Christian World Liberation Front

(CWLF) and an untold number of quasi-communal, highly localized, typically rural centres of neo-Christian worship and apostolic imitation (Balswick, 1974; Heinz, 1976; Richardson et al., 1979).

In addition, the 1960s produced a host of religious movements which defy simple categorization. From its modest origins in 1969, the Unification Church, led by the Rev. Sun Myung Moon, grew from 2,500 members in the United States and Canada to as many as 2 million members worldwide by the middle 1970s (Solomon, 1981).

The 1960s also produced a variety of Satanic and witchcraft movements. One of the best known was Anton LaVey's Church of Satan in San Francisco, founded in 1966. The Process Church, which was founded in England in 1963 and immigrated to the United States in the early 1970s, represented a somewhat milder and more eclectic mixture of Satanism and witchcraft (Bainbridge, 1978).

Finally, there were communes — as many as 3,000 of them — many with their own varieties of religious ritual and belief, ranging from revitalized monastic traditions handed down from the Middle Ages (e.g., Weston Priory) to totally innovative and self-consciously created versions of nature worship, self-help ideology and hedonism (Zablocki, 1980; Fracchia, 1979).

All told, the new religions of the 1960s and early 1970s appear to have initiated at least 3,000 local centres of activity, according to a detailed guide published in 1974 (the *Spiritual Community Guide*, an annual publication). In seedbeds such as the San Francisco Bay Area at least a fifth of the public took part in one or more of them at one time or another, while close to half expressed some attraction. In the Montreal area participation may have been even higher (Bird and Reimer, 1982). And judging from the Canadian and US surveys, the vast majority of the public had become aware of them by the middle 1970s and perhaps as many as 10 percent had been participants in at least one.

Several summary statistics demonstrate graphically the extent of religious movement activity in the 1960s as compared with the 1950s. One is a recent compilation based on the movements described in Melton's *Encyclopedia of American Religions* (Melton, 1978). This compilation is by no means complete, listing only 484 new religions, but it appears to be nearly comprehensive as far as formally organized groups are concerned. In all, 184 of these groups were founded in the 1960s, compared with only 68 in the 1950s (Stark et al., 1979). Another source is the *Encyclopedia of Associations* (1983), which lists more than 15,000 national membership organizations incorporated as non-profit associations, among which are over 700 religious organizations. Of these, 147 were founded in the 1960s, compared with 105 in the 1950s.

More impressive than the totals, however, were the shifts in *type* of organization — shifts pointing towards a decline in the activity of established denominations compared with other types of religion. The number of organizations founded by whole denominations, acting as corporate entities, increased only marginally, from 35 to 42 between the 1950s and 1960s; by comparison, those sponsored by special interests within denominations rose from 6 to 21, and new organizations not sponsored by denominations grew from 37 to 64. Also of interest is the fact that the number of new culturally defensive organizations — groups explicitly opposed to modernization and oriented towards a reassertion of fundamentalist religious and moral values — grew from 2 during 1950–59 to 9 during 1960–69. A count of mergers and schisms for the two periods (restricted to major denominational families — Lutheran, Methodist, Presbyterian and Baptist) shows that the number of new denominations emerging as splinter groups in each decade was about the same (11 versus 10, respectively), but the number of denominational mergers increased from 2 in the 1950s to 9 in the 1960s (data compiled from Melton, 1978; the figure on schisms is consistent with Stark and Bainbridge's, 1981, tabulation of 'American-born sects').

For Canada, as for the United States, there was a heightened degree of religious activity on the fringes of the major denominations. This activity is clearly evidenced in the results of the Canadian decennial censuses which report information on religious affiliations (*Canada Year Book*, 1981). In 1951 only 2.2 percent of the Canadian population listed 'other' religious affiliations (the remainder fell into nine major categories). By 1961 this figure had risen only modestly — to 2.9 percent. By comparison, the 1971 figure was 6.2 percent, more than twice that of 1961.

Thus, on all of these summary measures it can be seen that the 1960s were, indeed, a period of intense religious movement activity in comparison with the 1950s, not just in the few more esoteric youth movements which captured the attention of the press, but in mergers, schisms and newly formed non-profit religious organizations and interest groups.

Irruption in the social fabric
What were the sources of this religious activity? Specific answers can be given for specific movements or types of movements. The Process Church, the Children of God, the Unification Church and other movements with highly authoritarian leadership structures, for example, appear to have capitalized on the availability of drug

addicts and dope users. Jesus People, Krishnas and Nichiren Shoshu Buddhists may have relied heavily on personal networks for evangelization and recruitment (Snow et al., 1980; Stark and Bainbridge, 1980). Testimonials by musicians, actors and other public figures appear to have given impetus to movements such as TM and *est*. Vatican II may have been the decisive event in spawning the Catholic pentecostal movement; and similar reforms, mergers or ecumenical efforts may have been the immediate source of the various fundamentalist movements within Protestantism. All of these explanations may be true, and yet the fact that such a variety of movements occurred when they did and took the forms they did still begs for an interpretation which reflects broader changes occurring in the rest of the society. Particularly if the near-simultaneous emergence of movements as different as TM and the Creation Research Society is to be understood not as a mere coincidence, but as an interrelated shift in religious orientation, a more holistic approach must be taken. The place to begin is with the larger social processes which were shaping the society in the 1960s.

This period was characterized by broad social changes in the United States and Canada. In the United States the population rose from 181 million in 1960 to 205 million in 1970; the percentage of the population between the ages of 14 and 24 rose from 15.2 to 19.6 percent; and median family income (factoring out inflation) increased from $13,774 to $18,444 (*US Statistical Abstract*, 1981). Canada exhibited similar patterns. Its population rose from 18.2 million in 1961 to 21.6 million in 1971; persons in their twenties made up 13.5 percent of the population in 1966 but 16.1 percent in 1971; and family incomes (in constant 1971 dollars) rose from $7,093 in 1961 to $10,368 in 1971 (*Canada Year Book*, 1981).

These trends have all been posited as sources of the religious unrest of the period. Population growth, resulting in an overabundant cohort of young people, allegedly created a better defined stage in the life-cycle during which youth could experiment with deviant religious orientations (Keniston, 1971). Urbanization left the churches in 'suburban captivity' (Winter, 1962), causing them to lose appeal to the larger metropolis, and nurtured a 'subculture' of diversity, ideological pluralism and individual autonomy, all of which were conducive to new religions. The shift of population to western states and provinces, particularly California, was associated with being non-religious and therefore with being available for recruitment to new religions. And affluence changed people's social status, making them uncomfortable with the churches, and giving them new opportunities to engage in religious experimentation.

In comparison with the 1950s, however, there is only partial support for the idea that these trends were sufficiently more pronounced in the 1960s to have made the difference between the two decades in levels of religious unrest. Population in the United States actually grew faster between 1950 and 1960 (from 152.3 million to 180.7 million) than it did the following decade. The same was true in Canada. The percentages living in Standard Metropolitan Statistical Areas (SMSAs) in the United States also grew at about the same rate in the 1950s (from 56.1 to 63.0 percent) as in the 1960s. Gross domestic product per capita did in fact grow more slowly in the earlier period (only 1.4 percent annually), but median family income grew from $10,008 to $13,774, and the percentage of households with annual incomes over $10,000 (constant dollars) grew dramatically, from 50 to 68 percent, compared with a change from 68 to 79 percent during the 1960s. The only real difference was that the percentage of young people in the population did not grow in the 1950s as it did in the 1960s — indeed, in the United States it declined slightly, from 16.0 to 15.2 percent. But it is difficult to understand precisely how this difference could have contributed to the religious movements of the 1960s unless another important social change is considered.

That change is the growth of science and technology and, with it, the tremendous increase in advanced education. At the close of the second world war the United States sought to continue the policy of expansion in higher education that had been initiated in the 1890s, and simultaneously to relieve the strain imposed on the economy from the sudden return to civilian status of its armed forces, by passing the GI Bill, permitting veterans to attend college at government expense. More importantly, the experience of the second world war confirmed the importance of science and technology to the nation's defences, evidenced most clearly in the Manhattan Project and more generally in the development of aviation and submarine technologies. This dependence was dramatized further in the 1950s, first by the Soviet Union's success in developing atomic weapons, then in 1957 by its entry into the era of space exploration, and increasingly during this period by the reconstruction of a competitive world economy in which technology figured as an important factor. By 1965 the United States produced $27.2 billion of goods annually for export (15 percent of the world total), and of this figure 64 percent was in technologically intensive industries such as chemicals, aircraft, telecommunications, computers, electronics and scientific instruments. Canada was (and has remained) a close partner of the United States in international trade, with more than two-thirds of its imports and exports involving her southern neighbour. Also by 1965, the United States had 500,000

R & D scientists in the labour force, the highest proportion of any country in the world, and spent 2.9 percent of its total gross national product on R & D, up from 1.5 percent in 1955.

Bringing about this level of activity in science and technology — and sustaining it — required a vast expansion in the educational system. In 1950, 2.6 million persons in the United States were enrolled in higher education; by 1960 there were 3.6 million; and by 1970 the figure was 8.6 million, an increase of 5 million (139 percent) in a single decade. Not only did the overall increase in numbers of young people (16.2 million of age 18–24 in 1960; 24.4 million in 1970) contribute to this growth, but the *proportion* of young people enrolled also rose dramatically — from 16.6 percent in 1950 to 22.3 percent in 1960, to 35.2 percent in 1970. The growth in expenditures for higher education was equally dramatic: $2.2 billion in 1950, $5.6 billion in 1960, $23.4 billion in 1970. For Canada the pattern was much the same: enrolments in higher education increased from 128,600 in 1961 to 323,000 in 1971; and expenditures on education (at all levels) rose from $1.7 billion in 1960 to $7.7 billion in 1970 (*Canada Year Book*, 1981).

Culturally, the expansion of science, technology and higher education was accompanied by dramatic increases in egalitarian sentiments, as reflected by declining levels of race prejudice, anti-Semitism and prejudice against women, and by growing support for civil liberties in areas such as freedom of speech for communists, atheists and homosexuals (Wuthnow, 1976a; 1982b). Over the same period, there was a sharp liberalization of attitudes concerning divorce, premarital sexuality and abortion; a shift towards independent and liberal orientations in politics; and rising support for welfare spending and environmental protection. Many of these specific attitudes appeared to be rooted in a shift towards worldviews influenced by social scientific and collectivist symbolism (Wuthnow, 1976a; Bibby, 1979). Most studies showed strong differences in attitudes, values and life-styles between persons with college educations or employed in the professions and persons of lower educational or occupational attainment, leading many observers to speculate that a 'new class', comprised of knowledge workers and professionals, had come into being, with distinctive outlooks and social programmes which could have drastic effects on the course of the society (Kristol, 1978; Bell, 1979; Gouldner, 1979).

In religion, dominant trends in participation, in belief, in the status of clergy, in clergy–laity relations, in the composition of denominations, in differences between youth and older people and in the relations between religion and educational attainment itself all bore the imprint of the expanding educational system. After as much as a century of steady increase as a percentage of the population, church membership in the United States had begun to edge downward (Jacquet, 1982; Gallup, 1982); from a peak around 1958 at 49 percent during a typical week, it declined steadily to 40 percent in 1971. In belief and attitudes, the percentage who felt the influence of religion to be increasing dropped from 69 percent in 1957 to 14 percent in 1969; 81 percent said religion could answer all or most of 'today's problems' in 1957, compared with 62 percent in 1974; and according to two Detroit Area surveys, in 1958 and 1971, the percentage who said they had recently become less interested in religion rose from 7 to 30 percent, while the proportion who were sure of God's existence dropped from 68 to 48 percent (Duncan et al., 1973). In Canada, the one measure of belief available over this period — belief in life after death — showed a decline from 68 percent in 1960 to 55 percent in 1969 (Bibby, 1979).

By other indications, also, the influence of religion was declining. As scientific and technical books made up larger and larger shares of the publishing industry, religious publications declined accordingly — sales in the United States (as a proportion of all books and pamphlets sold) fell from 6.8 percent in 1954 to 4.5 percent in 1972; new religious books published in the United States fell from 6.8 percent of the total in 1950–55 to 5.6 percent in 1968–72 and in Canada from 6.9 to 5.3 percent (Wuthnow, 1977). The relation between charitable giving to religion and to education in the United States revealed a similar pattern: in 1955 about $4.50 was donated to religion for every dollar donated to education; by 1970 this ratio was down to $2.90 (calculated from figures reported in *Public Opinion*, 1982: 25). With the expansion of higher education, US masters degrees in religion and theology dropped from 2.2 percent of the total in 1955 to 1.1 percent in 1975; more abruptly, doctorates in religion dropped from 2.8 percent of all doctorates to 1.4 percent between 1960 and 1970 alone. The proportion of clergy in the US labour force fell only slightly, from 0.30 percent in 1960 to 0.27 percent in 1970; but their representation as members of the knowledgeable, professional elite fell in relative terms owing to the growth in other professions — from 4.2 percent of the professional–technical category in 1950 to 2.2 percent in 1970 (Hunter, 1983b).

Because of the relatively high levels of educational attainment of clergy, the differences in social, political and moral attitudes evident in the general public between the better educated and the less educated were also reflected in differences between clergy and laity, evoking internal tensions within many denominations, as Hadden (1969), Quinley (1974) and others have shown (reviewed in Hunter 1983b). Among laity themselves, denominations with only a small fraction of educated members in the 1950s found themselves composed of as many as a quarter or a third of college-educated persons by the early 1970s (McKinney and Roof, 1982). These changes would have been even more dramatic had it not been for the fact that younger people left the churches in droves during the 1960s — according to most studies, because of disagreements with the Church's position on birth control (in the case of Catholics), exposure to the counter-culture and new attitudes toward sexual conduct, all of which were particularly prominent among young people who had been to college during the 1960s (Greeley, 1979; Wuthnow, 1976a; 1978a; 1983b).

Notably, not only did higher education play a direct or indirect role in all of these trends, but the *relation* between religious commitment and educational attainment itself underwent a significant change. This change was particularly evident in church attendance. Studies conducted during the 1950s generally concluded that college-educated persons were considerably *more likely* to participate in organized religion than the less educated, even though they might not subscribe as strongly to conservative beliefs or engage as frequently in private devotional practices — if for no other reason than the fact that middle-class people were 'joiners' in all types of organizations to a greater extent than working-class people (Goode, 1980; Marty et al., 1968: 212–13). By the end of the 1960s, however, that pattern had begun to change. Gallup studies showed a gradual decline in church attendance at all levels, but especially at the college-educated level. Between 1969 and 1970, church attendance among the college-educated fell abruptly by 6 percentage points, while comparable figures for other education levels remained constant. Thus, the better educated were no longer the most religiously active.

On matters of belief, somewhat the same changes occurred. Studies in the 1950s showed the better educated to hold about the same levels of belief as the less educated, or moderately lower levels; by the early 1970s the educated had dropped dramatically below the less educated. For instance, between 1957 and 1974 the percentages in Gallup polls who thought religion could answer all or most of today's problems fell by just 6 points among those with only grade-school educations, but by 26 points among those with at least some college education (Gallup, 1981)

In short, whereas there had been virtual unanimity (or relatively minor differences) among the educated and less educated on religious matters in the 1950s, by the early 1970s there was a clear education gap in US religion. The better educated still went to church about as often as anyone else (though not more often), but they were less likely to hold strongly to the traditional tenets of their faith. And from other studies it can be inferred that they differed from the less educated on a wide range of social, political and moral issues as well. Moreover, the better educated now constituted a far larger minority — and in some cases a majority — of their denominations than they had in the 1950s. As a whole, they were younger, were likely to have received their education during the turbulent years of the 1960s, were better educated than their own parents and often had the sympathetic ear of their pastors, whose level of education was similar to their own.

The ramifications of these developments were far-reaching for the churches and figured as a major factor in all of the religious movements described thus far. It was the better educated among laity and clergy who pushed the churches to become active in the civil rights movement, who later organized students against the Vietnam war, who favoured greater co-operation between persons of different faiths and between different denominations, and, in all likelihood, who pushed more actively for denominational mergers and the adoption of theologically liberal confessions (cf. Hoge, 1976). Less is known about the supporters of splinter groups, new fundamentalist movements and movements opposed to liberal theology and denominational mergers, but they were often located geographically in rural sectors of the midwest and south (i.e., areas with lower educational levels), were led by older, less educated, conservative clergy, and from most of the anecdotal evidence appear to have been supported by older, less educated church members.

The role of education in the 'new religions' was also pronounced and has been documented in great detail. Those who actively participated in movements such as TM, Zen and yoga, and those who expressed attraction to them, were significantly better educated than average (Wuthnow, 1978a). More generally, it was the better educated young people, particularly those whose campus experiences had exposed them to the counter-culture, who defected from conventional religious beliefs and practices and who adopted worldviews conducive to joining the new religions (Wuthnow, 1976a; Aidala, 1983). The major exceptions to this pattern were the Jesus people groups and more authoritarian movements such as the Unification Church, but even these movements often recruited indirectly from the educational system by picking up its dropouts — young people not making the grade, young people who were victims of campus isolation, cut off from families and in many cases victims of alcohol or bad drug experiences.

The net result of the 1960s, therefore, was to create a new basis of social division along educational lines, a division which cut through established religious organizations and set the stage for movements and counter-movements which would realign religious loyalties. To the extent that education has been closely connected with income, prestige, power and privilege, it has always served as a basis of social differentiation, but the 1960s was a time of veritable revolution in the educational system and, more importantly, in the role which higher education came to play in the economy at large, particularly in relation to the rise of technology and the professions, and in the positioning of North America in the larger world economy. It was as if the very basis of social order underwent a transition — from industrial to 'post-industrial' society, as it was sometimes described, or, more accurately, from a society rooted in heavy industry, agriculture, old money and traditional regional and ethnic cleavages to one in which levels of education — including the cultural orientations, professionalized occupations and access to mobility and power which were dependent on education — came to be a major new basis of social order (cf. Bell, 1973; Campbell, 1982; Wuthnow, 1978b, 1982a).

As with all such fundamental social transitions, the process of transformation was itself fraught with considerable strain — strain which became manifest on overcrowded campuses, in generational tensions between young people and their parents, and even in government policy, as evidenced in the crisis which surrounded the Vietnam war. In religion, denominations which had been organized along regional, ethnic and doctrinal lines suddenly faced internal cleavages within their ranks, leading some to work for movements aimed at transcending the traditional lines of organizational division, others to resist these changes and seek the security of like-minded persons with similar cultural and theological outlooks, and still others to abandon previous religious affiliations entirely in order to experiment with new opportunities for spiritual exploration.

A period of consolidation and reaction
If the 1960s was a decade of social and religious upheaval, the period from about 1973 to the early years of the 1980s was primarily a time of consolidation — of continuity in the major educational and religious patterns established in the 1960s — and of reaction to this consolidation on the part of groups whose life-styles were increasingly threatened and who found the resources with which to mobilize as the larger society shifted once again to more centristic policies and sought to correct the course it had of necessity adopted during the major transition years of the 1960s. Continuity and consolidation can be seen both in religion and in the relations between religion and the educational system.

Within conventional religion, aggregate indices of religious strength were virtually constant during this period. Church membership fell from 62 percent of the total population in 1974 to 61 percent in 1975 and remained there till the end of the decade (Jacquet, 1982). There were 797 religious non-profit associations in 1980, compared with 806 in 1970 (*Encyclopedia of Associations*, 1983). Overall, this figure represented a somewhat smaller proportion of *all* non-profit associations, but even the proportion remained constant from 1973 to 1980. In 1980, 2,055 new religious books were published, representing 4.8 percent of all new books, compared with 5.0 percent in 1970 (*US Statistical Abstract*, 1981). In sales, religious books actually made up a slightly larger share of the total in 1980 (10.3 percent) than in 1970 (9.2 percent) (Dessauer, 1981). Religious contributions remained absolutely constant throughout the decade, at 1.0 percent of personal income. And church attendance during a typical week in 1982 was 41 percent, compared with 40 percent in 1971 and 42 percent in 1970 (Gallup, 1982).

Measures of religious beliefs and attitudes also pointed towards a levelling out in the 1970s, after the dramatic slumps of the late 1960s. Whereas only 14 percent of the public thought religion's influence was increasing in 1970, this figure had risen to 31 percent by 1974 and to 39 percent in 1975; in 1981 it was 38 percent (Gallup, 1982). Between 1973 and 1980 the proportion who indicated 'a great deal' or 'a lot' of confidence in the churches or organized religion held steady at 66 percent (Gallup, 1981). The number who felt religion could answer all or most of today's problems was 65 percent in 1981, compared with 52 percent in 1974 (Gallup, 1981).

Most of the new religions still in existence at the end of the decade had formed some time prior to 1972. Melton (1978), for example, reports 111 new religions between 1970 and 1977, most originating in 1970 or 1971, compared with a total of 184 for the 1960s. Data on these movements during the 1970s are difficult to obtain, but the general picture appears to be one of growth until 1975 or 1976, followed by stability or decline. It has already been seen that public familiarity with new religions seems to have grown at least till 1975, judging from the high figures reported for Canada in that year compared with the earlier California figures. Estimates of participation are limited primarily to US Gallup polls, since figures released by movements themselves have generally been discredited. In 1979, 4 percent of the public claimed to be involved with TM, 3 percent with yoga and 1 percent with other Eastern religions, exactly the same figures as in 1976 (Gallup, 1980: 34). A Gallup survey of teens that year showed that 4 percent were involved with TM, 6 percent with yoga and 3 percent with other Eastern religions.

The major development in the late 1970s with respect to the new religions was the emergence of a sweeping public reaction against them, resulting in several formally organized anti-cult movements (Shupe and Bromley, 1979; 1980). The sources of this reaction appear to have been chiefly the mass suicide of approximately 900 members of Jim Jones's People's Temple in Guyana in November 1978, an event which captured North American newspaper headlines for weeks and evoked widespread revulsion (Hall, 1981; Richardson, 1980), and, secondarily, the growing fear that movements such as the Unification Church might have been engaged in brainwashing as part of their recruitment tactics (Shupe and Bromley, 1981). Polls demonstrated an overwhelmingly negative view of the Unification Church. The attitude toward 'cults' more generally was evidenced by a 1981 Gallup poll showing that 30 percent of the US public would not like to have cults or sects as neighbours, the highest number for any group asked about (Gallup, 1982). Unlike nearly all other studies of intolerance, moreover, negative sentiments towards cults ran higher among the *better educated* than among the less educated.

During the latter half of the 1970s and first half of the 1980s the most visible new religious movements, by all indications, were the conservative, culturally defensive movements of which fundamentalist preacher Jerry Falwell's Moral Majority was the leading example (Fackre, 1982; Hill and Owen, 1982; Kater, 1982; Liebman and Wuthnow, 1983). Although Moral Majority succeeded in popularizing a unique blend of evangelical piety and conservative moral politics, it was but one feature of a more general constellation of movements in both of these areas. Evangelicalism, for its part, became the leading news story of 1976 following Southern Baptist Jimmy Carter's successful bid for the presidency. In that year, the Gallup poll — using a combination of questions about fundamentalist views of the Bible, conversion and proselytization — estimated that 19 percent of the public were evangelicals (the number who self-identified themselves as such ran upwards of 30 percent). Four years later, both the Gallup poll and the 1980 National Election Survey conducted by the University of Michigan estimated that evangelicals still comprised 19 percent of the public (Gallup, 1982).

If evangelicalism as a whole was not growing, however, there was nevertheless remarkable growth within particular evangelical denominations, and evangelicals were rapidly expanding their activities in a number of strategic areas. Between 1971 and 1980 the Church of God grew by 37.3 percent and the Southern Baptist Convention by 12.4 percent, for example, compared with net losses in most mainline denominations (Briggs, 1982). By 1980 expenditures for religious television programming, virtually all of which was concentrated among evangelicals, had risen to $600 million annually, up from only $50 million in 1970. Oral Roberts took in $60 million, Pat Robertson $58 million, Jim Bakker $51 million and Jerry Falwell $50 million (*Los Angeles Times*, 25 February 1980). And evangelicals were by far the heaviest viewers of these programmes: according to a poll taken in late 1981, 63 percent of all evangelicals (compared with 32 percent of the nation) claimed to have watched a religious television programme within the *past week* (Gallup, 1982: 46). Evangelicals were also increasingly active in the founding of Christian schools. Between 1971 and 1978 alone, there was a 47 percent increase in the number of Protestant private schools, a 95 percent increase in pupils enrolled and a 116 percent increase in teachers; all told, there were more than one million pupils in these schools in 1978 (*US Statistical Abstract*, 1981: 148). Most notably, there was also a resurgence of interest in political affairs among evangelicals. After 1976 the tendency of evangelicals to remove themselves from politics, which had been noted for nearly fifty years, was reversed, and all major studies showed that evangelicals were more likely to be registered voters, more likely to vote, more supportive of churches speaking out on political issues, more supportive of pastors who actually spoke out, and at least as involved in civic groups as non-evangelicals of similar social background and geographic location (Wuthnow, 1983a).

The Moral Majority was built on an infrastructure of evangelical support, and nearly all of its leaders at the state level were Independent Baptist clergy. It succeeded where other efforts with similar objectives had failed, largely because it was able to rely on the pre-existing networks and organizational skills of these pastors at the local level (Liebman, 1983). By 1981, more than half of the US public was familiar with it and 5 percent were either members or expressed willingness to become members (Gallup, 1982: 170). Among evangelicals, the latter figure was 14 percent and about a quarter expressed favourable views of the movement. A survey of evangelical college students conducted a few months later showed that, even there, about a quarter favoured the movement (Hunter, 1982).

Through national telecasts, direct mail solicitation, local rallies and door-to-door campaigns Moral Majority raised funds to distribute literature and a monthly publication, *Moral Majority Report*; it co-operated with other organizations involved in lobbying and electioneering, claimed to have registered some 4 million new evangelical voters, and publicized its conservative views on issues such as school prayer, pornography, homosexuality, equal rights for women, abortion and national defence. How much it actually succeeded in accomplishing its goals in these areas, and how much it merely rode in on the crest of a larger tide of conservative sentiment, remain matters of debate. Nevertheless, studies conducted during the 1980 election showed that there were indeed thousands of new evangelical voters — in the south alone almost *half* of the evangelicals who had not voted in 1976 did so in 1980, compared with only a sixth of the non-evangelicals (Smidt, 1982) — and large minorities (in some cases majorities) expressed opinions which were compatible with the Moral Majority platform (Simpson, 1983).

Other religious movements which also expressed overtly conservative political orientations included Christian Voice, organized in 1979 as a lobbying effort, and Religious Roundtable (also 1979), a leadership forum to co-ordinate activities among the many evangelical movements operating in politics on a smaller scale. Indeed, local newspapers had begun documenting literally dozens of such movements around the country during the 1978 elections and these efforts continued in both the 1980 and 1982 elections. At the national level, at least eight culturally defensive religious movements had appeared between 1970 and 1974, and between 1975 and 1982 another 19 came into existence (*Encyclopedia of Associations*, 1983). These included a number of specifically anti-abortion movements such as the Christian Action Council (1975), Prayers for Life (1977) and Family America (1979), as well as an even larger number of movements with broader concerns regarding threats to the family, changes in sex roles and opposition to the proposed Equal Rights Amendment which was designed to guarantee gender equality. Among these were Life Action Ministries (1971), the Apostolate for Family Consecration (1975), Concerned Women of America (1979) and the National Pro-Family Coalition (1980).

Some of the conservative movements of the 1970s, like those in the 1960s, were organized within religious bodies and were evoked mainly by concerns about liberalism in theology or in official religious policies. One such movement was the Fellowship of Concerned Churchmen (1973), organized in the Episcopal Church to oppose the ordination of women and maintain 'traditional conservatism'. Another was the Committee of Catholics Who Care (1978), whose purposes included guarding the traditional mass, identifying moral irregularities among priests and opposing sex education in parochial schools. Three movements were organized by evangelicals with the specific aims of applying biblical ethics to television and boycotting sponsors of programmes who did not conform to these standards — the National Federation for Decency (1977), Clean Up TV Campaign (1978) and Coalition for Better Television (1981). Finally, a number of movements emerged with broad political objectives, such as combating federal interference in religious expression, bringing about national repentance, introducing conservative biblical interpretations into the process of government and encouraging conservative Christians to take a more active role in politics.

As in the past, the new religious movements on the right were also accompanied by parallel movements and counter-movements on the left. In the middle 1970s a number of such movements were prompted by the larger push for ratification of the Equal Rights Amendment (ERA), among which were Priests for Equality (1975), Catholic Women for the ERA (1974), Religious Committee for the ERA (1976) and Mormons for ERA (1979). Towards the end of this period, most of the new movements on the left were organized specifically in opposition to Moral Majority and similar groups. Among these were Moral Alternatives (1980), Voice of Reason (1980), People for the American Way (1980) and the Committee for American Principles (1981). These were generally not specifically religious organizations, but involved clergy from liberal denominations in leadership roles in order to counter the influence of religious leaders in the conservative movements (for descriptions, see Heinz, 1983; and Hunter, 1983a).

The main contours of this more recent episode of religious movements can be understood by again turning to the broader developments in the society, particularly the on-going reorganization of the society around science, technology and advanced education, and the effects of these on religious commitments. By 1980, 32 percent of the adult population (over age 25) had completed at least some college education, compared with 21 percent in 1970. Total enrolments in higher education rose from 8.6 million in 1970 to 12.1 million in 1980; the proportion of young people age 18–24 who were in school rose from 35 to 40 percent; and expenditures for higher education increased from $23.4 billion to $50.7 billion. Two-thirds of US exports were still in high technology industries; these were the principal areas in which the United States enjoyed a favourable export–import balance, and some of these industries had grown dramatically — aircraft, up 108 percent since 1970; telecommunications, up 119 percent; computers, up 248 percent; and aerospace products, up 383 percent. Overall, total expenditures for R & D had risen by 22.3 percent after inflation, and an increasing share of these expenditures was being borne by the private sector (*US Statistical Abstract*, 1981; National Science Board, 1981). In short, the 'knowledge sector' played an even greater role in US society in 1980 than it had in 1970.

The 'education gap' in social attitudes and religion which had been evident in 1970 was also still an important factor a decade later. One of the biggest differences between the better and less educated was in the proportion who viewed the Bible as the literal word of God. According to a 1981 Gallup survey, only 21 percent of the college-educated thought of the Bible this way, compared with 56 percent of the grade-school-educated (Gallup, 1982). Conversely, the proportions who identified themselves as 'religiously liberal' were 45 and 14 percent, respectively. These differences also had ramifications for the manner in which people from different educational strata viewed the churches and issues within the church. For example, 47 percent of the college-educated thought it acceptable for homosexuals to be hired as clergy, compared with only 17 percent of those with grade-school educations. As another example, 48 percent of the college-educated Roman Catholics polled in 1976 said they approved of women being ordained as priests, compared with only 28 percent of the non-college group; three-quarters of the former (78 percent) said they approved of the changes in the Church since Vatican II, compared with about half (57 percent) of the latter (Gallup, 1978). More generally, polls taken around 1980 and 1981 still showed huge differences between the educated and less educated on a wide variety of social and political issues. For example, most polls on attitudes towards abortion showed nearly twice as much support among those with college educations as among the non-college sector, and similar differences existed on questions about pornography, homosexuality, living up to strict moral standards and trying to obey God (Gallup Organization, 1982; Simpson, 1983; Ladd, 1979).

Within the more liberal mainline denominations, a disproportionate number of the laity had become college-educated by the 1980s; pastors and official church policies supported the views of these members; and the better educated were leaving other churches to join these denominations, while the less educated shifted memberships to more conservative churches. Based on estimates from Gallup surveys in 1979, approximately 66 percent of all Episcopalians had been to college, as had 50 percent of all Presbyterians, 50 percent of United Church of Christ members and 42 percent of United Methodist Church members. By comparison, 33 percent of the total national sample had been to college; the proportion among largely evangelical Southern Baptists was only 25 percent; and among all persons holding evangelical beliefs it was a mere 19 percent (calculated from figures reported in Gallup, 1982). As for the views of clergy, the evidence from studies in liberal mainline denominations pointed strongly towards greater compatibility with their college-educated parishioners than with the less educated (Wuthnow, 1979; Johnson,

1983). In contrast, surveys of clergy in theologically conservative denominations with smaller proportions of college-educated members generally showed much more conservative orientations on political and moral issues (Wuthnow, 1979; Luidens, 1978; Guth, 1983).

It is perhaps not surprising, therefore, that studies of denominational switching among US Protestants showed a strong educational factor in the directionality of this switching. The extent of switching overall was such that only about half of those in the late 1970s who presently belonged to any of the major denominations had grown up in that denomination; and those who switched from mainline denominations to more liberal denominations were about twice as likely to have had a college education as those who stayed put, while those who switched into more conservative groups had about average levels of education (Roof and Hadaway, 1979).

Given these patterns, the social sources of conservative movements such as Moral Majority become more readily apparent. It was by and large the less educated segment of the population which was, in a sense, disenfranchised by liberal theological currents in the churches; and it was they — even though they may have remained active in their churches and been largely satisfied with their spiritual care — who turned to movements like Moral Majority to express their sentiments on morality and politics. Several types of evidence support this interpretation. First, the platform of Moral Majority and similar groups which emerged in 1979 and 1980 was virtually the mirror opposite of liberal views supported by the college-educated laity and clergy in mainline denominations — anti-abortion, anti-pornography, anti-homosexuality, anti-ERA — and this platform was shared most extensively among the less educated strata (Simpson, 1983; Yinger and Cutler, 1982). Second, it has already been seen that overt support for Moral Majority was disproportionately higher among evangelicals than non-evangelicals; and that evangelicals were generally less educated on average than non-evangelicals. The same data show that non-college-educated persons were about as likely to approve of Moral Majority as to disapprove of it, whereas college-educated people were three times as likely to disapprove as to approve (Gallup, 1982: 62). And finally, even in local areas and within single denominations, it was the less educated who supported Moral Majority and its platform more than the better educated (Guth, 1983; Shupe and Stacey, 1983; Patel et al., 1982).

Conclusion

The rising influence of science and technology in North America, and with it the expanding role of higher education, appears to have been a decisive factor in the religious movements that frequented this continent with growing intensity after the second world war, reaching a climax in the late 1960s, and producing movements and counter-movements which continued to arouse zeal a decade later. As the educational institution grew, both from the input of the 'baby boom' generation and from conscious efforts to upgrade the technical skills of the work-force, movements occurred within established religious organizations to bring them into line with newer, more liberal theological interpretations, with values which downplayed particularistic ethnic and doctrinal distinctions, and with attitudes of egalitarianism, tolerance and social concern on secular issues. These movements were opposed by counter-tendencies involving the formation of sectarian offshoots, splinter groups and interest groups concerned with protecting traditional morality and values. By the end of the 1960s, these movements within the established religious institutions had not only intensified but had been joined by hundreds of movements outside these institutions which appealed to the better educated segments of the younger generation.

The next decade saw a diminution of religious movement activity, as the rate of growth in technology and education slowed, as new power alignments within religious organizations solidified, and as people shifted loyalties to find religious organizations more in keeping with their own educational and occupational positions. With the consolidation of orientations in the religious mainstream which reflected the dominance of the better educated strata, there was also a proliferation of independent conservative movements oriented towards the restoration of traditional morality and attitudes towards government.

While education plays a prominent role in this interpretation, its effects should not be understood simply as the inevitable consequences of long-term modernizing tendencies, of which education has generally been regarded as a significant feature. The impetus towards rapid expansion in the education system was ultimately the economic position which the United States and Canada assumed in international affairs following the second world war, a position of dominance that could be sustained only through continuous technological innovation involving heavy expenditures for R & D; and, secondarily, this expansion was nurtured because of defence requirements and a more general political climate in the international system towards the fostering of education. The postwar period, in short, was a time of transition from a largely industrial mode of production among advanced countries in the world economy to one in which technology and education were increasingly the vital components. The urgency in making this transition led to an unusually rapid rate of expansion in the educational system during the 1960s and involved the federal government in a decisive way.

As with any such major transition, the new basis of support and power led to a significant new cleavage in social status between those who participated in it and those who did not — the college-educated sector and the non-college-educated sector. This cleavage, while embodying the cultural values associated with higher education for many decades, was nevertheless more than a matter of culture and cognition alone, determining among other things the type of occupation one was likely to obtain, where one would live, how different one might be from one's forebears, and how one might feel about governmental programmes and social reforms. With respect to religion, these cleavages cut across traditional modes of denominational organization which had largely been constructed along regional and ethnic lines prior to the second world war. Accordingly, tensions developed *within* religious bodies that had formerly existed primarily between them, resulting in movements aimed at reforming these bodies, and re-organizing them through outright mergers or co-operative ventures, and in counter-movements supported by those who wished to retain the traditional modes of organization. In the process, many became disaffected with established religious organizations entirely and either adopted their own private religions or joined new religious movements.

References

Aidala, Angela A. (1983) 'Worldviews, Ideologies and Social Experimentation: Clarification and Replication of 'The Consciousness Reformation', *Journal for the Scientific Study of Religion*, 22(3), 44–59.

Alfred, Randall H. (1976) 'The Church of Satan', pp. 180–202 in Charles Y. Glock and Robert N. Bellah (eds), *The New Religious Consciousness*. Berkeley and Los Angeles: University of California Press.

Back, Kurt W. (1972) *Beyond Words: The Story of Sensitivity Training and the Encounter Movement*. Baltimore: Penguin.

Bainbridge, William Sims (1978) *Satan's Power: A Deviant Psychotherapy Cult*. Berkeley and Los Angeles: University of California Press.

Balswick, Jack D. (1974) 'The Jesus People Movement: A Generational Interpretation', *Journal of Social Issues*, 30(3), 23–42.

Barstow, Robbins W. (1951) *Christian Faith in Action: The Founding of the National Council of the Churches of Christ in the United States of America*. New York: National Council of Churches.

Bell, Daniel (1973) *The Coming of Post-industrial Society*. New York: Harper & Row.

——— (1979) 'The New Class: A Muddled Concept', *Society*, 3, 15–23.

Bibby, Reginald W. (1979) 'Religion and Modernity: The Canadian Case', *Journal for the Scientific Study of Religion*, 18(1), 1–17.

Bird, Frederick and Bill Reimer (1982) 'Participation Rates in New Religious and Para-religious Movements', *Journal for the Scientific Study of Religion*, 21(1), 1–14.

Briggs, Kenneth (1982) 'Church Growth Lags Far Behind that of US', *New York Times*, 24 September.

Campbell, Colin (1982) 'The New Religious Movements, the New Spirituality and Post-industrial Society', pp. 232–42 in Eileen Barker (ed.), *New Religious Movements: A*

Perspective for Understanding Society. New York: Edwin Mellen Press.

Canada Year Book (1981) Ottawa: Ministry of Information.

Daner, Francine J. (1976) *The American Children of Krisna: A Study of the Hare Krisna Movement*. New York: Holt, Rinehart and Winston.

Dessauer, John P. (1981) 'Book-buying Patterns in the '70s Showed Real Gains — Mostly Through Retailers', *Publishers Weekly*, 221 (2 April), 37–9.

Duncan, Otis Dudley, Howard Schuman and Beverly Duncan (1973) *Social Change in a Metropolitan Community*. New York: Russell Sage Foundation.

Encyclopedia of Associations (1983) (17th edn). Detroit: Gale.

Fackre, Gabriel (1982) *The Religious Right and Christian Faith*. Grand Rapids, Mich.: Eerdmans.

Fracchia, Charles A. (1979) *Living Together Alone: The New American Monasticism*. New York: Harper & Row.

Gallup, George, Jr (1978) *Religion in America, 1978*. Princeton: Princeton Religion Research Center.

—— (1980) *Religion in America, 1979–80*. Princeton: Princeton Religion Research Center.

—— (1981) *Religion in America, 1981*. Princeton: Princeton Religion Research Center.

—— (1982) *Religion in America, 1982*. Princeton: Princeton Religion Research Center.

Gallup Organization (1982) *The Robert Schuller Survey of Self-Esteem*. Princeton: Gallup Organization, Inc.

Glock, Charles Y. and Robert N. Bellah (eds) (1976) *The New Religious Consciousness*. Berkeley and Los Angeles: University of California Press.

Goode, Erich (1980) *Social Class and Church Participation*. New York: Arno Press.

Gouldner, Alvin W. (1979) *The New Intelligentsia*. New York: Seabury Press.

Greeley, Andrew M. (1979) *Crisis in the Church*. Chicago: Thomas More Press.

Guth, James L. (1983) 'Southern Baptist Clergy: Vanguard of the Christian Right?' in Robert Liebman and Robert Wuthnow (eds), *The New Christian Right: Mobilization and Legitimation*. New York: Aldine.

Hadden, Jeffrey K. (1969) *The Gathering Storm in the Churches*. Garden City, NY: Doubleday.

Hall, John R. (1981) 'The Apocalypse at Jonestown', pp. 171–90 in Thomas Robbins and Dick Anthony (eds), *In Gods We Trust*. New Brunswick, NJ: Transaction Books.

Heinz, Donald (1976) 'The Christian World Liberation Front', pp. 143–61 in Charles Y. Glock and Robert N. Bellah (eds), *The New Religious Consciousness*. Berkeley and Los Angeles: University of California Press.

—— (1983) 'The Struggle to Define America', in Robert Liebman and Robert Wuthnow (eds), *The New Christian Right: Mobilization and Legitimation*. New York: Aldine.

Hill, Samuel S. and Dennis E. Owen (1982) *The New Religious Political Right in America*. Nashville: Abingdon.

Hoge, Dean R. (1976) *Division in the Protestant House*. Philadelphia: Westminster.

Hogg, W. Richie (1977) 'The Role of American Protestantism in World Mission', pp. 354–502 in R. Pierce Beaver (ed.), *American Missions in Bicentennial Perspective*. South Pasadena, Cal.: William Carey Library.

Hunter, James Davison (1982) 'Evangelicals and Political Civility: The Coming Generation'. Unpublished paper presented at the annual meeting of the Society for the Scientific Study of Religion, Providence, RI.

—— (1983a) 'The Liberal Reaction', in Robert Liebman and Robert Wuthnow (eds), *The New Christian Right: Mobilization and Legitimation*. New York: Aldine.

26   Robert Wuthnow

—— (1983b) 'Religion and the New Class: Religious Elites in Advanced Industrial Society'. Unpublished paper.

Jacquet, Constant H., Jr (ed.) (1982) *Yearbook of American and Canadian Churches, 1982*. Nashville: Abington.

Johnson, Roger A. (ed.) (1983) *Views from the Pews*. Philadelphia: Fortress Press.

Judah, J. Stillson (1974) *Hare Krishna and the Counterculture*. New York: John Wiley.

Kater, John L., Jr (1982) *Christians on the Right: The Moral Majority in Perspective*. New York: Seabury.

Keniston, Kenneth (1971) *Youth and Dissent*. New York: Harcourt Brace Jovanovich.

Kristol, Irving (1978) *Two Cheers for Capitalism*. New York: Basic Books.

Ladd, Everett Carll, Jr (1979) 'Pursuing the New Class: Social Theory and Survey Data', pp. 101–22 in B. Bruce-Briggs (ed.), *The New Class?* New Brunswick, NJ: Transaction Books.

Lane, Ralph Jr (1976) 'Catholic Charismatic Renewal', pp. 162–79 in Charles Y. Glock and Robert N. Bellah (eds), *The New Religious Consciousness*. Berkeley and Los Angeles: University of California Press.

Liebman, Robert (1983) 'Mobilizing the Moral Majority', in Robert Liebman and Robert Wuthnow (eds), *The New Christian Right: Mobilization and Legitimation*. New York: Aldine.

—— and Robert Wuthnow (eds) (1983) *The New Christian Right: Mobilization and Legitimation*. New York: Aldine.

Lofland, John (1978) *Doomsday Cult* (rev. edn). New York: Irvington.

Luidens, Donald Alan (1978) *Organizational Goals, Power, and Effectiveness: Desires and Perceptions in a Protestant Denomination*. Unpublished PhD dissertation, Rutgers University.

Malko, George (1970) *Scientology: The Now Religion*. New York: Delta Books.

Marty, Martin E., Stuart E. Rosenberg, and Andrew M. Greeley (1968) *What Do We Believe? The Stance of Religion in America*. New York: Meredith Press.

McGuire, Meredith (1982) *Pentecostal Catholics*. Philadelphia: Temple University Press.

McKinney, William and Wade Clark Roof (1982) 'A Social Profile of American Religious Groups', pp. 267–73 in Constant H. Jacquet, Jr (ed.), *Yearbook of American and Canadian Churches*. Nashville: Abington.

Melton, J. Gordon (1978) *Encyclopedia of American Religions* (2 vols). Wilmington, NC: McGrath.

Moore, John A. (1974) 'Creationism in California', *Daedalus*, 103, 173–89.

National Science Board (1978) *Science Indicators, 1978: Report of the National Science Board, 1978*. Washington, DC: National Science Foundation.

—— (1981) *Science Indicators, 1980: Report of the National Science Board, 1981*. Washington, DC: National Science Foundation.

Needleman, Jacob (1970) *The New Religions*. Garden City, NY: Doubleday.

Nelkin, Dorothy (1979) 'Creation Versus Evolution: The California Controversy', pp. 213–26 in Dorothy Nelkin (ed.), *Controversy*. Beverly Hills, Cal.: Sage.

Page, Ann L. and Donald A. Clelland (1978) 'The Kanawha County Textbook Controversy: A Study of the Politics of Life Style Concern', *Social Forces*, 57, 265–81.

Patel, Kant, Denny Pilant and Gary Rose (1982) 'The Politics of the New Right: A Study of Born-again Christians in a Border State'. Unpublished paper presented at the annual meeting of the Society for the Scientific Study of Religion, Providence, RI.

Quinley, Harold (1974) *The Prophetic Clergy*. New York: John Wiley.

Richardson, James T. (1980) 'People's Temple and Jonestown: A Corrective Comparison and Critique'. *Journal for the Scientific Study of Religion*, 19(3), 239–54.

——, Mary W. Stewart and Robert B. Simmonds (1979) *Organized Miracles: A Study of a Contemporary, Youth, Communal, Fundamentalist Organization*. New Brunswick, NJ: Transaction Books.

Robbins, Thomas and Dick Anthony (eds) (1981) *In Gods We Trust: New Patterns of Religious Pluralism in America*. New Brunswick, NJ: Transaction Books.

Robbins, Thomas, Dick Anthony and James Richardson (1978) 'Theory and Research on Today's "New Religions"'. *Sociological Analysis*, 39(2), 95–122.

Roof, Wade Clark and Christopher Kirk Hadaway (1979) 'Denominational Switching in the Seventies: Going Beyond Stark and Glock', *Journal for the Scientific Study of Religion*, 18(4), 363–78.

Shupe, Anson and David G. Bromley (1979) 'The Moonies and the Anti-cultists: Movement and Countermovement in Conflict', *Sociological Analysis* 40(4), 325–34.

—— (1980) *The New Vigilantes: Deprogrammers, Anti-cultists, and the New Religions*. Beverly Hills, Cal.: Sage.

—— (1981) 'Witches, Moonies, and Accusations of Evil', pp. 247–62 in Thomas Robbins and Dick Anthony (eds), *In Gods We Trust*. New Brunswick, NJ: Transaction Books.

Shupe, Anson and William Stacey (1983) 'The Moral Majority Constituency', in Robert Liebman and Robert Wuthnow (eds), *The New Christian Right: Mobilization and Legitimation*. New York: Aldine.

Simpson, John H. (1983) 'Moral Issues and Status Politics', in Robert Liebman and Robert Wuthnow (eds), *The New Christian Right: Mobilization and Legitimation*. New York: Aldine.

Smidt, Corwin (1982) '"Born Again" Politics: The Political Attitudes and Behavior of Evangelical Christians in the South'. Unpublished paper presented at the 1982 Citadel Symposium on Southern Politics, Charleston, SC.

Snow, David A., Louis A. Zurcher, Jr and Sheldon Ekland-Olson (1980) 'Social Networks and Social Movements: A Microstructural Approach to Differential Recruitment', *American Sociological Review*, 45(5), 787–801.

Solomon, Trudy (1981) 'Integrating the "Moonie" Experience: A Survey of Ex-members of the Unification Church', pp. 275–96 in Thomas Robbins and Dick Anthony (eds), *In Gods We Trust*. New Brunswick, NJ: Transaction Books.

Spiritual Community Guide (1974) ed. Parmatma Singh. San Rafael, Cal.: Spiritual Community Publications.

Stark, Rodney and William Sims Bainbridge (1980) 'Networks of Faith: Recruitment to Cults and Sects', *American Journal of Sociology*, 85(6), 1376–95.

—— (1981) 'American-born Sects: Initial Findings', *Journal for the Scientific Study of Religion*, 20(2), 130–49.

Stark, Rodney, William Sims Bainbridge and Daniel P. Doyle (1979) 'Cults of America: A Reconnaissance in Space and Time', *Sociological Analysis* 40(4), 347–60.

Stone, Donald (1976) 'The Human Potential Movement', pp. 93–115 in Charles Y. Glock and Robert N. Bellah (eds), *The New Religious Consciousness*. Berkeley and Los Angeles: University of California Press.

Tipton, Steven M. (1982) *Getting Saved from the Sixties*. Berkeley and Los Angeles: University of California Press.

Tobey, Alan (1976) 'The Summer Solstice of the Healthy–Happy–Holy Organization', pp. 5–30 in Charles Y. Glock and Robert N. Bellah (eds), *The New Religious*

28   Robert Wuthnow

Consciousness. Berkeley and Los Angeles: University of California Press.
US Statistical Abstract (1981)   Washington, DC: US Department of Commerce, Bureau of the Census.
Winter, Gibson (1962)   *The Suburban Captivity of the Churches*. New York: Macmillan.
Wuthnow, Robert (1976a)   *The Consciousness Reformation*. Berkeley and Los Angeles: University of California Press.
—— (1976b)   'Recent Patterns of Secularization: A Problem of Generations?' *American Sociological Review*, 41(5), 850–67.
—— (1977)   'A Longitudinal, Cross-national Indicator of Cultural Religious Commitment', *Journal for the Scientific Study of Religion*, 16(1), 87–99.
—— (1978a)   *Experimentation in American Religion*. Berkeley and Los Angeles: University of California Press.
—— (1978b)   'Religious Movements and the Transition in World Order', pp. 63–79 in Jacob Needleman and George Baker (eds), *Understanding the New Religions*. New York: Seabury Press.
—— (1979)   'The Current Moral Climate: What Pastors Think', *Theology Today*, 36(2), 239–50.
—— (1980)   'World Order and Religious Movements', pp. 57–75 in Albert Bergesen (ed.), *Studies of the Modern World-System*. New York: Academic Press.
—— (1982a)   'The Moral Crisis in American Capitalism', *Harvard Business Review*, 60(2), 76–84.
—— (1982b)   'Anti-Semitism and Stereotyping', pp. 137–87 in Arthur G. Miller (ed.), *In the Eye of the Beholder: Prejudice and Stereotyping*. New York: Praeger.
—— (1983a)   'The Political Rebirth of American Evangelicals', in Robert Liebman and Robert Wuthnow (eds), *The New Christian Right: Mobilization and Legitimation*. New York: Aldine.
—— (1983b)   'Sources of Confessional Unity and Diversity', in Roger A. Johnson (ed.), *Views from the Pews*. Philadelphia: Fortress Press.
Yinger, J. Milton and Steven Cutler (1982)   'The Moral Majority: A Major Force or a Symptom of the Times?' Unpublished paper presented at the annual meeting of the Society for the Scientific Study of Religion, Providence, RI.
Zablocki, Benjamin (1980)   *Alienation and Charisma: A Study of Contemporary American Communes*. New York: Free Press.
Zaretsky, Irving I. and Mark P. Leone (eds) (1973)   *Religious Movements in Contemporary America*. Princeton: Princeton University Press.

2

New religious movements in Western Europe

James A. Beckford and Martine Levasseur

Introduction
The speed and scope of the social changes that have taken place in most Western European countries since the end of the second world war may be less massive than·those registered in some other parts of the world, but this is not to say that rapid social changes have not made their effects felt. This chapter will show how some of the young adults who have been especially affected by these changes have responded by joining various new religious movements (NRMs). A prominent theme will be a comparison between today's NRMs and those transmitted to Europe from the United States in the late nineteenth and early twentieth centuries.

Since the topic for discussion is only one small aspect of life in a densely populated area divided into numerous national and cultural groupings, it is essential to be clear about the intended meaning of some key terms. 'New religious movements' is a problematic term. For present purposes, it refers to organized attempts to mobilize human and material resources for the purpose of spreading new ideas and sensibilities of a religious nature. They are therefore intentional, collective and historically specific. Some, like the Charismatic Renewal movement, or the movement for the preservation of the Tridentine Mass, are currents within much larger religious organizations. But for present purposes attention will be focused only on NRMs which operate independently of other religious bodies.

In Western European countries, where there is a special relationship of an historical and/or constitutional nature between the state and one or more Christian Churches, there has always been a rich vocabulary for describing religious groups which depart from the Churches' practices. 'Sects', 'cults', 'heresies', 'nonconformity' and 'deviations' are all terms conveying a mixture of doctrinal, historical, cultural and social judgements of relative 'abnormality'. It is particularly important, therefore, to insist that the use of 'NRM' be free from such judgements.[1] Accordingly, no evaluative importance is attached here to distinctions which might be made between such things as Christian and non-Christian movements; Western and Asian spirituality; biblical and non-biblical sources of truth.

For present purposes, the following will be taken as representative NRMs: the Unification Church (UC) (the 'Moonies'), the International Society for Krishna Consciousness (ISKCON), Scientology, the Divine Light Mission (DLM), Transcendental Meditation (TM), the Children of God/Family of Love (COG/FOL), Nichiren Shoshu, and the Rajneesh Foundation. We recognize that, on the one hand, there are numerous candidates for addition to this list[2] and that, on the other, it already contains a problematic diversity of groups. But, provided we are not mistakenly thought to be making statements about all NRMs, or implying an unwarranted degree of homogeneity among those nominated, our chosen strategy will be acceptable. As it happens, most of the groups that we have nominated as NRMs display the defining characteristics of NRMs as stipulated by Bryan Wilson:

> . . . exotic provenance; new cultural lifestyle; a level of engagement markedly different from that of a traditional church Christianity; charismatic leadership; a following predominantly young and drawn in disproportionate measure from the better-educated and middle-class sections of society; social conspicuity; international operation; and emergence within the last decade and a half. (Wilson, 1981a: v)

Estimating the numerical strength of these movements is hazardous. It seems unlikely, however, that any one of them could truthfully lay claim to more than a few thousand members who were living and working full-time for its benefit in Europe. Moreover, the indications are that the rate of recruitment to full-time membership is declining in most movements. Scientology, TM and the Rajneesh movement have certainly 'processed' thousands of participants in their training or therapeutic sessions, but the quality of subsequent commitment to these movements is rarely strong or lasting for *most* participants. In the circumstances, then, the only safe conclusion is that none of the movements which try to recruit large numbers of full-time members has managed to retain more than a few thousand of them, while the movements which try to train and/or serve client-like participants have succeeded in attracting many thousands of them for brief periods only.

Limitations on space prevent us from giving descriptions of the history, teachings and practices of NRMs. Readers are therefore referred to the growing body of secondary literature, of which the following are merely representative.

On the UC:	Barker (1978; 1981; 1984); Bromley and Shupe (1979); Kehrer (1981)
On ISKON:	Judah (1974); Daner (1976); Rochford (1982); Carey (1983)

On Scientology: Wallis (1976a); Straus (1976); Whitehead
                    (1974)
On DLM: Price (1979); Downton (1979); Derks (1980)
On TM: Forem (1973); Bainbridge and Jackson (1981)
On COG/FOL: Wallis (1976b, 1981; 1984); Davis and
                    Richardson (1976)
On Nichiren Shoshu: White (1970); Snow (1976); Hashimoto and
                    McPherson (1976)
On Rajneesh: Hummel and Hardin (1983)

General surveys of NRMs, some from a critical point of view, include: Haack (1979); Mildenberger (1979); Woodrow (1977); Berger and Hexel (1981); Beckford (1985); *Social Compass* 30 (1), 1983; *Concilium* 181, 1983; *Conscience et Liberté* 23, 1982. Useful bibliographies of social scientific studies of NRMs can be found in: Barker (1982): Beckford and Richardson (1983); Universitätsbibliothek Tübingen (1981).

Fewer difficulties arise from the imposition on our survey of a time-scale beginning with the aftermath of the second world war, for it was only in the 1950s and 1960s that these distinctively new movements came to light in Western Europe. Of course, the whole history of Christianity could be written in terms of the periodic rise and fall of new religious movements, with the seventeenth and nineteenth centuries being particularly fruitful periods for innovation in both Protestantism and Catholicism. And in many respects the so-called new movements represent variations on themes already observed in earlier religious changes.

But a qualitative shift occurred in the postwar period. It was marked by changes in the provenance of new ideas and sentiments in religion; the social composition of NRMs; and the modes of their 'insertion' in society (Beckford, 1985). Each of these changes will be examined in detail later, but before then we shall outline the dimensions of wider social changes which have conditioned the rise of NRMs. They are necessarily a deliberate selection from the vast number of changes that have occurred in the postwar era. Their combined effect has been to produce a largely youthful set of sympathizers with the NRMs imported from the United States in the 1960s and 1970s.

Aspects of social change

Of the whole myriad of social changes affecting Western Europe in the past four decades, special prominence must be given to the rapid improvements made in the *means of communication*. In particular, the relative cheapness, ease and enhanced effectiveness of the printed and broadcast media have made it possible for would-be social movements of all kinds to reach a truly mass audience without incurring prohibitive costs or labour time. The increased efficiency of systems for information-storage, -retrieval and -transmission has enabled movement organizers to capitalize on the advances in printing technology. And the growing ease of transport for persons and goods over both short and long distances has helped organizers to maximize the benefits of access to ever larger 'markets'. The result is a general increase in the visibility of NRMs.

These considerations all have a direct bearing on the practical conditions within which NRMs have been organized. They emphasize the enhanced importance of 'movement organizations' (Zald and Ash, 1966) to an understanding of strategies for the growth of NRMs; in combination with changes in their market, these strategies help to account for the distinctiveness of today's NRMs compared with for example, nineteenth-century religious innovations. But comparison with their forebears shows that the changes are largely a matter of degree; for movements such as the Mormons (Arrington and Bitton, 1979), Christian Scientists (Wilson, 1961) and the Jehovah's Witnesses (Beckford, 1975a; 1975b) all made innovative use of various mass communications media in their formative years. In this respect, at least, today's NRMs are following in a tradition which could be traced back to the influence of religious innovations on the very origins of printing technology in the West. But, as Wilson (1981a) has emphasized, today's NRMs are novel in so far as they transcend the localized appeal and interest of earlier movements. This is clearly associated both with the central importance of young adults in NRMs and with the mass media's preoccupations with such people.

While changes in the conditions affecting the practical outreach of NRMs are important, they should not be artificially separated from concurrent changes in their *markets*. For there is no doubt that, in all the countries of Western Europe, although with varied consequences, a host of demographic, social and cultural changes have helped to provide a specific type of audience for today's NRMs.

In demographic terms, Western Europe experienced a 'baby boom' between approximately 1950 and 1965, giving rise to unprecedentedly large numbers of young adults in the 1970s and early 1980s. Members of NRMs are drawn very largely from this segment of the population. The age-cohort 18–24 at the end of the 1970s does not, however, represent a significantly larger proportion of the total population of most countries than it did thirty years earlier. This is largely due to the slow rate of decline in the birth rate after the baby-boom years and to the steadily increasing size of the population over the age of 60 throughout the twentieth century.

As a proportion of the population, then, young adults in Western Europe have not grown markedly in the postwar period. But their socio-cultural salience and distinctiveness have increased greatly. This is more important than the bare demographic facts would suggest, and is connected with the fact that young people are disproportionately concentrated in urban and metropolitan areas. It is also related to the commercial importance of youth and young adults as major producers and consumers of goods and services marketed for mass consumption.

Moreover, changes in educational patterns and in the structure of European economies have tended to make the dominant cohorts of young adults more responsive to new ideas than were earlier generations. It is almost a sociological commonplace that adolescents and young adults are among the people most deeply affected by rapid social change because they are aware simultaneously of the past and of the new opportunities becoming available, or being denied, to them (Keniston, 1963: 169). In the light of the 'student movement' of the late 1960s, it was therefore tempting to use such terms as 'youth counter-culture', 'youth contra-culture' (Yinger, 1960) or 'youth subculture' in order to capture the distinctiveness of the ideological and social position of youth. And, although serious problems beset the use of such terms (see Smith, 1976), they at least served the useful purpose of sensitizing observers to the radical shifts that had undoubtedly occurred since the second world war in the demographic, economic, political and cultural importance of the cohort of young adults in most Western countries. Wuthnow's chapter in this volume (Chapter 1 above) elaborates further on the link between the massive expansion of the sphere of higher education after the second world war and the receptiveness of well-educated young people to various kinds of NRM.

Moreover, the counter-culture took place against a background of major structural changes in Western societies, and the pace of such change did not slacken in the 1970s. Even the onset of worldwide economic recession in the mid-1970s, deepening in the early 1980s, did not significantly affect the pace of change. There is also reason to believe that the experience, or the expectation, of declining affluence in the West may have actually enhanced the appeal of some counter-cultural themes, especially among the middle-ageing cohort. This theme is sensitively explored, for example, in Léger and Hervieu's (1983) study of the attractions of back-to-the-land communities with religious overtones for well-educated dropouts from the liberal and caring professions in France. The attraction is said to derive from the perceived contradiction between their personal expectations of being able to bring about a more humane social order and the reality of bureaucratic and political obstructions to constructive change. In the search for a compensatory ethic, these disenchanted idealists are drawn towards intentional communities celebrating utopianism and apocalypticism. Today's young adults are therefore faced with the echoes of the counter-culture, with hostile reactions to it as well as with unremitting social change. (For a comparison with the United States, see Tipton, 1982 and Lasch, 1984.)

For the sake of convenience, the salient effects and indicators of change among young adults can be summarized as follows: their exposure to formal education is longer; their commitment to the prospect of life-long marriages, occupations and places of residence is weaker; the age at which such commitments are made (if ever) is getting higher (and, incidentally, closer to early twentieth century patterns); their willingness to experiment with new life-styles and patterns of sexual relationship is stronger; their rates of participation in traditional politics, religion and trade union activities are lower; their rates of geographical mobility are higher; their spending power is greater; their openness to moral relativism is more pronounced; their exposure to influences from other countries and cultures is more extensive; and their experience of unemployment is more frequent and longer-lasting.

All these features of the generational distinctiveness of young adults in the late 1960s and 1970s can be interpreted as likely to increase responsiveness to NRMs. This does not necessarily mean a *positive* response: it simply means an opportunity and a readiness to take account of the messages and activities of NRMs. In fact, there are good grounds for believing that, compared with the generation of those who participated in the widespread agitations among young people in the late 1960s, today's young adults are ideologically more diverse but also more conservative on balance. This is an important consideration, because it highlights the fact that, although they are experiencing no fewer basic changes in their societies, their interpretations of this experience are different. This has led some commentators to account for the growth of NRMs as part of a reaction *against* the ideological disturbances of the 1960s (see Robbins and Anthony, 1972; Foss and Larkin, 1976; Pilarzyk, 1978). There is some confirmation here of Mannheim's (1952) view that discontinuities between successive generations of youth indicate a lack of stability and high rates of social change.

A number of the changes which have taken place in the *social institutions* of Western European societies have also facilitated the growth of NRMs. The contributions have usually been indirect and have merely helped to provide conditions conducive to their growth.

It goes without saying that these changes have also led to other, and possibly more important, developments in fields other than religion.

Interrelated changes in science, education, technology and the employment market have all conspired to increase the length of full-time education and to encourage the idea that recurrent and continuing education, retraining, serial careers and early retirement are appropriate to modern conditions of life. This is associated with long-term shifts towards the growing dominance of the service sector of the economy, higher rates of female participation in the labour force, more intense competition in world markets, and increasing opportunity/necessity for part-time employment. When these changes (and others) are combined with the steadily progressing rates of unemployment, underemployment and disguised unemployment that many countries have endured since the early 1970s, a picture emerges of increasingly varied and uncertain conditions of work. The effects are experienced differently by different age-groups, but one of the main effects on young adults is to undermine the culturally sanctioned sense of continuity between education and life-long careers. It is precisely in the late teens and early twenties that the full realization of their precarious position in the modern employment market occurs.

In all, then, diverse signs of the emergence of an increasingly salient and distinctive 'constituency' of young adults in economic status, life-style, culture and politics have become apparent in the recent past. This is reflected in the growing popularity of experimental forms of recreation, sexual relationships, marriage, households and child-rearing patterns. Although experimenters are doubtless in the minority, the trickle-down effect on their peers is still producing changing outlooks and opinions. Indeed, the fact that 'liberated' outlooks have coincided with an economic recession may serve to polarize opinion and practice between the more and the less conventional among young adults. This distinction is refracted in complex ways within and between NRMs.

While some young adults respond to rapid social change with an eagerness to tap what they see as the positive advantages of liberation from the constraints of tradition and convention, others respond more ambivalently. Rapid social change may, for example, be dismissed as mere 'illusion', or as a disguise of the timeless verities which transcend the appearance of things. Alternatively, it may simply be accepted for what it allegedly is — something to be lived with to the best advantage of the 'aware' individual. It may also be anathematized as the work of the Devil. NRMs in Western Europe cater for the whole gamut of such responses (cf. Tipton, 1982).

At this point, it is essential to interject a note of caution against unwarranted inferences from the information about rapid social change and the growth of NRMs in Western Europe. The latter certainly make sense in the light of the former. But the relationship between them must be firmly set in the context of other phenomena associated with young adults in the postwar era. It must be emphasized, for example, that only a *minute* percentage of young adults has ever joined NRMs and that an even more minute percentage has remained in membership for longer than, say, one year. By contrast, considerably larger percentages of young adults have taken drugs on a regular basis; the crime rate for young adults is higher than for any other age-group; the rate of deaths from violence is higher among young adults than among other age-groups; and their divorce rate outstrips that for other age-groups. Viewed in the light of these comparisons, the affinity between young adults and NRMs assumes a different significance. Membership of NRMs is only one small, though highly publicized, aspect of their response to rapid social change. The overwhelming majority of young people in Western Europe have never had anything to do with NRMs.

The Provenance of NRMs
Any attempt to characterize the NRMs under consideration in terms of their provenance must come to terms with the fact that, despite the diversity of their cultural origins, the imprint of American culture is unmistakable. Of course, the source of some movements actually lies in the United States. But even those which, like ISKCON, DLM and TM, originated in Asia have been transmitted to Europe via the United States. Scientology and COG/FOL are the two most prominent US inventions, but the other movements had all been cultivated to some extent in the United States before being trans-mitted to Europe (and elsewhere). (Nichiren Shoshu is something of an anomaly, since it is the overseas wing of a massive new religion of Japan, the Soka Gakkai (see White, 1970; Snow, 1976). It is largely directed from Japan, but the form of its overseas outreach is nevertheless heavily influenced by the experience gained in the early missions to the United States.)

Only the Rajneesh Foundation has successfully made the trans-ition from Asia to Western Europe without the mediation of the United States. This unusual pattern can be explained, first, in terms of its founder's slowness to respond to the advantages of encouraging the formation of centres for therapy and meditation outside India and, second, in terms of the fact that many Europeans had partici-pated in the ashrams originally founded in India by the Bhagwan Shree Rajneesh; on return to Europe, they therefore constituted a ready-made basis for the cultivation of their guru's particular styles of meditation and therapy. Only later did Rajneesh and his close associates take the step of transferring the centre of their movement's gravity to the United States — first in New Jersey and then in Oregon.

Hummel and Hardin have argued that the US influence on most NRMs originating in Asia 'worked against their chances of success' (1983: 23) in Europe. The commercialization and public relations methods, in combination with other adaptations designed specifically to meet the socio-cultural conditions of the United States, are cited as prime factors in reducing the appeal of such movements in Western Europe. (The Rajneesh movement is correctly perceived to be an anomaly in this respect.) But it is debatable whether US influences have been as counter-productive for Asian movements in general as Hummel and Hardin imply. Waldenfels (1981), for example, is more circumspect about this claim. Certainly, we should examine the consequences of these influences in more detail.

First, implantation in Europe of these NRMs was, in most cases, directed from the United States. The amount of unplanned, 'spontaneous' growth from the New to the Old World was small in comparison with the scale of planned expansion. Moreover, the implantation was managed and supervised by personnel who were either American or had been prepared for this task in the United States. The extent of leadership by 'indigenous' personnel is nowadays growing, but it varies considerably from movement to movement.

Second, the extent of material or decision-making autonomy enjoyed by European 'branches' of US dominated NRMs is variable, but in no case has any European branch permanently severed connections with its US 'parent' organization. On the contrary, the tendency appears to be for a closer integration of the European 'periphery' with the US 'centres', thereby reproducing the structure of the dominant economic and political relations between Western states.

Third, NRMs in Europe have followed the example set by their US counterparts in remaining separate from other groups or movements.[3] Each movement has recruited its own members and has retained them with varying degrees of success and in varying modes of affiliation. Exclusive and full-time commitment has, until recently, been the normal requirement for members of the UC, ISKCON, DLM and COG/FOL. It has been possible for the practitioners of Scientology, TM, Rajneesh and Nichiren Shoshu, however, to participate simultaneously in the activities of other religious and spiritual groups, although such eclecticism may not have been encouraged or welcomed. And, despite a small amount of mobility between NRMs, there is no sign that their boundaries are being weakened or supplanted by coalitions. It is only for the sake of mutual protection that some movements have made common cause on issues strictly limited to legal and/or publicity matters.

Finally, although in most NRMs there is a circulation of members (usually leaders) between groups in Europe as well as between European and US groups, it is only among the COG/FOL that the distinctively 'national' character of each European branch has been eroded. In no case has there been a policy of enticing European recruits to migrate permanently to the United States. On the other hand, some movements have provided members with the opportunity to travel widely throughout the world on business associated with creating new groups, sustaining existing groups and imposing a measure of cross-national uniformity on all groups. In this way, NRMs may be contributing towards distinctively cross-national cultures.

One of the intriguing questions raised by the US 'mediation' of so many NRMs originating in Asia is whether their development in Europe would, or could, have occurred in its absence. The political and cultural disturbances which occurred among European students in the 1960s, and the widespread popularity of the commune movement in the 1970s, seem to indicate that at least *some* European societies might also have sustained religious innovations among youth without US help. Indeed, studies of contemporary youth culture emphasize the relative creativity of youth in some European countries (see Martin, 1981; Hebdige, 1979; Hall and Jefferson, 1976). But it remains doubtful whether such indigenous religious growths would have prospered to the same extent unless the funds already generated by NRMs in the United States had been available.[4] In other words, Europe on its own may well have provided the occasion, but not the means, for the development of Asian NRMs.

In addition to sharing some features of the ethos of an earlier generation of US sects, today's NRMs also share with them a social status bordering on that of outcasts. This is especially notable in predominantly Catholic countries but is also true of Protestant countries where NRMs have generally enjoyed better fortunes. Another similarity concerns their organizational structure, which typically dispenses with clear-cut distinctions between laity and clergy.

On the other hand, today's NRMs display some sharp differences from their forebears. With the exception of Scientology, their intellectual orientation is less cognitive and more mystical; their economic bases are more diverse and innovative; they tend to depart more widely from mainstream Christian teachings; and their more or less simultaneous implantation in Europe was achieved more quickly and securely, although it is too early to judge whether their potential for growth in the long term will be greater. The most important difference lies, however, in their social composition.

Social composition of NRMs in Western Europe

In two major respects the social composition of today's NRMs differs from that of earlier sectarian groups originating in the United States. On the one hand, the age of the vast majority of members is lower, and on the other, their mode of belonging to the movements tends to be more exclusive of other commitments. A number of subsidiary implications follow from these major differences.

As in several other respects, however, it must be quickly pointed out that Scientology and the Rajneesh movement are partial exceptions to both generalizations. For, while the modal age of their members is probably in the mid-thirties, and not therefore very different from that of some earlier sectarian movements, the *range* of their ages is much wider. This is partly a function of the fact that Scientology has been operating in Europe since the early 1950s and that, consequently, some of its practitioners have aged beyond early adulthood. But another important consideration concerns the fact that the practice of both movements is more easily combined with the full round of 'normal' adult roles and statuses. As a result, Scientologists and followers of the Bhagwan, most of whom are recruited during their late twenties and thirties, find it less difficult than do their counterparts in some other movements to remain in membership through middle age.

The age of members in the other NRMs under consideration tends to fall within the range 20–35. This is certainly true for the overwhelming majority of recruits at the time of recruitment, but each movement is now beginning to acquire a growing number of older members who have remained active for ten years or more. There are grounds for believing that, since a large proportion of recruits leave their movements after only a year or two, a process of polarization between an ageing minority and a continually young, but changing, majority is setting in. If this indeed proves to be the case, it may have serious consequences for authority patterns and, in the longer term, for recruitment prospects. At the same time, of course, the increasing number of middle-aged members will generate more pressing needs for ways of integrating their children into the movements. In combination, then, age polarization, high turnover rates among young recruits and the growth of a generation of members' children will (and in some cases are already beginning to) put pressure on NRMs to modify some of their existing practices and dispositions. Evidence of this is clearly visible in ISKCON, the UC and the COG/FOL.

At present, however, the typical European members of NRMs other than Scientology and the Rajneesh group are white, unmarried, young adults who are slightly more likely to be male than female. As such, they may not differ greatly from the first generation of recruits to US sectarian movements such as the Seventh-Day Adventists, the Jehovah's Witnesses and the Christian Scientists, which began operating in Western Europe in the late nineteenth century. There is a major difference between them, however, in terms of social class and status. Their nineteenth-century predecessors were much more likely to have been drawn from working class or lower middle-class backgrounds characterized by manual or minor service occupations, elementary education and residence in rented accommodation. In contrast, in keeping with large-scale transformations of the economic structure of most Western societies and, in particular, with the proportional increase in the levels of education, material consumption, leisure time and property ownership, the recruits to today's NRMs are drawn typically from middle-class backgrounds (see Campbell, 1978).

The young adult members of NRMs in Europe (as in the United States) tend to have completed secondary education in school and to have had some exposure to further or higher education; they come from families enjoying material comforts and security; their prospects for entering well-paid professions or occupations are generally good at the time of recruitment; and they possess small amounts of personal property or cash savings. Many are accustomed to foreign travel and have been exposed to the influence of foreign cultures. An interest in fine arts and humanistic philosophies has often been cultivated at home and/or school. In short, their 'life chances' tend to be better than average. They are not, therefore, representative of their peers; and they certainly do not conform with the stereotype of recruits to the older wave of sectarian movements. Ironically, and in sharp contrast to the experience of nineteenth-century NRMs, it is their relatively *privileged* social background which has helped to place the members of today's NRMs at the centre of controversy in so many countries (Beckford, 1983a; 1985).

A close connection exists between the social composition of NRMs and the typical modes of participating in them. By no stretch of the imagination, for example, can they be termed 'congregational' religions. They do not offer religious services on a regular basis to any neighbourhood, nor do they provide them in the main for particular families. Rather, membership and participation are largely individual undertakings entered into by unattached young adults on a voluntary basis. Of course, intense relationships with other members may be formed within NRMs, but it is as individuals that most recruits are inducted. The number of family groups recruited as such to NRMs is much smaller than is the case for most other European religious groups. This has consequences for the rate and manner of defection and for the subsequent experiences of defectors (Beckford, 1985).

It is also worth noting that, to the best of our knowledge, no significant relations exist between any NRM and ethnic or national minorities. This is to say, no movement has managed to recruit disproportionately from such a source. There are signs to indicate, however, that ISKCON is beginning to attract sponsors, patrons and clients for its ritual services among urban Hindu populations in the UK (Carey, 1983). But they can hardly share the designation 'members' with the young native-born Europeans who adopt the monastic style of life. Rather, the growth of support from Hindu migrants to Europe reflects a fortuitous and mutually convenient accommodation between two different minorities.

Insertion in society
Given that the NRMs under consideration originate outside Europe and that their appeal has been very largely to a small segment of the population in any country, it is important to ask questions about their strategies for survival and expansion. How, for example, do they manage to maintain the work of disseminating their distinctive teachings? How do they manage to ensure the production and reproduction of the material necessities for this work? And, how are the movements' diverse activities related to those of other social institutions, official agencies and voluntary associations? For the sake of convenience, we shall refer to these, and allied, questions as aspects of the ways in which NRMs are 'inserted in society' (Beckford, 1985). Under this heading we shall consider the interrelatedness of their teachings, ideology, organization, social composition, material resources and treatment at the hands of outsiders.

Rather than typify or classify NRMs in terms of any particular mode of insertion in society, we shall describe three ideal-typical positions towards which movements have tended to gravitate. In practice, of course, NRMs may combine tendencies towards more than one ideal-type.

The refuge
In their different ways, reflecting different philosophies and experiences, movements such as ISKCON, the DLM and COG/FOL are inserted in their host societies in the form of a refuge. That is, they

offer and they reproduce a safe place (physically and intellectually) in which fully initiated members can feel secure from the evil and/or illusory character of life in the 'outside' world. Indeed, one of the features of this mode of insertion is the accentuation of all manner of boundaries separating the inner from the outer, the inside from the outside, the saved from the lost, the enlightened from the ignorant, etc. Salvation and enlightenment are held to be conditional upon the maintenance of these boundaries. Social and psychological mechanisms of insulation and isolation are employed to this end. At the same time, however, the social conditions in which the refuge can be effective have to be continually reproduced. Members are to be recruited; the message is to be disseminated; purity is to be preserved; and members are to be fed, sheltered and reinforced in their convictions and commitments.

ISKCON's mode of reproduction, for example, centres on the disciplined orientation of Temple-based communities towards the production and sale of religious goods and services to the public. In turn, personal contacts with the public and the literature that is disseminated serve as the main channel for attracting new members, supporters, clients, etc. Members of COG/FOL also display a more flexible and pragmatic pattern of small-group residence under the distant control of the founder/leader, David 'Moses' Berg, nowadays. They support themselves and their missionary work by a bewildering variety of strategies, including begging, selling literature, performing public entertainments, administering a regular system of tithing for members and supporters, radio broadcasting and acquiring property from wealthy recruits. Likewise, the DLM has changed its strategy more than once and is currently using a combination of residential ashrams and more loosely structured groups of non-resident members. Some residents are employed full-time in administering the movement's affairs, while others with 'outside' jobs contribute their salary to communal funds. The non-resident members are expected to offer financial support.

Reform
The primary characteristic of the reforming mode of insertion is the capacity or preparedness to bring distinctive teachings about the possibility of radical improvements to bear on existing socio-cultural structures. NRMs which have adopted this position include the UC, Scientology and Synanon.

The reforming strategy of the UC, for example, turns on the creation and sustenance of an exemplary 'hallowed universe' which, it is believed, can serve as the leaven of a regenerated societal order. It therefore involves some of the insulating and isolating mechanisms associated with the creation of a refuge. But, crucially, this is expected largely to serve the further purpose of facilitating appropriate changes in all social arrangements. The movement's intrinsically sacred character is matched by a sacred mission to inspire, by example, social transformation.

Scientology is a movement with an entirely different, and doubtless incompatible, ideology, but, like the UC, it has inserted itself in societies in such a way as to facilitate not only its internal development but also the application of its precepts and practices in all spheres of life. There is less inclination to establish an exemplary hallowed universe and more determination to infiltrate or influence existing groups and institutions with a view to reforming practices in accordance with Scientology's metaphysical foundation and psychosocial strategies.

What the UC and Scientology have in common is primarily a capacity to achieve their very different goals through the institutional structures of the wider society. Indeed, many of their activities appear to be designed to give them an entrée into, for example, education, organized religion, mental health and politics. In order to do this, a plethora of specialized branches and agencies may be formed; ambitious programmes of reform may be launched; and alliances may be struck with outside groups. As a result, such movements usually lead a far more public existence than do those tending towards the refuge position. One of the corollaries of this is that they develop a strong sensitivity towards the need for a good public image and for effective public relations.

The other side of this coin is that, in some countries, the search for 'social relevance' and active engagement in matters of public dispute lead some movements into frequent litigation, if not litigiousness. The strength of their legal departments is a fair indicator of the importance attached to a reforming influence on public life, regardless of doctrines which may suggest a strong degree of detachment from such things.

A further corollary of the tendency towards a reforming mode of social insertion is the diversification of their economic bases. They tend to rely heavily on enrolment of members as a source of income, and there may be a provision for the existence of communal elites. But at the same time, it is common practice to form extensive business operations in such fields as publishing, marketing, real estate and the sale of therapeutic services. Members are normally the sole operators of these businesses, although the services of specialized professionals may also be engaged as the occasion demands. This diversity of activity increases the likelihood of conflict with all kinds of state agencies for enforcing regulations and laws (see

Beckford, 1983b; 1985; Robbins, 1981; Kelley, 1982). It is also a cause for concern among private citizens and groups of anti-cultists.

Release
Some NRMs have adopted a mode of insertion in society which depends mainly upon the provision of a service to their clients. They offer to release people from conditions allegedly obstructing the full realization of their human potential. This entails diagnosing the source of the obstruction, identifying the resources for overcoming it and inculcating ways of achieving the desired release. These activities may be conducted through a variety of channels ranging from mail-order sales of literature and the mass-instruction of conference delegates, to the intensive cultivation of skills and sensitivities on residential courses. TM, Erhard Seminars Training (*est*), and the Rajneesh Foundation are currently the most visible NRMs offering a release service to clients in Western Europe, but a large number of smaller groups are also in operation. And some aspects of Scientology suggest that it tends towards combining the reform with the release mode of insertion. There are grounds for thinking that more people are active, though less visible, in movements offering release than in those offering refuge and reform (see Beckford, 1984).

Regardless of their particular teachings, movements which tend towards the release mode of insertion in society are organized in such a way as to produce a constant supply of clients. That is, the service must be efficiently marketed, and, if necessary, follow-up services must also be supplied. The organization is under pressure to remain open to new clients and to be able to supply a service of constant quality.

The distinction between staff members and clients (or members) is probably less sharp in this mode of social insertion than in the others because periods of work in the movement-organization are a common aspect of participation. That is, staff work may be required as a condition of participation in such communal activities as therapy sessions, meditation or retreats (as in the Rajneesh movement). Alternatively, it may be a practical way for members to earn enough money to pay for their continuing involvement in the movement (as in TM and Scientology). This flexibility and fluidity make movements offering a release service particularly attractive to young adults who wish to combine their religious and spiritual activities with jobs or courses of education in the outside world. Indeed, some of these movements aim to improve their participants' effectiveness in virtually any sphere of activity and are therefore perfectly compatible with the conduct of all kinds of careers.

Public response: the case of France
The capacity for growth of NRMs in Europe depends partly on their modes of 'insertion in society' and partly on the public responses that are thereby elicited. Public response reflects many complex factors and is an important aid to understanding the movements' varying fortunes in different countries. The broad outlines of public response in Britain, France and the Federal Republic of Germany have been discussed elsewhere (Beckford 1981; 1983a; 1983b; 1985; Hardin and Kehrer 1982). This section will focus in detail on the case of France and in particular on the French state's response to public pressure for more effective control over the activities of NRMs.

During the twenty years or more after the first of the present wave of NRMs took root in France, the state barely reacted officially to the problems that they posed, in spite of repeated complaints from groups such as the Association for the Defence of the Family and the Individual (ADFI) and in spite of pressure from public opinion and the mass media.

Before 1982 only one important measure had been taken, namely, the notification to Sun Myung Moon, leader of the Unification Church, that he was forbidden to reside on French soil. But in 1982 the new Socialist government decided, in view of the lack of 'objective' information on the subject, and in face of mounting pressure from the public, to ask a parliamentary 'député', Monsieur Alain Vivien, to conduct a fact-finding inquiry. His brief was to examine the problems posed by sects, as well as their legal and financial standing, and to suggest measures which would protect the freedom of association within sects while also preserving the basic freedoms of individuals.[5] The Vivien Report[6] was allegedly delivered in February 1983 but was not made public by the Minister of the Interior until 1985.

The report's aim was clear: the overriding concern was for information and not repression. There was no question of attacking sects but of simply clarifying their legal position in French society. Actually, there was a choice to be made. On the one hand, sects could be straightforward, non-profit associations under the law of 1901, which gives them the right to raise funds required for their operations but also imposes the obligation to be 'socially useful'. On the other hand, sects could declare that they are religions and must then seek the status of 'congregations', which could be granted to them following an inquiry by the Interior Ministry. The inquiry could require that they make their financial records open to inspection.

What the report seemed to want was for the sects to respect the existing law in its entirety — something that was apparently not being done. The nine proposals made by the Vivien Report all tend in this direction. Their explicit aim is to ask the state to see that the law is respected in order to preclude situations in which citizens would be tempted to take the law into their own hands.

1. The first proposal[7] is for the creation of an interministerial structure of co-ordination under the direction of a leading civil servant appointed by the Prime Minister. Since the phenomenon of sects is especially complex, all ministers would have to give thought to the problems in question. The Ministry of the Budget would be concerned with the openness to public inspection of the finances of NRMs and of their subsidiaries; the Interior Ministry, with the problem of whether NRMs would have the status of civil or cultural associations; the Ministries of Solidarity, Social Affairs and Labour, with respect to the laws on paid holidays and workers' rights; and the Ministry of Education with problems of schooling and of the private schools within the movements.

2. The second proposal is 'to issue warnings and impartial information about sects'. It is envisaged that, with the assistance of parents' associations, technical files would be drawn up on sects and on the progress of members. These files would be made available to social workers, teachers and parents' associations.

3. The third proposal is in favour of 'an open-minded laicity' in the schools. This arises from the separation of church and state, which has led to laicity within the educational system and has opened the way for a kind of neutrality on religious and philosophical issues which, in turn, threatens to produce a total ignorance about morality and philosophy among children. The moral and religious battlements must no longer be the preserve of sectarian groups. A way of teaching the Rights of Man in school must be worked out if children and young people are to have the moral and spiritual means of making choices.

4. The fourth proposal is 'to go beyond the nation's horizons'. This has to do with making it possible for associations which specialize in handling the NRM phenomenon across the world to get together and to exchange information. If the sects are international, it is only proper to organize thinking and co-ordinated action with other countries.

The idea of creating an international legal agency must be capable of preventing movements that are guilty of crimes and already under prosecution from simply turning to countries showing a better, warmer welcome.

5. The fifth proposal is connected with information for the public at large and, above all, with control over the mass media by means of the High Commission for Audio-Visual Communication. In this way, news items linked with sects should never be taken out of their context; i.e., they should not allow news to be turned into advertizing

material. This proposal includes the possibility of transmitting information and preventative broadcasts.

6. The sixth proposal is for 'mediation'. This concerns setting up regional organisms in the form of associations of volunteers from different backgrounds in order to assist relations between families and their children in NRMs and to prevent acts of violence like kidnapping children and deprogramming movement members. Among other things, these associations would be expected to become neutral places where a child would be sheltered from outside pressures and able to choose his or her own way of life. Another duty for this structure would be to follow the re-entry into society of those cultists who wanted to re-establish a social life for themselves.

7. The seventh proposal is to modify the rules of the social security system so that ex-members of sects would be covered.

8. The eighth proposal is to assist French people abroad by not leaving members who had left their home country entirely to their own devices if they wished to defect from an NRM and return home.

9. The ninth proposal is to assert the rights of children as human beings: they do not have to be the unconditional property of their 'cult family'. Another problem to be sorted out concerns children whose births in sectarian movements are not officially registered. (This is a frequent problem with the Children of God.) The child's right to schooling is reaffirmed in this proposal, as is the problem raised by the private schools within the sects which do not allow children to grow up with a capacity for making comparisons.

These are, then, what could be called the first reactions of one part of the French state to the problems of NRMs. In fact, however, NRMs do not present a clear danger to the state, nor have they ever sought to defy it. Bearing in mind the need to protect the freedom of thought, the government's task is not easy, and, as upholder of the constitution, the state cannot run the risk of being seen to be anti-constitutional.

The real opposition to sects in France lies with the families of members, with the anti-cult organizations such as ADFI and with the public opinion moulded by the mass media. The bipolarity of family and sect-family is symptomatic. On the one hand are the families, which claim to uphold order and the institutions of society, and on the other are groupings which replace them to the extent of calling themselves 'the new family'. This is a clash between two centripetal forces. In the wider society, families are considered to be the basic building-blocks because it is through them that traditions, laws and beliefs are transmitted, and they are necessary conditions of societal reproduction. Belonging to an NRM seems to imply both a rejection of the family and a questioning of its social role.

There can be no non-violent relations between families and NRMs. The family defines itself as the victim of an attempt to misappropriate one of its offspring intended to keep the wider society going. Its role is to invest in education and thereby to reproduce a whole cultural system of which it is a trustee. By rejecting this role of link in a genealogical family, the sect member rejects the investment made in him or her and, as a result, in the family as well. Public opinion cannot understand this attitude, so it can only talk in terms of abductions, black magic and brainwashing. It all has to do with the abduction of minors; and families have met it with equal violence, as kidnappings and deprogrammings have shown. The cry of families is, 'Is the state willing to protect families?' This seems to be the nub of the matter in France, and it raises interesting questions about the actual role of the family in the reproduction of institutions today.

Conclusion

NRMs have been a recurrent feature of European cultures and societies. A suspicious or hostile public response to them has also been common. But today's NRMs present several features which distinguish their situation from that of their predecessors.

The fact that a number of ostensibly similar movements developed at roughly the same time, were exported from the same country and attracted followers from the same narrow social stratum, created the widespread impression that they amounted to an organized conspiracy against traditional values and social institutions. The public response to recent NRMs in Europe has therefore been unusually uniform and co-ordinated (see Beckford, 1981; 1983a; 1985; Hardin and Kehrer, 1982).

Indeed, in 1984 a report to the European Parliament from its Committee on Youth, Culture, Education, Information and Sport on 'the activity of certain new religious movements within the European Community'[8] actually proposed that member state governments should exchange information and co-ordinate their policies for dealing with the problems generated by NRMs. Its rapporteur, Richard Cottrell, MEP for Bristol, encouraged governments and other competent authorities to adopt a uniform 'voluntary code' in terms of which NRMs would be encouraged, among other things, to deter people under 18 from making vows of long-term commitments; to allow a probationary period of not less than six months; to guarantee access to members by their family and friends; to urge recruits to complete courses of education or training; to publish full financial accounts; to avoid deceptive means of recruitment; and to refrain from recruiting young people while they are in foreign countries.

Following publication of the draft report in August 1983, various organizations lobbied for its rejection. In particular, the Conseil de la Fédération Protestante de France wrote to every member of the European Parliament pointing out that religious freedom was indivisible; that it was impossible to locate a clear dividing line between Churches and 'sects'; and that problems associated with NRMs could be handled satisfactorily within the terms of laws already existing in each member country. These views were repeated in a similar letter written by the General Secretary of the Executive Committee of the British Council of Churches. And a sub-committee of the Second Chamber of the Dutch Parliament warned the European Parliament that its own investigation of NRMs,[9] which eventually appeared in June 1984, would not support Cottrell's interpretations and proposals. Caution and moderation were urged on MEPs. Yet, the report was accepted with many amendments[10] after a debate on 22 May 1984: 98 votes were cast in favour, 28 against, with 27 abstentions.

There are grounds for believing that the long-term socio-cultural significance of today's NRMs lies less in their intended contributions to religious and spiritual life than in the unintended consequences of their activities for the clarification of the limits of toleration. For, partly through litigation and partly through public controversies, NRMs are helping to define the practical boundaries of acceptable and unacceptable conduct in a supposedly secular age. The fact that some of them profess no interest in the affairs of this world is immaterial in this respect. It is simply an irony of their position: spiritual renunciation inadvertently clarifies the unwritten criteria of social acceptability.

At the same time, the controversial NRMs are also helping to trace the limits of state involvement in the control of religion (see Beckford, 1983b). Official agencies of numerous European states have been caught in the cross-fire between the critics and the defenders of NRMs. The states' dilemma stems partly from the fact that some of the movements represent forms of religiosity which were not envisaged when existing laws and statutes regarding religion were enacted. They therefore challenge prevailing definitions of religion for legal purposes. Another aspect of the states' dilemma concerns the extent to which their responsibility for the welfare of citizens extends into the sphere of religiously motivated conduct. The practices of some NRMs run counter to the patterns of social life favoured by the policies of welfare states, especially in the fields of family relations and child-rearing. Finally, some NRMs cause embarrassment to states by taking an active part in politics and/or profit-making businesses. Fiscal systems and, in some cases, historic arrangements of church–state relations are thereby confronted with phenomena which are seen to threaten the traditional patterns. The relative insignificance of NRMs in Europe in terms of the number of their adherents should not, therefore, be allowed to obscure the importance of the probably unintended challenges that they represent for prevailing notions of 'normal' or 'acceptable' conduct and of defensible attempts by states to control the affairs of religious groups. The fate of NRMs may be taken as an interesting indicator of social changes taking place in the structure of European societies.

Notes

1. The complexity of the definitional problems is increased when it is borne in mind that in some languages other than English the groups nominated above as 'NRMs' may be designated quite differently. In French, for example, they may be called 'new religious sects' or simply 'sects', thereby reproducing an age-old practice of distinguishing between the dominant Catholic institutions and smaller, separatist groups. This tendency to take for granted the Catholic hegemony can even lead to a conceptual opposition between 'sect' and 'religion' *tout court* (see Morelli, 1983). In German and Dutch, on the other hand, the youthfulness of participants in NRMs is emphasized in terms meaning 'youth religions' or 'youth sects'. Waldenfels (1981) and Hardin (1983) discuss these terminological subtleties at greater length.

2. Hardin (1983) has pointed out that in West Germany there seems to be an official consensus that only eight movements qualify as 'youth sects'. They are TM, Ananda Marga, UC, ISKCON, COG/FOL, Scientology, Rajneesh and DLM.

3. A partial exception must be made for attempts by the UC and COG/FOL to infiltrate, and take over, existing religious groups as a tactic for making swift progress in recruitment: see, for example, Hardin and Kuner (1981: 134). The tactic seems never to have been successful.

4. Hardin and Kuner (1981: 130–1), for example, document the reliance of Moonies in Germany on funds from the United States for the expansion of missionary work.

5. Letter of authorization for the inquiry from the Prime Minister, Monsieur Pierre Mauroy, to Alain Vivien, Député for the Hauts de Seine constituency.

6. *Les Sectes en France: Expression de la Liberté morale ou Facteurs de Manipulations?* Delivered to the Assemblée Nationale on 9 April 1985.

7. The following information about Alain Vivien's proposals is not the verbatim text of his report; it merely summarizes its contents in the form in which they were leaked to the public over a two-year period and which turned out to be faithful to the report in its published form.

8. The final report is dated 22 March 1984 and bears the reference PE 82.322/fin.

9. 'Overheid en nieuwe religieuze bewegingen' (Tweede Kamer, vergaderjaar 1983–1984, 16 635, no. 4). This report of a subcommittee of the Dutch Parliament's Committee on Public Health earned a doctorate of law for the chief investigator, Tobias Witeveen.

10. The title of the Resolution, as passed by the European Parliament, was amended to: 'Resolution on a common approach by the Member States of the European

Community towards various infringements of the law by the new organizations operating under the protection afforded to religious bodies'. For the text of the debate, see *Official Journal of the European Communities. Debates of the European Parliament*, 22 May 1984, no. 1-314/34-74: 114–16. For the amendments and the Resolution, see *Official Journal of the European Communities*, C Series, 2 July 1984, no. C 172/40-43.

References

Arrington, L. J. and D. Bitton (1979) *The Mormon Experience*. London: Allen & Unwin.

Bainbridge, W. S. and D. H. Jackson (1981) 'The Rise and Decline of Transcendental Meditation', pp. 135–58 in Bryan R. Wilson (ed.), *The Social Impact of New Religious Movements*. New York: Rose of Sharon Press.

Barker, Eileen V. (1978) 'Living the Divine Principle: Inside the Reverend Moon's Church in Britain', *Archives de sciences sociales des religions* (Paris), 45(1), 75–93.

—— (1981) 'Who'd be a Moonie?', pp. 59–96 in Bryan R. Wilson (ed.), *The Social Impact of New Religious Movements*. New York: Rose of Sharon Press.

—— (ed.) (1982) *New Religious Movements: A Perspective for Understanding Society*. New York and Toronto: Edwin Mellen Press.

—— (1984) *Becoming a Moonie*. Oxford: Basil Blackwell.

Beckford, James A. (1975a) *The Trumpet of Prophecy. A Sociological Analysis of Jehovah's Witnesses*. Oxford: Basil Blackwell.

—— (1975b) 'Organization, Ideology and Recruitment: The Structure of the Watchtower Movement', *Sociological Review* (Keele), 23(4), 893–909.

—— (1981) 'Cults, Controversy and Control: A Comparative Analysis of the Problems Posed by New Religious Movements in the Federal Republic of Germany and France', *Sociological Analysis* (Connecticut), 42(3), 249–64.

—— (1983a) 'The Public Response to New Religious Movements in Britain', *Social Compass* (Louvain), 30(1), 49–62.

—— (1983b) 'The State and Control of New Religious Movements', *Acts of the 17th International Conference for the Sociology of Religion*. London: CISR.

—— (1984) 'Holistic Imagery and Ethics in New Religious and Healing Movements', *Social Compass* (Louvain), 31(2–3), 259–72.

—— 1985 *Cult Controversies. The Societal Response to New Religious Movements*. London: Tavistock Publications.

—— and James T. Richardson (1983) 'A Bibliography of Social Scientific Studies of New Religious Movements', *Social Compass* (Louvain), 30(1), 111–35.

Berger, H. and P. Hexel, (1981) *Ursachen und Wirkungen gesellschaftlicher Verweigerung junger Menschen unter besonderer Berücksichtigung der 'Jugendreligionen'*. Vienna: European Centre for Social Welfare and Research.

Bromley, D. G. and A. D. Shupe, Jr (1979) *The Moonies in America*. Beverly Hills: Sage.

Campbell, Colin B. (1978) 'The Secret Religion of the Educated Classes', *Sociological Analysis* (Connecticut), 39(2), 146–56.

Carey, Seán (1983) 'The Hare Krishna Movement and Hindus in Britain', *New Community* (London), 10(3), 477–86.

Daner, Francine (1976) *The American Children of Krisna. A Study of the Hare Krisna Movement*. New York: Holt, Rinehart & Winston.

Davis, Rex and James T. Richardson (1976) 'The Organization and Functioning of the Children of God', *Sociological Analysis* (Connecticut), 37(4), 320–41.

Derks, Frans (1980) 'Differences in Social Isolation between Members of Two New Religious Movements, in *Proceedings of the Colloquy of European Psychologists of Religion*. Nijmegen: University of Nijmegen.

Downton, James V., Jr (1979) *Sacred Journeys: The Conversion of Young Americans to Divine Light Mission*. New York: Columbia University Press.

Eliade, Mircea (1969) *Initiations, rites et sociétés secrètes*. Paris: Gallimard.

Forem, Jack (1973) *Transcendental Meditation*. New York: Dutton.

Foss, D. and R. Larkin (1976) 'From "The Gates of Eden" to "Day of the Locust": An Analysis of the Dissident Youth Movement of the 1960s and Its Heirs in the 1970s — the Post-movement Groups', *Theory and Society* (Amsterdam), 3, 45–64.

Haack, Friedrich-Wilhelm (1979) *Jugendreligionen. Ursachen, Trends, Reaktionen*. Munich: Claudius Verlag.

Hall, Stuart and Tony Jefferson (eds) (1976) *Resistance through Rituals. Youth Subcultures in Post-war Britain*. London: Hutchinson.

Hardin, Bert (1983) 'Quelques aspects du phénomène des nouveaux mouvements religieux en République Fédérale d'Allemagne', *Social Compass* (Louvain), 30(1), 13–32.

—— and Günter Kehrer (1982) 'Some Social Factors affecting the Rejection of New Belief Systems', pp. 267–83 in Eileen V. Barker (ed.), *New Religious Movements: A Perspective for Understanding Society*. New York: Edwin Mellen Press.

—— and Wolfgang Kuner (1981) 'Entstehung und Entwicklung der Vereinigungskirche in der Bundesrepublik Deutschland' pp. 129–70 in Günter Kehrer (ed.), *Das Entstehen einer neuen Religion: das Beispiel der Vereinigungskirche*. Munich: Kosel Verlag.

Hashimoto, Hideo and William McPherson (1976) 'Rise and Decline of Soka Gakkai, Japan and the United States', *Review of Religious Research* (New York), 17(2), 82–92.

Hebdige, Dick (1979) *Subculture. The Meaning of Style*. London: Methuen.

Hummel, Reinhart and Bert Hardin (1983) 'Asiatic Religions in Europe', *Concilium* (Paris), 181, 23–8.

Judah, J. Stillson (1974) *Hare Krishna and the Counterculture*. New York: John Wiley.

Kehrer, Günter (ed.) (1981) *Das Entstehen einer neuen Religion: das Beispiel der Vereinigungskirche*. Munich: Kosel Verlag.

Kelley, Dean M. (ed.) (1982) *Government Intervention in Religious Affairs*. New York: Pilgrim Press.

Keniston, Kenneth (1963) 'Social Change and Youth in America', in E. Erikson (ed.), *Youth, Change and Challenge*. New York: Basic Books.

Lasch, Christopher (1984) *The Minimal Self. Psychic Survival in Troubled Times*. New York: W. W. Norton.

Léger, Danièle and Bertrand Hervieu (1983) *Des communautés pour les temps difficiles*. Paris: Le Centurion.

Levasseur, Martine (1985) *Ethnographie d'une secte: l'Association internationale pour la Conscience de Krishna*. Paris: Editions Lidis.

Mannheim, Karl (1952) 'Sociological Problems of Generations', in P. Kecskemeti (ed.), *Essays on the Sociology of Knowledge*. London: Routledge & Kegan Paul.

Martin, Bernice (1981) *A Sociology of Contemporary Cultural Change*. Oxford: Basil Blackwell.

Mildenberger, Michael (1979) *Die religiöse Revolte. Jugend zwischen Flucht und Aufbruch*. Frankfurt am Main: Fischer Verlag.

Morelli, Anne (1983) 'A propos des sectes religieuses en Belgique. Les recherches à l'Université de Bruxelles', *Social Compass* (Louvain), 30(1), 137–41.

Pilarzyk, T. (1978) 'Conversion and Alternation Processes in the Youth Culture', *Pacific Sociological Review* (Eugene, Oregon), 21(4), 379–405.

Price, Maeve (1979) 'The Divine Light Mission as a Social Organization', *Sociological Review* (Keele), 27(2), 279–96.

Robbins, Thomas (1981) 'Church, State and Cult', *Sociological Analysis* (Connecticut), 43(3) 209–26.

—— and Dick Anthony (1972) 'Getting Straight with Meher Baba: A Study of Drug-Rehabilitation, Mysticism and Post-Adolescent Role-Conflict', *Journal for the Scientific Study of Religion* (Connecticut), 11(2), 122–40.

Rochford, Burke, Jr (1982) 'Recruitment Strategies, Ideology, and Organization in the Hare Krishna Movement', *Social Problems*, 29(4) 399–410.

Smith, David (1976) 'The Concept of Youth Culture. A Re-evaluation', *Youth and Society* (Beverly Hills), 7(4), 347–66.

Snow, David A. (1976) 'The Nichiren Shoshu Buddhist Movement in America: A Sociological Examination of its Value Orientation, Recruitment Efforts, and Spread'. Unpublished PhD dissertation, University of California at Los Angeles.

Straus, Roger (1976) 'Changing Oneself: Seekers and the Creative Transformation of Life Experience', pp. 252–73 in John Lofland (ed.), *Doing Social Life*. New York: John Wiley.

Tipton, Steven (1982) *Getting Saved from the Sixties*. Berkeley: University of California Press.

Universitätsbibliothek Tübingen (1981) *Neuerwerbungen: Theologie und allgemeine Religionswissenschaft. Sondernummer: 'Neue religiöse Bewegungen'* (*'Jugendreligionen'*). Tübingen: University of Tübingen.

Waldenfels, Hans (1981) 'Zur Entwicklung und Beurteilung der neureligiösen Bewegungen in der Bundesrepublik Deutschland', *Zeitschrift für Missionswissenschaft und Religionswissenschaft*, 65(2), 103–20.

Wallis, Roy (1976a) *The Road to Total Freedom. A Sociological Analysis of Scientology*. London: Heinemann.

—— (1976b) 'Observations on the Children of God', *Sociological Review* (Keele), 24(4), 807–29.

—— (1981) 'Yesterday's Children: Cultural and Structural Changes in a New Religious Movement', pp. 97–132 in Bryan R. Wilson (ed.), *The Social Impact of New Religious Movements*. New York: Rose of Sharon Press.

—— (1984) *The Elementary Forms of the New Religious Life*. London: Routledge & Kegan Paul.

White, James R. (1970) *The Soka Gakkai and Mass Society*. Stanford: Stanford University Press.

Whitehead, Harriet (1974) 'Reasonably Fantastic: Some Perspectives on Scientology, Science Fiction and Occultism', pp. 547–87 in Irving Zaretsky and Mark Leone (eds), *Religious Movements in Contemporary America*. Princeton: Princeton University Press.

Wilson, Bryan R. (1961) *Sects and Society*. London: Heinemann.

—— (1975) 'American Religious Sects in Europe', pp. 107–22 in C. W. E. Bigsby (ed.), *Superculture: American Popular Culture and Europe*. London: Paul Elek.

—— (ed.) (1967) *Patterns of Sectarianism*. London: Heinemann.

—— (ed.) (1981a) *The Social Impact of New Religious Movements*. New York: Rose of Sharon Press.

—— (1981b)   'Time, Generation and Sectarianism', pp. 217–34 in Bryan R. Wilson (ed.), *The Social Impact of New Religious Movements*. New York: Rose of Sharon Press.

Woodrow, Alain (1977)   *Les nouvelles sectes*. Paris: Seuil.

Yinger, J. Milton (1960)   'Contraculture and Subculture', *American Sociological Review*, 25, 625–35.

Zald, M.N. and R. Ash (1966)   'Social Movement Organizations: Growth, Decay and Change', *Social Forces* (Chapel Hill), 44, 327–41.

3
The development of millennialistic thought in Japan's new religions: from Tenrikyō to Honmichi

*Susumu Shimazono**

If a new religious movement is to have millennialistic ideas,[1] one or both of the following conditions must be met: (1) traditions of millennialistic ideas must already exist or be imported; and (2) a millennialistic worldview must be created. The first condition can be broken down into various levels. On the least systematized level, vague and amorphous images of catastrophes or ideal states of affairs exist, such as a big flood or an abundant harvest. They are found in folklore and are called *yonaori* (world renewal) in Japan.[2] At the opposite pole, there are highly refined and systematized traditions concerning the ultimate state of the world, based on articulated views of history and mankind. The millennialistic ideas of new religious movements are largely derived from these highly systematized millennialistic traditions. However, when these traditions do not exist or are weak, what is the source and salience of millennialism in new religious movements? They seem to inherit vague and amorphous millennialistic images from folklore, thus fulfilling the second condition for the formation of millennialism, that is, a millennialistic worldview. In large part, this worldview directly or indirectly reflects rapid social change.

Among Japan's new religions dating from the middle of the nineteenth century, we can find several groups which have a millennialistic inclination. Well-known examples are Tenrikyō, Maruyamakyō, Ōmoto, Soka Gakkai and Honmichi, a schism from Tenrikyō. The millennialistic ideas of these groups are heterogeneous and, generally speaking, unorganized.[3] This is because there is no firm tradition of systematic millennialism in Japan. In the earlier movements such as Tenrikyō and Maruyamakyō, in particular, millennialism is vague and amorphous, largely reflecting their perception of changing situations. In these groups, moreover, there is no messianism, and the founder or foundress is worshipped merely as a living *kami* (god), not as a divine king or queen. But the circumstances of the later movements are

---

* I am greatly indebted to Michael Newton for reading the first draft of this chapter and offering suggestions for its improvement.

different. Traditions of millennialistic ideas preceded them even though they had not been articulated in the forms previously developed by other new religions. The millennialism of the new movements was nevertheless based on these foundations. In some cases systematic millennialistic ideas were eventually formed, as happened in Honmichi. This is a rare case in which an indigenous messianism was also created. In this chapter I shall investigate how amorphous millennialism developed into systematic millennialism in conjunction with messianism in the course of the transformation of Tenrikyō into Honmichi.[4]

An important condition for the formation of millennialism is a millennialistic worldview which can be seen in part as a reaction to rapid social change. Before millennialism is established as a system of thought, millennialistic ideas depend largely on this type of worldview. In order to elucidate the contents of millennialistic ideas in Tenrikyō and early Honmichi, it is therefore necessary to analyse how these ideas reflected believers' worldviews at different historical junctures. I shall describe the believers' worldviews in the following three ways:

(a) Perception of the total society, that is, how they perceive the society with which they believe they share a common destiny (mankind, nation, tribe, etc.). This will be called 'perception of the societal situation'. For example, when the societal situation is perceived as dangerous, believers expect some supernatural power to overcome the crisis, and millennialism is likely to develop with this expectation.

(b) Perception of the movement itself, that is, how they perceive the situation of their own movement or group which is believed to embody the earthly manifestation of supernatural power. This will be called 'perception of the group's situation'. For example, when a movement spreads very fast, and various miracles are believed to be changing the destiny of many believers, it is likely that members will also expect transformations of the whole society.

(c) Perception of the relationship between a movement and the wider society (government, police, mass media, established religions, etc.). This will be called 'perception of the relational position'. For example, when a movement is persecuted, the persecution is recognized as a symptom of the confrontation between god and some evil power, and there is an expectation of an imminent catastrophe as a result.

In the following sections, the histories of Tenrikyō and Honmichi in their early phases are first sketched, and then the processes whereby the millennialistic ideas in each group were formed and transformed are analysed.[5]

The formation of Tenrikyō
Tenrikyō[6] was founded by Nakayama Miki (1798–1887), the wife of a farmer in Yamato province. She was born in Sanmaiden village (now part of Tenri City), the daughter of a rich farmer. At the age of 13[7] she was married to Nakayama Zenbei, the first son of a rich farmer in Shōyashiki village (now another part of Tenri City). Miki's religious career began when she was 40 years old. In the autumn of 1837 her only son Shūji, then 17, developed a severe pain in his leg when working in the fields and could not work any more. Miki, very anxious about her son's illness, asked a *yamabushi* (mountain ascetic) called Nakano Ichibei to offer prayers for Shūji. This seems to have been effective initially, and Miki eventually became a devout believer of Ichibei's cult. However, Shūji's pain recurred again and again, and it became evident that the disease could not be cured easily. A year after the onset of the illness, Ichibei was invited to the Nakayamas' house, and a shamanistic ritual was performed to cure Shūji's recurrent problem. In the ritual Miki insisted that she was possessed by the original and genuine God (*moto no kami, jitsu no kami*), later called Tenri-Ō-no-Mikoto, God the Parent, or Tsuki-Hi (Moon and Sun). After three days of violent and continuous possession, Miki believed that she had become the 'Shrine of God' with a great mission to save mankind.

According to Tenrikyō doctrine, the last day of her possession was the beginning of the new religion, Tenrikyō. Members believe that from that day on the Creator came to earth and revealed His will directly to mankind. In fact, however, Miki's belief was not recognized by anybody for more than ten years and was regarded as a kind of madness which would lead the family to ruin. It was not until 1862, when Miki was 65 years old, that believers began to form a group.

As the number of members increased, the group gradually became an organized body with its own identity. First, a system called *sazuke* was initiated. This was a system for giving devout believers the capacity to reveal God's will or perform magical prayers. Only a few people were ever qualified to reveal God's will, and after about 1870 only the latter qualification was bestowed. Eventually the term *sazuke* came to mean the magical prayers themselves.

Between 1866 and 1867 the first scripture in a 'counting song' style, Mikagura-uta, was composed. In a mild and pleasant tone reflecting the folk songs of those days, the believers were instructed in daily practices and attitudes. Then a ritual called *tsutome*, which consists of dances, gestures and the chanting of Mikagura-uta, was developed. Later, *tsutome* became the central practice of the religion. Moreover, some people called *toritsugi* began to take on the role of giving instruction to those who visited Miki for the first time. Their teachings formed a set of doctrines which later became the practical part of Tenrikyō's doctrinal system.

The contents of these initial doctrines are as follows. Human beings are children of God the Parent for they were created by Him (or Her). The world is the body of God, and human bodies are lent to men by God. Only the mind belongs to each person, and when he (or she) uses it incorrectly, *hokori* (dust) piles up around it. This dust is the cause of disease and of other misfortunes. Dust, or misuse of the mind, is of eight kinds: miserliness, covetousness, hatred, self-love, enmity, anger, avarice and arrogance. Men can stop piling up dust by turning their minds to God and getting rid of the dust which has already collected by reflecting on themselves (*sange*), by practising *tsutome* and service work (*hinokishin*), and by proselytizing (*nioigake*). It was taught that diseases would then be cured and other misfortunes would vanish. Man does not experience life on earth only once, but is reborn again and again. Thus, dust piled up in one lifetime influences the next life. This connection is called *in'nen* (cause and effect). If diseases or misfortunes afflict a life lived in virtue, it is because of the *in'nen* from a previous life (or lives). One should, and can, get rid of this by more self-reflection and religious practice than is strictly necessary for removing the dust accumulated in one's present life.

Beginning in 1869, the second year of the Meiji Restoration, Miki started writing a new scripture named Ofudesaki and she continued writing it intermittently until 1882. It is written in *tanka* (a traditional Japanese poem of 31 syllables) style. Because Miki wrote these verses when possessed by God, the scripture is full of God's words expressed in the first person and is not a systematic statement of doctrine; rather, it reveals God's will concerning concrete problems of the present moment. It is often difficult to know what is meant, however, for the expression tends to be vague and allusive.

One type of situation which is covered in Ofudesaki is when the movement is oppressed and interfered with from the outside. Oppression and interference directed towards the community of believers surrounding Miki gradually increased as the group grew bigger and as the administrative system of the Meiji government became firmly established. In 1874 the Nara prefectural government and the Nara Middle Teaching Academy (the local office for propagating Tennoist and Shintoist ideology through all the religious bodies) interfered in Tenri's activities. The following year the police also began to interfere. Miki was arrested nine times before her death. Miki's God spoke with fierce indignation against this interference and oppression.

Meanwhile, Shūji and other leading believers sought approval for their activities from the authorities by getting a licence for a public bath, registering as a suborganization of a traditional Buddhist temple, and so on. Miki, regarding these efforts as unfaithful compromises, issued strong warnings against them. Nor was this the only instance of such warnings, for she also warned throughout most of the Ofudesaki against the irreligious actions and attitudes of those around her. In her opinion, the followers were motivated too much by worldly concerns and too little by faith in God. She suggested that there was great hope for the future and implored them to mend their ways and deepen their faith.

Miki believed that the most fundamental doctrine of her religion was the story of the creation and the growth of mankind (it can be called the 'Heilsgeschichte' of Tenrikyō). Although part of it is also alluded to briefly in the Ofudesaki, she created another scripture called the Kōki, or the Doroumi-kōki, in order systematically to state the myth in full detail. She told the story to some educated believers and dictated it to them several times between 1881 and 1887, leaving several variations. The outline of the story is as follows. 'Originally, this world was an immense expanse of muddy waters. Tsuki-Hi, God the Parent, found this chaotic condition unbearably tasteless and thought of creating human beings so that He might share their joy by seeing their *yōkigurashi* (joyous life).' (Tenrikyō Church Headquarters, 1972a: 25) He therefore chose nine aquatic animals as materials for creating human beings. From these materials 999,999 (or 900,099,999) human foetuses were created and delivered to the place where the house of the Nakayama family stood. Eight of those nine aquatic animals were also gods, and so the original God was simultaneously conceived of in three ways: as one, God the Parent; as two, Tsuki-Hi (Moon and Sun); and as ten, two plus eight. The ten gods each protect various functions of the human body, representing the sun, the moon and the stars, and they are also the substance of popular gods, buddhas and bodhisattvas.

The foetuses were then born in various places which had not yet been formed as land in the Yamato area and throughout Japan. At first they grew to only three inches in height and then died. But as they were reborn several times they grew to five feet in height. Meanwhile, the whole world — heaven and earth, land and sea — was formed, and mankind began to dwell on land. Those who were originally born in Yamato lived in Japan, while others lived in other countries. By this time 990,000 (or 900,090,000) years had passed. During the further period of 9,999 years God indirectly gave mankind various cultures. Following this period of preparatory education, in accordance with the original promise, God descended to earth and started Tenrikyō. It was believed that the *kanrodai* (nectar stand) would be built at the place of human creation, and that, by taking the nectar (*kanro*) which would fall on it, men could live their full span of life, that is, up to 115 years. The *kanrodai* would be made of 13 hexagonal stones piled up about eight feet high. After the first model of the *kanrodai* was constructed in 1873, the location of the true *kanrodai* was determined in 1875. Miki walked around the garden of her house, and when her feet stopped as if attracted by the earth she believed she had found the place of human creation. In 1881 the bottom two pieces of the genuine *kanrodai* were made and erected, but the next year the local police removed and confiscated them. After that incident Miki did not order the making of the genuine *kanrodai*. After her death another wooden model was constructed, and now the third one stands at the centre of the shrine of the Tenrikyō Church Headquarters. Every month a mask dance symbolizing human creation (*kagura zutome*) is performed around this model *kanrodai*.

As the group grew larger, Miki came to be worshipped as the sole 'Living God', representing God's will on earth (see Shimazono, 1979, 1981). The members believed that all important problems should be resolved in accordance with her divine will. There were also occasions, however, when someone substituted for her in relating God's will to the believers. For a while Miki's fifth daughter Kokan played this role most frequently, but in Miki's last years Iburi Izō (1833–1907), one of the earliest followers, monopolized it. After Miki's death in 1887, this role became very important. Izō then became the spiritual leader of the whole group. As *tenkeisha* (the revealed one), he was the sole person to mediate God's will to mankind. He also monopolized the role of conferring *sazuke* on the believers and was called *honseki* (the true seat). On the other hand, the leader of the group's secular aspects was called *shimbashira* (the central pillar) or *kanchō* (superintendent). Makayama Shin'nosuke (1866–1944), a son of Miki's third daughter, who had been adopted into Miki's family, performed this role. Thus there were two complementary leaders in Tenrikyō at this time. During Izō's 20-year period as the *honseki* the group grew so rapidly that, according to one source, the number of believers reached about 1,242,000 by 1907 (Tenrikyō Dōyūsha, 1929).

Izō's revelations were collected by others and called the Osashizu. The Osashizu are of two kinds: '*sashizu* for questions', giving answers to concrete questions about troubles with the authorities, permission for opening branch churches and so on; and '*sashizu* of the fixed time', delivered at a special hour of the night, giving directions about what the faithful should believe and how they should act. Like the

Ofudesaki, the Osashizu does not give a systematic presentation of the doctrine and is for the most part vague and allusive, although some passages touch on fundamental problems of doctrine. One such important problem is how to explain the death of the Foundress. Miki died when she was 90 years old, although she herself had forecast that she would live to be 115. There had to be an explanation, therefore, for her premature death. Izō's answer in the Osashizu is in two parts: (1) she died early because she loved her 'children' (men), and (2) she would live in her 'house', that is, in the Headquarters' shrine, and continue to work in the world. This doctrine is called 'the doctrine of the Foundress's further life' (*zonmei no ri*). Though it did not answer the question completely, it did greatly mitigate the shock caused to the believers by her death.

One of the consequences of this answer was that the role of Izō himself was limited to a certain extent; for, according to this doctrine, it is still the Foundress who mediates God's power and will on earth, and Izō is only her proxy. Since the organizational management of the Church was basically in the hands of the superintendent and other leading believers, Izō's role was confined to correcting their decisions from the spiritual viewpoint. 'The doctrine of the Foundress's further life' and this limitation on Izō's power are closely related to each other.

Izō played his corrective role most effectively in connection with the problem of how to cope with public authorities. There had been, as we saw earlier, a lot of oppression and interference by public authorities during Miki's lifetime. In 1888, a year after her death, the group received official approval as Shintō Tenri Kyōkai, albeit in the unsatisfactory form of being assigned to Shintō Honkyoku, one of the Shintō sects (*kyōha shintō*) embracing miscellaneous religious groups. Oppression and interference did not stop, however, and as the organization spread rapidly throughout the whole country, the government in 1896 issued an order limiting Tenrikyō's activities (the so-called 'secret official order of the Ministry of Home Affairs'), which caused local Tenrikyō organizations considerable trouble. The leading believers took various measures to stop or mitigate the problem, and from 1899 onwards their efforts were concentrated on getting official approval as an *independent* Shintō sect. The way to gain approval often involved doctrinal changes and restrictions on activities. Izō handled such measures from the spiritual viewpoint, but when tension arose between secular logic and religious logic, Miki stuck to religious logic and did not permit compromises. Izō, on the other hand, suggesting religious logic, sometimes did permit compromises. The Ofudesaki was filled with the sense of tension between God's will and men's worldly thinking, but in the Osashizu, even though the tension was still an important theme, its character was somewhat softened.

Izō died in 1907, and the status of *honseki* was handed over to Ueda Naraito (1863-1937). But she could not live up to her leadership role in the Church as 'the revealed one', and in 1918 even the role of conferring *sazuke* was transferred to Nakayama Shin'nosuke's wife Tamae. Since then, the position of the highest authority of the Church has been monopolized by the head of the Nakayama family. Meanwhile the government gave official approval to Tenrikyō as an independent sect in 1908, and the tension between the group and the wider society was greatly reduced (Tenrikyō Dōyūsha, 1929).[8]

The formation of Honmichi
Honmichi[9] was founded by a Tenrikyō missionary, Ōnishi Aijirō (1881-1958). Aijirō was the third son of Kishioka, a farmer in Uda village in Nara Prefecture. The Kishioka family had been rich farmers of high standing in the Tokugawa period, but by the time Aijirō was born they had lost a lot of their land and had sunk to the status of middle-class farmers. Since the third son could not inherit the family's lands, and since Aijirō had a talent for learning, he became an elementary school teacher. In 1899, when he was 19 years old, he entered the Nara Prefecture Normal School in order to gain a higher qualification while living in Nara City as a boarding student.

About this time the Kishioka family fell victim to some unfortunate events. In 1897, after the second son's serious hypochondria, the first son, Sentarō, developed an eye disorder and soon lost his sight. In 1898 their mother, Kisa, began to suffer severe pain from a tumour in the womb, and from then on the pain was recurrent. Out of the agony of his disease Sentarō developed faith in Tenrikyō and exhorted Aijirō to have faith too. During the summer vacation of Aijirō's first year in the Normal School, Kisa's condition became grave. Aijirō began to have deep faith in Tenrikyō as a result of an experience in which his mother's pain was alleviated by his prayer; but Kisa died shortly afterwards. Aijirō thought that her death revealed that the Kishioka family had bad karma (*in'nen*) and that consequently he had to devote his life to Tenrikyō and eliminate bad karma.

After official approval for the Tenrikyō movement in 1888, proselytization has been conducted through its churches. Every follower belongs to a church and is required to increase the members of the church through proselytization. When a believer (or, rather, a missionary) converts a certain number of people and gains the qualification of a priest (*kyōshi*), he can then start a new church and become its head (*kyōkaichō*). Thus, a 'child' church is born from a 'parent' church. Because a child church is a suborganization under the guidance of a parent church, the creation of a new church by a successful missionary does not jeopardize the parent church's prosperity. It is the ideal of a missionary to devote all of his (or her) life to the propagation of the church, donating all property and abandoning any profession; to establish a new church by his efforts; and to 'give birth' to as many child churches as possible. To attain this, a missionary often goes to a distant place by himself or with only his immediate family, and in extreme poverty looks for new converts.

Aijirō belonged to the Nara Shikyōkai (branch church) in Nara City, but he left the Normal School in December 1900 and began travelling for the purpose of proselytization without telling his father anything about it. He went to An'naka, a town in Gunma Prefecture, and made a few converts. In late 1903 he came back to Nara in order to be married to a member of Nara Shikyōkai, Ōnishi Toh, thereby becoming a member of the Ōnishi family. (Hereafter Aijirō will be called Ōnishi.) Then he was ordered by the head of Nara Shikyōkai to do more proselytization in and around Yamaguchi City. There were already some members in Yamaguchi City, and in 1895 Yamaguchi Fukyōjo (propagation office) was established. He was appointed the head of Yamaguchi Fukyōjo but later went to Hanaoka (now in Kudumatsu City) with his wife and mother-in-law to start 'solitary proselytization' again.

Ōnishi had to come back to Yamaguchi Fukyōjo in 1907 after about two years of proselytization because of Yamaguchi prefectural government's new policy of religious regulation. He then proselytized in Yamaguchi City for seven years while working for four years as an officer of the Tenrikyō Church Association in the Chūgoku District. This work took up a lot of time and money and did not help the task of proselytization. As a missionary Ōnishi was unlucky because, for reasons beyond his control, he had to move several times and could not devote his time to proselytization. Since he was not a successful missionary, and members of Yamaguchi Fukyōjo were far fewer than was expected by the Nara Shikyōkai, he must have felt alienated from Nara Shikyōkai.

It was against this background that in 1913, when he was 33 years old, Ōnishi believed that he received a revelation from God, which gave him an understanding of fundamental truth. This happened at a time when he had confined himself to his house for six months and had been reflecting on himself and on the seemingly incurable diseases of some members of his church. He came to believe that he himself was the 'revealed one' (*tenkeisha*) who should reign over the whole Tenrikyō organization. On 15 August, wearing nothing, Ōnishi and his wife began walking round and round in one room, bearing their children on their backs. After several hours Ōnishi's feet came to a halt as if attracted by the floor. He believed that it was God's affirmation that he himself was the *kanrodai*. Present-day Honmichi members celebrate this event annually on 15 August as the foundation day of their religion.

As we saw earlier, the *kanrodai* in Tenrikyō is a stone stand which is meant to be set on the place of human creation. But Ōnishi believed that there must also be a human *kanrodai* (*nin no kanrodai*) along with the stone *kanrodai*, and that, since he himself was the human *kanrodai*, he should become the spiritual leader of Tenrikyō. Moreover, his revelation held that, because the Foundress was to have lived on earth only until she was 115 years old, or in other words until 1912, and not eternally, as Tenrikyō doctrine taught, there should be another revealed leader after 1912 and that it was he himself. Although these ideas were quite strange and heretical from the viewpoint of orthodox Tenrikyō doctrines, Ōnishi believed that many passages in the Ofudesaki and the Osashizu predicted the advent of a human *kanrodai*.

Following his revelation, it was not Ōnishi's intention to challenge the Tenrikyō Church. Until 1922, in fact, he merely sent *tankas* (named Kanrodai-kōki) expressing his new ideas to the leaders of the Church. However, the established Tenrikyō organization, naturally, could not tolerate keeping a missionary with such ideas. Ōnishi accepted Nara Shikyōkai's proposal in 1914 that he should resign as head of the Yamaguchi Senkyōjo (propagation office) and leave the Church. The Ōnishi family lost contact with members of the Church and fell into extreme poverty. With virtually no belongings, they went back to Nara Prefecture where their relatives and acquaintances lived, and eked out a living in a small hut at Tsuji in Makimuku village until 1917. After the birth of their fourth child, Ōnishi found a job in a hospital and then in a taxation office, and in 1920 he became an elementary school teacher in Iwaki village, Takenouchi, and was assured of a stable livelihood.

In June 1920, a Tenrikyō missionary who had read the *tankas* that Ōnishi had sent to the local churches came to join him. At last, here was a sympathizer from outside his family; and from that time on, more and more Tenrikyō missionaries and believers, hearing of his revelation, came to him. In 1923 four followers were sent to Tenri City (then Tanbaichi Town) to visit the headquarters of Tenrikyō and the homes of church staff in order to persuade them that Ōnishi should become the leader of the Church. In 1924 he resigned from the school to devote himself full-time to religious activities again after a lapse of 11 years.

By 1925, when the number of Ōnishi's followers exceeded several

Japan's new religions 65

hundred, a new religious organization was rapidly taking shape. The group was called 'Tenri Kenkyūkai' (Tenri Study Association), and was not intended to be an independent religious organization outside Tenrikyō's but, rather, to be a study group for Tenrikyō's scriptures, especially the Osashizu, and to spread their correct interpretation within the Tenrikyō organization. However, because Tenrikyō dismissed the priests and excluded from its churches those followers who joined in Tenri Kenkyūkai's activities, it in fact became an independent organization from Tenrikyō.

Meanwhile, Ōnishi began to believe that the great remaking of the whole world was imminent. The apparent reason for this idea was the development in 1925 of a serious mental disorder in his first son, Yoshinobu, who was then 18 years old. Ōnishi thought that this disease was God's message that the catastrophe hinted at in the Ofudesaki and the Osashizu was approaching. At the end of 1925 he therefore left Takenouchi for Ujiyamada (now Ise City) with his wife and a few upper-level staff on a mission connected with the anticipated catastrophe. For more than a year, he wrote *tankas* called Iwato-Kōki and sent them to Takenouchi, one after another. Most of these *tankas* were precepts for the believers' daily life, but in some there are words hinting at the imminence of some grave events.

From September to December 1927, Ōnishi worked on a pamphlet called *Kenkyū Shiryō (Study Data)* with Nakai Ginjirō and Nakagawa Kiroku, both of whom were retired naval officers and the most important leaders of the group at the time. Expecting a detailed investigation by the police in the immediate future, they intended the pamphlet to inform the public authorities of their ideas about the future. The pamphlet, details of which will be discussed below, criticized the Tennō regime and warned people about a massive transformation of Japan and the world which was believed to be imminent according to their interpretation of the Ofudesaki and the Osashizu.

In early 1928 Ōnishi moved with his wife and Nakai from Ujiyamada to a follower's house in Nagoya and concealed their whereabouts, perhaps so that his arrest would be postponed for as long as possible. Meanwhile, Yoshinobu's illness became more serious, and Ōnishi was more and more convinced that the catastrophe was about to occur. On 12 March Ōnishi sent the *Study Data* to Takenouchi, and as soon as Yoshinobu saw it he gave orders for it to be taken to the Nara prefectural government. On 22 March the staff in Takenouchi took a copy to the neighbouring Takada police station and then delivered copies to the Nara prefectural government; to police stations, prefectural governments and elected representatives in various places; and to all the ministries, embassies and legations in Tokyo. This action was later called the *uchidashi* (campaign).

As the government was drawing up stringent regulations concerning anti-government movements (for example, the enactment of the 'Law for the Maintenance of Public Peace' in 1925), it naturally took strict measures against Ōnishi's whole organization. On the legal grounds that delivery of the pamphlet was a crime of *lèse majesté*, 467 believers were arrested, of whom 180 were prosecuted alongside Ōnishi and his wife. All the activities of Tenri Kenkyūkai were temporarily prohibited in what has come to be called the 'Tenri Kenkyūkai incident'. Tenri Kenkyūkai argued in court that they did not intend to overturn the state but simply to foretell and warn against future events. In the first and the second trials Ōnishi was found guilty and sentenced to four years of penal servitude, but the Supreme Court decided in 1930, on the evidence of a mental examination, that Ōnishi was not guilty by reason of diminished capacity for judgement. Devout followers took this decision as proof that their beliefs and actions were correct.

As a result of this incident, the Tenri Kenkyūkai organization at first suffered serious damage, not only because many followers were arrested, but also because activities in Takenouchi were brought to a halt, and newspapers attacked the group in sensational articles reporting the incident. But soon after the Supreme Court's acquittal, the organization recovered and became active again. The headquarters was shifted to Osaka and facilities were rapidly expanded there, as well as in other places.

In this process the group became more like an independent religious body, and by 1934 it claimed 10,000 followers. It was probably about this time that a short doctrinal book, *Kyōgi Ippan* (*An Outline of the Doctrine*), written by Ōnishi himself, began to be used as the text for the introductory lecture course. The first three and the last sections teach the basic doctrines of Tenrikyō such as creation and the protection of human beings by God; the eight dusts and *in'nen* karma; the fourth and fifth sections, entitled 'Three Steps of the Way' and 'Solely for *Kanrodai*', teach Ōnishi's original doctrines. In the 'Solely for *Kanrodai*' section it is asserted that there is not only the stone *kanrodai* but also a human *kanrodai*, and that this human *kanrodai* will accomplish the 'Way'. It is also hinted that the human *kanrodai* is Ōnishi himself. 'Three Steps of the Way' explains the process of the Way as initiated by Nakayama Miki and completed by Ōnishi in three stages. The first step, occurring from the Foundress's first possession until her death, was the 'Way of the Prototype', a state full of difficulties representing a model for the true Way. The second step, the 25-year period from the Foundress's death to Ōnishi's revelation, is called the 'Way of Reason', a provisional stage of compromising with the world and preparing for the next step. The third step, beginning with Ōnishi's revelation, was the *honmichi* (True Way), namely, the genuine Way in which the goals of mankind will be attained. Based on this idea, the name of the group was changed from Tenri Kenkyūkai to Tenri Honmichi.

However, this period of attracting converts and giving instruction in doctrines did not last long. In 1936 Ōnishi's wife Toh developed a kidney disease, and in 1937, when her body became paralysed on one side, the group's activities again turned to the outside. A new propagation campaign was launched in June 1937, and in September three leading believers moved to Tenri City for about a year, visiting Tenrikyō Headquarters and trying to convert its leaders. In early 1938 Toh's disease took a serious turn which made Ōnishi all the more convinced that a catastrophe was imminent. Ōnishi and other leaders therefore planned a second public campaign, and from July to September seven pamphlets entitled *Shoshin* (*Letters*) were written by Iwata Gen'emon, Koura Yoshio and Ōnishi Aiko (Ōnishi's daughter). About 9 million copies were printed and were delivered to police stations, military police offices, politicians and prominent men of the time. In addition, when Toh's condition became dangerous on 3 August, Koura wrote a pamphlet entitled *Yūkoku no Shi ni Tsugu* (*An Announcement for the Patriots*) and sent copies to two leading newspaper companies in Osaka.

These pamphlets claim to explain the events of 1928 and to correct the public's misunderstandings. Although it is true that they refer to these events, the main contents are a repetition of the *Study Data*. 'The Fifth Letter' and 'The Sixth Letter' are, respectively, concerned with Ōnishi's detailed autobiography and *An Outline of the Doctrine*. The history of Tenrikyō and the relationship between Tenrikyō and Honmichi are described and explained in 'The Second Letter' and 'The Seventh Letter'. As a whole, however, the style of the pamphlets is more objective and the argument is clearer than in the *Study Data*.

The government, which had just crushed two big new religions, Ōmoto and Hitonomichi in 1936 and 1937, used the publication of these pamphlets as a pretext for taking strong repressive measures against Honmichi. On 21 November 1938, 346 leading believers and Ōnishi himself were arrested, and 237 were prosecuted for violating the 'Law for the Maintenance of Public Peace' and for committing the crime of *lèse majesté*. The Ministry of Home Affairs prohibited all activities of Tenri Honmichi and ordered its dissolution in September 1939 in what has come to be known as the 'Tenri Honmichi incident'. The result was that Honmichi was unable to conduct any religious activities for about six years. In the first and second trials of Ōnishi and a few leading believers, all were found guilty and Ōnishi was sentenced to penal servitude for life. But while they were on trial in the Supreme Court, the second world war ended.

Along with many prisoners accused of political crimes and thought 'dangerous' to the state, Ōnishi was released in September 1945. He and other believers were finally acquitted in March 1946, and a few days before that, in accordance with the new Religious Corporation Ordinance, the group had received official recognition for the first time as a religious corporation. Following the Tenri Honmichi incident the government had ordered the disposal of the group's properties, and the Ōnishi family had moved to Hagoromo Town in the southern part of Osaka Prefecture, which became the location of the group's new headquarters. Membership increased steadily, reaching about 230,000 members in 1954 and about 300,000 members in 1980.

I shall not describe the history of Honmichi in the postwar period, but one point needs to be raised: namely, the problem of the succession of 'charisma', in the Weberian sense. As early as 1932, when his first son Yoshinobu died, Ōnishi told some of the leading believers about his death and about his successors: he said he would not live to be a 100 years old; he would be born again and again eternally in the Ōnishi family as the human *kanrodai*; and until the reborn *kanrodai* reached maturity, proxies (*tegawari*) designated by him should take his place. After release from gaol he designated his first daughter Aiko and his second son Masanori as, respectively, *kyoshu* (teaching head) and *kanshu* (superintendent) and as two proxies. Ōnishi himself retired from major activities soon after his release, and when he died in November 1958 Aiko and Masanori were already venerated by the followers. When Aiko and Masanori died in 1966 and 1971, they were succeeded by Masanori's first and second sons, Motooki and Masataka. Meanwhile, in 1962, in the Headquarters at Hagoromo, a group called Mirokukai developed in support of Ōnishi's second daughter, Tama, who claimed that she was the reborn Foundress and that she should be the successor of the human *kanrodai*. The governing body, rejecting her claim, expelled the group, which then formed a new religious body named Honbushin (True Construction). Soon after this 'Mirokukai incident' the leaders of Honmichi announced that the *kanrodai* had already been reborn as one of Masanori's sons, and they later revealed that this reborn *kanrodai* is Masanori's sixth son, Yasuhiko, who was born in 1960. At present, followers of Honmichi are looking forward to the day when the reborn *kanrodai* will receive his revelation from God.

Millennialism in Tenrikyō
Three periods can be discerned in the development of millennialism in Tenrikyō: (1) the period represented by the Mikagura-uta, the earliest stage in the formation of the group; (2) the period represented by the Ofudesaki and the Kōki, the stage when the group's identity was established; and (3) the period represented by the Osashizu, about twenty years after the Foundress's death. The periods after the Osashizu will not be discussed, for there was no literature with millennialistic ideas to guide the whole group, and no activity connected with millennialism was undertaken by most of the group.

Mikagura-uta
In the Mikagura-uta, millennialism is still very vague and amorphous. It is true that there are words predicting the coming of the ideal world by God's power.

Tong! Tong! Tong! The beginning of the dancing at New Year: How delightful it is!
Second, This marvellous construction once it is started: How lively it is!
Third, Nourishment will be put on you.
Fourth, The World will change to prosperity,
Fifth, If all come and follow Me,
Sixth, I will cut off the root of rebellion.
Seventh, If you help others who are suffering,
Eighth, I will cut off the root of illness.
Ninth, If you keep your mind determined,
Tenth, Peace shall reign everywhere.[10]

(Chapter II)

Though it does not indicate clearly when the ideal world will come, it seems that the shift to the ideal world is already under way and the goal near at hand. However, the coming of this ideal world is not conceived as accompanying a fundamental change in the present order of the world. The shift is smooth, and the ideal world is the extension of present village life. The 'joyous life' consists of such images as abundant harvests, sound health and the end of social disorders. It is not completely different from the present state.

This vagueness in the millennialism is inherited from the folkloric concept of *yonaori* (world renewal), and the manner in which Mikagura-uta is sung to the accompaniment of various simple instruments with slow dances and gestures is reminiscent of rural folk festivals.

(a) How, then, did this vague and amorphous millennialism reflect the contemporary worldview? The societal situation is perceived quite optimistically, but the political trends are not grasped or clearly represented. There is just a vague, optimistic expectation for the future of village life in the Yamato district:

Third,	Keep the mind of a three-year-old child!
Fourth,	Then, a rich harvest.
Fifth,	The providences shall come forth.
Sixth,	Unlimited abundance everywhere.
Seventh,	If you grow and reap whatever you wish,
Eighth,	Yamato will be blessed with a rich harvest
Ninth,	Now come hither and follow Me!
Tenth,	Then the full harvest will become fixed.

(Chapter I)

The Mikagura-uta was composed at a time when rapid social change was just beginning. The political change known as the Meiji Restoration was anticipated, but wars, social disorders and economic suppression had not yet deeply touched the farmers' lives. Most of the people were still living a quiet and orderly village life. They hoped for a better life, but not for a world greatly different from the contemporary one. In 1867 people's hope for change exploded in the form of mass pilgrimages to the Ise shrine from all over the country (*Eejanaika*). The Mikagura-uta reflects the kind of hopeful perception of the societal situation that was shared by a wide range of people.

(b) The movement itself had just started. People who had not been acquainted with each other formed a new community and voluntarily worked together to build a shrine (*tsutome-basho*). The community was expanding rapidly, and the members were experiencing miracles one after another. The future of the community was full of possibilities, and the Mikagura-uta expresses a bright perception of the group's situation:

Second,	This marvellous place for the Service,
	Though I ask no one to build,
Third,	All gathering together from the world,
	The construction has been accomplished.
	How miraculous it is!
Fourth,	With much effort, you have followed Me thus far;
	True salvation will begin from now.

(Chapter III)

(c) Following Nakayama Miki's possession by God in 1838, her faith was accepted at first only by a few people around her. But in the late 1860s, when she was invariably surrounded by her followers, including influential farmers from neighbouring villages, she did not feel so isolated. It is true that in certain passages a sense of tension with the external world is expressed:

First,   Whatever others may say;
         God is watching, so be at ease!
Third,   All of you close to Me,
         Watch whatever God acts and works!
Fourth, Night and day, dong! chang! we perform the
         service;
         The neighbors may feel it noisy and annoying.
Fifth,   As I am always in haste to save you,
         Quickly become joyful and come to Me!
Sixth,   Villagers I wish to save at once,
         But they do not understand My heart.

(Chapter IV)

On the whole, however, there are not many passages with such a tone of tension. Moreover these passages are not closely connected with ideas concerning millennialism.

Thus, Mikagura-uta reflects a bright outlook on all three levels, and this is in a sense conducive to the formation of millennialism. But, at the same time, an important component of millennialism is lacking: namely, the sense of crisis. This is partly why millennialism in the Mikagura-uta is very vague and amorphous.

The Ofudesaki and the Kōki

The vague and amorphous expectations characteristic of the Mikagura-uta can still be found in the first part of the Ofudesaki, but the optimistic tone of the Ofudesaki gradually fades away. There are more and more phrases expressing a keen awareness of the distance between the ideal state of affairs and the actual one, which is filled with various evils. There are also many phrases forecasting a drastic turn from the present bad state of affairs to a good one. As we have already seen, the Ofudesaki was written in order to show God's will concerning the concrete problems of the moment; and the more critical the situation, the more drastic and the more total the impending change was thought to be. Thus, millennialism is better articulated in the Ofudesaki than in the Mikagura-uta.

For example, the verses referring to the construction of the *kanrodai* predict the coming of the ideal world, a world fundamentally different from the contemporary one:

If only you have finished the sweeping of your mental dust, I will work
remarkable salvation. 98[11]
You shall be saved according to the true sincerity of your mind. You shall
not fall ill, die or become weakened.   99
By this salvation I, God, intend single-heartedly to fill the natural term of
human life at one hundred and fifteen years.   100

(Part III)

> I set up the Kanrodai as the evidence that I created human beings at this place.   9
> If only this Stand is completed, and every Prayer shall be heard.   10
> Before that time the sweeping of the dust of human hearts must be accomplished throughout the whole world.   11
>
>   (Part XVIII)

These words correspond to the actual construction of the *kanrodai*. Some followers believed that they really watched nectar falling to earth, and Miki herself, at least for a period, believed that the *kanrodai* would be completed and that the ideal world would be ushered in during her lifetime.

Phrases predicting the great change and, in turn, demanding faithfulness are found not only in passages related to the *kanrodai* but almost everywhere in the Ofudesaki (see Shimazono, 1981). The composition of Kōki and the performance of the *tsutome* (service) are also referred to as preconditions for the coming of the ideal world. Words like 'until now' and 'henceforth' appear many times, showing that the present was considered an important point of change.

It may be asked, however, whether all the changes referred to in the Ofudesaki represent millennialistic ideas. Some predictions are concerned too narrowly with the future of the Nakayama family to be called millennialistic, and, on the whole, phrases expressing the nature of the change are vague and fragmentary. One typically vague expression is the metaphor of the 'way' (or road):

> Do not despair of your present way, whatever kind of way it may be! Look forward with delight to the main road [true way] ahead of you!   37
>
>   (Part III)

Moreover, the timing of the ultimate change is not clearly and consistently stated. Sometimes the change is pictured as occurring in the remote future, an interpretation adopted by Tenrikyō today for most of the verses concerning change. However, we can say that all predictions of change found in the Ofudesaki arise from a more or less millennialistic mood. How then is this millennialistic mood related to the perception of the contemporary situation?

(a) Two pair-concepts, foreigners *v.* Japanese and the high mountain *v.* the bottom of the valleys, are used to express the perception of the societal situation. It was, according to the Ofudesaki, against God's will that the 'foreigners' and the 'high mountain' dominated the 'Japanese' and the 'bottom of the valleys':

> Until now the foreigners have managed the Japanese[12] as they please. The sorrow of God was so severe that I could not find any way to clear it away.   86

Henceforth the Japanese will lead the foreigners. All of you, be aware and expect it! 87
They are the root and branches of the same tree. Branches may be broken, yet the root will grow prosperous. 88
Until now the foreigners have been said to be great; henceforth they shall only be broken. 89

(Part III)

Although until now those who are on the high mountains have done whatever they pleased, scolding noisily, 57
Henceforth, however high their position may be, those who are on the high mountains shall never be able to do as they please to those who are at the bottom of the valleys. 58

(Part XV)

'The high mountains' refer to political and religious rulers who are regarded as being heavily influenced by 'the foreigners'. Contemporary politics is considered bad because of the foreigners' influence. The right people are in powerless positions, and this bad state of affairs must change — these ideas represent the perception of the societal situation in the Ofudesaki. They imply criticism of the political reforms and economic instabilities around the time of the Meiji Restoration which made farmers' lives desperate. Rapid social change was beginning, and many farmers lost their land and had to leave their villages. Because the main cause of these undesirable changes was believed to be, and in a sense really was, the pressure of western countries, criticism of the societal situation takes the form of chauvinism.

The combination of millennialism and chauvinism is also very evident in Maruyamakyō and Ōmoto and is one of the common components of millennialism in Japan's new religions before the end of the second world war. In the case of Tenrikyō, the chauvinism was vague and general, for there is neither criticism of western customs nor references to specific policies.

(b) As the perception of the societal situation became more pessimistic, the perception of the group's own situation was hardly brimming with optimistic expectation. Even though the believers' community was still expanding rapidly, and God's presence was strongly felt, a trend contrary to God's will was observed in the obviously conciliatory attitudes of the leading believers towards oppression and interference. Miki thought that those around her did not have true faith and that this was both the cause and the result of the fact that God was not exercising his power fully.

Make haste in high spirits! Do you not know the expectation of Tsukihi? 49

I, Tsukihi, truly have a single-hearted desire to exhibit my omnipotence at once.   50
Although I, Tsukihi, care with so much true sincerity, the minds of you close to Me are yet as common as those of the world.   51

(Part VII)

Among those 'close to' Miki, she was most concerned for her son Shūji. Although, as the head of the Nakayama family, he naturally played an important role in the group's management, Miki doubted whether he had much faith in her God. One reason was that Shūji's leg pain, which had inspired Miki to create a new religion in the first place, had not been cured. For Miki, his misery was also a part of God's will, and human will, she thought, struggles against God's will. This situation had to change fundamentally:

I, Tsukihi, made you lame, though you had to that time no bodily defect at all. This has given you much trouble.   118
Therefore you are doubting whatever words I, Tsukihi, may say. But, it is natural.   120
This time I am preparing to clear up your innermost heart. This is the prime matter.   121
My regret which has piled up to the present is not slight, so it cannot be expressed by word of mouth.   126
Until now I have been passing through a mountainous regret. If only I can clear it all away this time,   127
Thereafter I will save you from any and every kind of disease or trouble, however serious it may be.   128

(Part XII)

The perception of the group's situation to the effect that God's benevolent power, through active life on earth, is not fully revealed leads to the formation of millennialism.

(c) The criticism of the upper stratum of society referred to above is related not only to the perception of the societal situation but also to that of the relationship between the religious movement and the rest of society. Typical expressions of the tension between the believers' community and society are 'regret', 'anger' and the 'return' of God. They appear again and again in verses written when the Nara Middle Teaching Academy ordered God's name to be changed and ritual properties were confiscated in 1874; and when the police removed two pieces of the stone *kanrodai* in 1882:

They rejected the name given by Tsukihi. What do you think of this deep regret of Mine?   70
Understand that the true anger and regret of Tsukihi is not slight!   71
Until now those who are on the high mountains have been rampant and managing everything as they please.   72

(Part VI)

But from now on, in their place I, Tsukihi, will reign as I intend. Copy whatever I, Tsukihi, will work. 41

(Part XVII)

Beginning with the perception that some external force is blocking the full realization of God's power, there is a swelling expectation of a great change which will get rid of the obstacle.

In the Ofudesaki, we can observe millennialistic ideas which are somewhat clearer than those in the Mikagura-uta. This means that there is a keen perception of the situation conducive to the formation of millennialism. These millennialistic ideas, however, were so heavily dependent on the perception of the situation that they could not be integrated into one system and so are expressed without a close, logical connection among them. Thus, this scripture does not form one organized millennialistic doctrine, but rather expresses in general nothing more than a millennialistic mood.

This will become clearer when comparing it with the Kōki[13] which was written at the same time as the Ofudesaki. The Kōki refers, though only briefly, to the future of mankind when the *kanrodai* is set up and the ideal world arrives, allowing men to live to be 115 years old. But it does not say that the coming of the ideal world is imminent, or that it will follow a catastrophic event. Moreover, it is difficult to draw the conclusion from what is written about the past in the Kōki that there will be a massive change in the near future. This scripture, mainly telling stories about human creation and God's intentions for it, as well as about God's protection of men's bodily functions, aims at confirming the harmonious relationship and oneness between God and men. Consequently, it says nothing about the tension or antagonism between God and men. Thus, the millennialistic mood of the Ofudesaki and the Kōki's guiding ideas fall into two different categories. This is evidence that Miki's ideas of millennialism and her basic view of mankind and of mankind's history were not integrated into one system of thought.

The Osashizu
The Osashizu is so voluminous that it is very difficult to analyse it thoroughly. I shall give only a rough outline for future study. There are, no doubt, expressions which can be called millennialistic, but, like those in the Ofudesaki, they are not systematic. Here, too, various ideas reflect different perceptions of the situation. The Osashizu has the same structure as that of the Ofudesaki in that it expresses God's will concerning the specific problems of the situation. The Osashizu basically imitates the Ofudesaki's style.

Generally speaking, however, the tension between God and men is less severe, and patience rather than resolution is exhorted in the

Osashizu. In the perception of the societal situation and of relationships between the movement and society, the tendency is to regard the crises as manageable; for, while Japan's industrial revolution was in progress and the two wars with China and Russia were being fought, Izō and others did not think that they were very dangerous. The catastrophe and the coming of the ideal world are conceived of as occurring in the distant future, and the process of change is seen as slow. But the difference between the Ofudesaki and the Osashizu is most conspicuous in the perception of the group's own situation. According to 'the doctrine of the Foundress's further life', the Foundress, who is the incarnation of supernatural power, though still alive and on earth, has hidden herself. Here is a latent awareness that supernatural power has ceased to be very active. Although the rapid increase of members is taken as evidence that the process initiated by the Foundress is on the way to its completion, there is also another conception of time: namely, that the greatest period of history lay in the past. Since the ideal world will be brought about only by the highest supernatural power, the Osashizu does not consider that it will occur in the near future.

Thus, although the Osashizu inherited millennialism from the Ofudesaki, the perception of the situation on various levels was not conducive to its further development. Consequently, millennialism in the Osashizu is no more refined than in the Ofudesaki.

Millennialism in Honmichi

As in the case of Tenrikyō, we can discern three periods in the development of millennialism in Honmichi: (1) from 1913, when Ōnishi came to believe that he himself was the human *kanrodai*, to 1923, when Ōnishi's belief was first propagated in Tenri City; (2) from 1923 to 1945, the period of the two 'campaigns' and the suppressions which immediately followed; and (3) from 1945, when the suppressed group was reorganized, to the present.

1913–1923

Although we do not have enough information for this period and must to some extent depend on conjecture, we can safely say that millennialism was only latent. Ōnishi's main concern was that he himself was the human *kanrodai* and that he should be the leader of Tenrikyō. According to the Ofudesaki, the *kanrodai* will be established at the coming of the ideal world, so we may infer that the human *kanrodai* will be the leader of the coming ideal world. Here is messianism, although not clearly expressed, and it is true that in the Ofudesaki, too, we can find messianism in its embryonic form:

This time, purifying the water, I desire to take in quickly the Shimbashira
(central pillar), who is to control the internal affairs. 56
The central pillar of those who are on the high mountains is a foreigner.
This is the prime cause of the anger of God. 57

(Part III)

In these verses Miki expresses, even if only vaguely, her wish to
establish a male leader for her group and also to make him the leader
of Japan or perhaps the world. However, this idea appears only in
fragments. The Shimbashira was conceived mostly as the leader of
the group and not as a messianic leader of the whole world. On the
other hand, Ōnishi's belief that he himself was the *kanrodai* was quite
likely to develop into messianism, for the image of the *kanrodai*
cannot be separated from the notion of the ideal world. Messianism is
not common in Japan's new religions; for, although founders and
foundresses are worshipped as living gods (see Shimazono, 1981),
they are not regarded as kings or queens of a coming ideal world. As
a sacred king there is already the Tennō, the Emperor of Japan, a
figure who is not easy to compete with (see Miyata, 1980). This lack
of messianism is closely connected with the fact that millennialism in
Japan was vague and unsystematic, yet Ōnishi's belief that he himself
was the *kanrodai* was capable of breaking through this limitation.

Ōnishi's outlook in this period, however, was so narrowly
restricted to the framework of Tenrikyō that the human *kanrodai* was
conceived only as the leader of the religion. Furthermore, the idea
that the transformation of the world was imminent was not yet clearly
developed. Of course, as an eager reader of the Ofudesaki and the
Osashizu, he might have taken special notice of millennialistic
passages in them, but he did not give expression to millennialistic
ideas in his own words or actions at this time. This indicates that his
own perception of the situation on any level was not likely to lead to
the formation of millennialism.

(a) In this period, while rapid industrialization and imperialistic
diplomacy were continuously causing both internal and international
political tension, it seems that Ōnishi, at least in the first part of the
period, paid little attention to the societal situation. Since he was
almost entirely preoccupied with the doctrinal system of Tenrikyō,
he was not very concerned with ideological problems concerning the
future course of the state and society. In the latter part of the period,
however, when he was working in a tax office and an elementary
school and had contact with many believers from various districts, he
might have paid closer attention to political affairs.

(b) As early as 1913, he held the idea that he himself was the
highest embodiment of the supernatural on earth. But it was only an
abstract idea. Until about 1920, in the absence of a believers'

community, he was most unlikely to have had a strong awareness of any substantial activity of supernatural power in the world at large. Only when a believers' community rapidly formed around him must he have perceived that a momentous change was imminent.

(c) After his revelation in 1913, he was extremely isolated in Tenrikyō. It might be the case that he regarded this isolation as a symptom of some grave crisis. However, there are no writings by him or stories about him which prove that this was how he saw the situation.

In sum, Ōnishi in this period took one step forward from the vague millennialism of the Ofudesaki towards a more systematic one in the sense that a messianic idea was constructed. However, because the millennialistic outlook was weak, a new millennialism, yet to find expression, remained merely latent.

1923–1945
This is the period when a fairly clear belief in millennialism was established, becoming the central component in the belief system of the whole group. The millennialism of this period was expressed mainly in three documents — *Study Data*, *Letters* and *An Announcement for the Patriots* — as well as in the group's actions during the two 'campaigns'. The millennialistic ideas which crystallized around 1928 and those from around 1938 are basically the same, although slight differences can be found. In *An Announcement for the Patriots*, the contents of the *Study Data* are skilfully summarized and itemized. I shall introduce the millennialistic ideas of Honmichi at this period by further summarizing them.[14]

(a) 'The central concern of this Way': this Way is not merely a religion, but the Way to the destiny of the whole world.

(b) 'The records of the Divine Age': the so-called Divine Age described in the *Kojiki* and *Nohon Shoki*, two ancient mythological texts, is not a story about the past, but prophecies. For example, Amaterasu-Ōmikami, the sun goddess who governs the world and who is considered the ancestor of the Tennō family, is in fact the Foundress Nakayama Miki; 'Iwato-gakure', a story in which Amaterasu hid from anger in a stone cave, is in fact the prophecy of the death of the Foundress; and the descent of the goddess's grandson, a story in which an ancestor of Tennō, Ninigi, descended to earth to reign over Japan or the world, is in fact a prophecy about the succession from Miki to Ōnishi, who will become the leader of the world. In the same way, the Paradise and the advent of Christ in Christianity, as well as the Land of Happiness and the advent of Maitreya in Buddhism, are all in fact prophecies about the impending divine world of the *kanrodai*.

(c) 'Our Tennō has no heavenly virtue': Tennō has no heavenly virtue to rule the country, the Emperor's insistence on divine origin is false, a mistake based on misinterpreting prophecies about the future as a story about his family in the past. People, realizing this, will not obey him in the future. Moreover, he must accept the return of God to earth and what it entails, for (the former) Tennō, opposing God's will, persecuted the Foundress.

(d) 'God's regret': the Foundress sacrificed herself in this world full of selfishness to save mankind, but she was persecuted and had to shorten her own life from 115 to 90 years. This is the cause of God's great regret, and rulers who are responsible for it must accept God's return to earth, that is, natural calamities and wars. In order to be saved, men should believe in, and rely on, God, who wishes to save people from these disasters.

(e) 'A great war will occur in the near future, and Japan will be placed in the ultimate predicament': when Japan is in the ultimate predicament, the human *kanrodai*, Ōnishi, will save her, for through him people can know God's will. Then, as the divine country (*shinkoku*), Japan will reign over the whole world.

(f) 'The Diet will not be able to govern the country': men's eternal peace can be attained only by divine rule.

(g) 'The construction of the *kanrodai*': this means the construction of paradise in this world under the rule of the human *kanrodai* with all the people in the world united as one. This is the purpose for which God made mankind.

The *Study Data* also predicts that the year 1928 is the 'year of Grace' when the great event will happen and all the people will then become equal.[15] And *Letters* maintains that the group's claims in the *Study Data* were proved correct by the acquittal pronounced by the Supreme Court. However, there is no reference in *Letters* to whether the prophecy of the great event in 1928 turned out to be true or not and, if not, why.

The two 'campaigns' were conceived to inform and warn rulers of the coming catastrophe, and the proselytization directed towards Tenrikyō had the same purpose. These were the collective actions of the whole group motivated by millennialism. With these actions and the three documents discussed above, a tradition of millennialistic ideas dating from the Mikagura-uta became a clear doctrine for the first time. Messianism, which was latent in the period 1913–23, became clear with the belief that the human *kanrodai* is the divine king of the impending ideal world. This concept occupies a unique position in Japan's history of ideas in that it boldly challenges the divine authority of Tennō.

The maturation of millennialistic ideas in this period was brought about by the keen critical perception of the situation shared by Ōnishi and others.

(a) The most important element was the perception of the societal situation, in which Japan was, internationally, in a very difficult position. Of course, this perception reflected the international situation and the political ideology dominant at that time. After the first world war Japan's international position was elevated, and the tension with the United States and other western countries became more and more serious. On the other hand, the aggressive policy against China was gradually escalated, turning into outright belligerency after 1931. In this position of international isolation, the government intensified internal control of the country. This policy was supported by the ideology that, in order to protect Japan from foreign countries, the people must become united under the reign of Tennō. Honmichi of this period modified this idea and incorporated it into its own set of teachings. In the process of modification and incorporation, a few leading believers played an important role as advisers to Ōnishi, for they had a great deal of knowledge about the political situation and about ideological problems as well as the ability to state their opinions about them in theoretical terms. Such ideas as the crisis of Japan and the illegitimacy of Tennō's reign were probably incorporated not by Ōnishi but by these believers. Without them, Honmichi might not have established a clear concept of millennialism.

The perception of the societal situation which was incorporated primarily by these believers and expressed in the three pamphlets, however, was not very wide in its scope. Although they asserted that the present ruler had no ability to rule, they said little about the consequences of this inability, that is, how people were suffering, how the society was changing for the worse and so forth. A short reference to the selfishness of ordinary people can be found, but only as an introduction to praising the great mercy of the Foundress. There is an indifference to social evils which is characteristic of Tenrikyō thinking after the Mikagura-uta. This is in sharp contrast to the perception of the societal situation in Ōmoto with its strong stance against social evils.

(b) The perception of the group's own situation, too, has much to do with the establishment of millennialism, although not as much as the perception of the societal situation. The rapid growth of the group after 1920 must have caused the believers to feel that a supernatural power was taking the world in hand. But it was the serious diseases of Ōnishi's son Yoshinobu, and his wife Toh, that sparked the launching of the two 'campaigns'. For Ōnishi and his followers, these diseases meant that some evil power or tendency had obstructed God's benevolent power. It was believed that this evil, which must have been conceived, at least unconsciously, as the cause of the long adversities of the Ōnishi family before 1920, would lead to catastrophe and would then disappear. As in the Ofudesaki, the perception that a benevolent supernatural power was very active in the world but not effective in the very centre of the group enhanced the idea that massive change was imminent.

(c) The relationship between millennialism and oppression of the group is not directly expressed in the three pamphlets. There are no references to the government's blocking of God's will or to prophecies that God will remove obstacles hindering the group. But we can surmise that, in fact, there was such a strong sense of tension between the group and the wider society that it motivated the articulation of millennialistic ideas. The two 'campaigns' were planned with the expectation that sooner or later there would be oppression, which was explicitly thought to be a chance to inform the public authorities of the group's teachings rather than the operation of some evil power or tendency. Yet behind such a thought there was a strong awareness of the coming crisis that would be caused by this oppression. It was this awareness that forced Ōnishi to go into hiding in 1927. Moreover, it is clearly stated that the persecution of the Foundress was an important cause of God's regret and retaliation. This means that the believers had a firm idea that the persecutors or the authorities represented evil.

Thus, the perception of the situation in Honmichi at this time was such as to precipitate the formation and the articulation of millennialism. Through this perception the vague millennialistic ideas that had crystallized since the Ofudesaki turned into a fairly clear concept with links to messianism. But it did not become an independent systematic idea at that time; that is, its contents still depended largely on the current worldviews, especially on the perception of the societal situation. In other words, the realization that Japan was in a crisis and Honmichi's central doctrine that Ōnishi was the human *kanrodai* are only contingently related, not integrated into one all-encompassing theoretical system. There is no fundamental explanation of why the crisis was deepening or why the final event was imminent. As was discussed earlier, we cannot conclude from the 'Heilsgeschichte' in the Kōki that a catastrophic change is imminent, because it says nothing about why and how the tension between God and mankind began and grew. In this respect Honmichi of this period added very little: it had neither a view of human beings nor a view of history which could become a basis for the development of millennialism, and the current millennialistic ideas, though fairly clear, did not evolve into systematic thought.

1945–present

There have been no dramatic events or drastic changes in doctrine in Honmichi during this period; yet, of course, there have been developments in various aspects, including doctrines. Indeed, much progress has been made in the systematization of the doctrines based on the scriptures from Tenrikyō and of ideas arising in the early days of Honmichi. The result of this systematization is presented in *An Outline of Honmichi*, published in 1972, where Honmichi's millennialistic ideas are stated in a logically consistent way. The basic contents of the prophecies and the assertions, however, do not differ from those of their predecessors. In the near future, a world war will occur and mankind will suffer a grave crisis; but by prayer (*muhonzutome*) performed around the human *kanrodai* at the place of human creation, the war will be ended, and those who follow the human *kanrodai* will be saved. As to the nature of future events, the main change is the disappearance of chauvinism and nationalism. A few new ideas which do not greatly affect the whole structure of millennialism are added concerning Honmichi's own history: that the two 'campaigns' were necessary in order to inform society of Honmichi and were preparatory actions for future events; that Japan's defeat in the second world war and the democratic reforms following surrender were fulfilments of prophecies in the scriptures; and so forth.

The most important characteristic of the millennialism in this period, however, is that it is firmly founded on the dualism of 'the unique Way of God' and 'the worldly and rational way', that is, on the antagonism between Honmichi itself and the wider society. The two main incidents of oppression are seen in the light of dualism. The 1928 incident, regarded as the result of the 'misunderstanding' of *Letters*, is now considered the inevitable consequence of profound antagonism between the two spheres. Just as the Foundress, according to Honmichi, was persecuted again and again, those who follow God are naturally persecuted by those rulers who oppose God. On the basis of this idea, harsh criticisms are directed against Tenrikyō which, they assume, has taken a compromising line with society since the Foundress's death. By withdrawing the Kōki and other scriptures, requesting governmental approval and providing various aid for the wars, Tenrikyō, they argue, has run counter to the 'Way of God' and degenerated into the 'way of man'.

Moreover, this dualism of 'the unique Way of God' and 'the worldly and rational way' is believed to have its basis in human nature. God gave human beings free will when creating them, and although He furnished the path for men's maturation, they abused this freedom of will and ran counter to the will of God. The impending catastrophe, in which men will be placed in a situation of grave danger, is the result of this abuse. Until men developed maturity, God permitted them, His children, to run counter to Him. But now that mankind has reached maturity, God will no longer permit men to commit profane actions. Furthermore, despite the fact that ultimate truth was revealed through the Foundress and the human *kanrodai*, man responded to it by committing acts of persecution. This heightened God's 'regret'. All these abuses by mankind will result in the coming catastrophe. Here the whole history of mankind is viewed from the perspective of the tension between God and men, and it is this perspective which has enabled millennialism to become a logically coherent system for the first time in a tradition dating from the Mikagura-uta.

On the other hand, actions based on millennialistic ideas are not extraordinary and one-off things but, rather, are embodied in daily activities. The construction of big shrines (*shinhaiden*) by service work (*hinokishin*), regarded as preparations for the coming catastrophe and the ideal world, have been the group's central activities in postwar Honmichi. The big shrines are, it is believed, places where people will be saved from the catastrophe and where believers will start to construct the ideal world. This routinization of millennialistic action, as well as the systematization of millennialistic thought, is closely connected with the institutionalization of the movement, whereby the group's situation and its relations with its social environment have become stabilized. Thus, both millennialistic ideas and actions tend to be independent of the current perception of the situation. In fact, although the perception of the societal situation has to some extent been conducive to the development of millennialism because of chronic international tension between the Western and Eastern blocs, the perception of the group's own situation in postwar Honmichi is not such as to elicit millennialism. This is because God's direct and immediate involvement in the world's affairs is felt to be weaker since Ōnishi's retirement and death. The tension between the movement and the external world has been lowered by the legal establishment of the freedom of religion. Yet, in spite of a situation unfavourable to millennialism, Honmichi has stuck firmly to it, chiefly because millennialistic ideas have become a systematized doctrine, and millennialistic actions have been routinized.

Conclusions
There is no influential tradition of systematic millennialism in Japan, but among new religions there are quite a few groups which display elements of millennialism, even if they are vague. The history of Tenrikyō and Honmichi shows how systematic millennialistic

doctrine can develop out of amorphous ideas. In Tenrikyō and Honmichi before the end of the second world war, as in most of the other new religions with elements of millennialism, millennialistic ideas were vague and largely dependent on the current worldview. Basically, their millennialism was simply the expression of a millennialistic perception of the situation and not a systematic doctrine.

We have not yet discussed why Nakayama Miki and Ōnishi Aijirō and those who followed them had a more acute perception of the situation than did others. Limitations of space prevent me from giving more than a single clue to the solution of this problem. Miki and Ōnishi tended to place great emphasis on the appearance both of God's power and of evil power or the tendency to obstruct God's power. This emphasis on the contrast between God's power and evil is due, at least partly, to their experience of long isolation at an early stage of their religious life. At the basis of all three aspects of their millennialistic worldviews, there is a keen sense of tension between their belief and the values of the wider society. But as long as this sense of tension could not be related to a firm view of mankind and history, millennialism remained vague.

In post-war Honmichi, however, millennialistic thought advanced beyond this limit, and a systematic millennialism was established. This unique process was accomplished, I assume, by the combination of the following three factors. (1) In the 1920s and the 1930s, when Honmichi grew rapidly and the basis of its doctrine was laid down, Japan's international relations were in a state of utmost tension. The dominant ideology at the time was itself millennialistic. Honmichi absorbed a great deal of the atmosphere of the age. (2) Honmichi was a schism from Tenrikyō, and most of its followers had been members of Tenrikyō. They were loyal to most of the Tenrikyō doctrines, opposing it only on one particular point. Thus, Honmichi could elaborate and refine Tenrikyō doctrines from one clear perspective, the problem of the divine leader. (3) For more than thirty years after Ōnishi had received his revelation, he and his religion were in continuous tension with society. Consequently, awareness of the severe tension with society became an essential part of Honmichi's thinking and helped the systematization of its millennialistic ideas.

Millennialism can be the expression of any traditional or imported view of mankind and history which puts an emphasis on the limitations and evils of human beings. But there are cases where such a view of mankind and history is formed only as a result of the work of millennialistic movements. Honmichi is an example of the latter. By further study of such cases, we shall be able to develop a deeper understanding of the structure and evolution of millennialistic thinking.

Notes

1. According to Yonina Talmon, millennialistic (millenarian) religious movements are those 'religious movements that expect imminent, total, ultimate, this-worldly, collective salvation' (Talmon, 1968).
2. Millennialistic traditions in Japan's folklore have been studied extensively by Noboru Miyata (1975a; 1975b; 1980).
3. This point is discussed in Yasumaru and Hirota (1966) and Miyata (1980).
4. Yasumaru and Hirota (1966) is the only existing study of the refinement of the folkloric millennialistic tradition into organized thought in new religions.
5. Few references are made in this chapter to the historical background of the movements. A handy introduction in English is Murakami (1980).
6. English-language works on Tenrikyō's history, doctrines and religious activities include van Straelen (1957); Tenrikyō Overseas Mission Department (1966); Tenrikyō Church Headquarters (1967; 1972a); and Ellwood (1982). Tenrikyō scriptures in English translation are Tenrikyō Church Headquarters (1971; 1972b). *Osashizu* and *Kōki* can be read only in Japanese, in Tenrikyō Kyōkai Honbu (1948–49) and Nakayama (1957).
7. Age is reckoned in this chapter in the traditional Japanese way of counting the years of one's age, that is, counting a fraction of a year as one full year.
8. In the same source, the number of believers in 1928 is given as more than 4 million. On the other hand, the statistics for 1980 show about 2,592,000 believers (Bunkachō, 1982). It is unlikely that believers decreased dramatically between 1928 and 1980; the statistics for 1928 seem to be highly exaggerated.
9. As far as I know, there have been no studies of Honmichi in English. Honmichi Kyōgibu (1972), Murakami (1974) and Umehara (1977) give descriptions in Japanese of Honmichi's history. Three important pamphlets from Honmichi in the early Shōwa period (*Study Data, Letters* and *An Announcement for the Patriots*) are reprinted in Tanigawa et al. (1971). I am greatly indebted to Murakami's work.
10. For the Mikagura-uta and the Ofudesaki I used the English translations published by the Tenrikyō Church Headquarters (1972b; 1971).
11. The number is that of each *tanka* in each Part.
12. In the original translation by the Tenrikyō Church Headquarters, 'foreigners' and 'Japanese' are 'the people of the region where My teachings spread later' and 'the people of the region where My teachings spread early'. Corresponding Japanese words are simply *kara* and *nihon*.
13. As to the relationship between Ofudesaki and Kōki, see Shimazono (1981; 1982).
14. In the summary of *An Announcement for the Patriots* there are eight items, the first of which — general remarks on God — is omitted here, for it has little to do with millennialism.
15. Mass pilgrimages to the Ise shrine occurred about every 60 years in the Tokugawa period, giving rise to a folk belief that God gives men abundant benefits at this interval. 1928 was the sixty-first year after 1867 when a big mass pilgrimage called 'Eejanaika' had occurred.

References

Bunkachō (The Cultural Agency) (1982) *Shūkyō Nenkan Shōwa 56 nenban* (*The Yearbook of Religions, 1981*). Tokyo: Gyōsei.
Ellwood, Robert S., Jr (1982) *Tenrikyō Pilgrimage Faith*. Tenri: Oyasato Research Institute, Tenri University.

Honmichi Kyōgibu (1972)   *Honmichi Gaikan (An Outline of Honmichi)*. Takaishi: Honmichi Kyōgibu.

Lins, Ulrich (1976)   *Die Ōmoto-Bewegung und der radikale Nationalismus in Japan*. Munich and Vienna: R. Oldenburg Verlag.

Miyata, Noboru (1975a)   *Miroku Shinkō no Kenkyū (A Study on Miroku (Maitrēya) Belief)* (rev. edn). Tokyo: Miraisha.

—— (1975b)   *Kinsei no Hayarigami (Fashionable Gods in the Tokugawa Period)*. Tokyo: Hyōronsha.

—— (1980)   *Mirai e no Inori: Miroku (Prayer to the Future: Miroku (Maitrēya))*. Tokyo: Kosei Shuppansha.

Murakami, Shigeyoshi (1974)   *Honmichi Fukei Jiken (The Incident of Lèse Majesté of Honmichi)*. Tokyo: Kōdansha.

—— (1980)   *Japanese Religion in the Modern Century*, trans. H. Byron Earhart. Tokyo: University of Tokyo Press.

Nakayama, Shōzen (1957)   *Kōki no Kenkyū (A Study on Kōki)*. Tenri: Tenrikyō Dōyūsha.

Shimazono, Susumu (1979)   'The Living Kami Idea in the New Religions of Japan', *Japanese Journal of Religious Studies*, 6(3), 389–412

—— (1981)   'Shinshūkyō no Shūkyōishiki to Seiten' ('Religious Consciousness in New Religions and the Scriptures'), pp. 298–312 in Ikeda Hidetoshi et al. (eds), *Nihonjin no Shūkyō no Ayumi (Steps in Japanese Religious History)*. Tokyo: Daigaku Kyōikusha.

—— (1982)   'Tenrikyō ni Okeru Kyūsaishi Shinwa' ('The Heilsgeschichte in Tenrikyō'). *Tetsugaku Shisō Ronsō* (University of Tsukuba, Department of Philosophy), 1, 17–28.

Talmon, Yonina (1968)   'Millenarism', in *International Encyclopedia of Social Sciences*, Vol. 9. New York: Macmillan and Free Press.

Tanigawa, Ken'ichi et al. (eds) (1971)   *Nihon Shomin Seikatsu Shiryō Shūsei*. 18: *Minkan Shūkyō (Materials for the Common People's Life in Japan*. Vol. 18: *Popular Religions)*. Tokyo: San'ichi shobō.

Tenrikyō Church Headquarters (1967)   *Life of Oyasama, the Foundress of Tenrikyō*. Tenri: Tenrikyō Church Headquarters.

—— (1971)   *Ofudesaki: The Tip of the Divine Writing Brush*. Tenri: Tenrikyō Church Headquarters.

—— (1972a)   *The Doctrine of Tenrikyō*. Tenri: Tenrikyō Church Headquarters.

—— (1972b)   *Mikagura-uta: The Songs for the Tsutome*. Tenri: Tenrikyō Church Headquarters.

Tenrikyō Dōyūsha (ed.) (1929)   *Tenrikyō Kōyō, Shōwa Yonenban (The Elements of Tenrikyō)*. Tenri: Tenrikyō Dōyūsha.

Tenrikyō Kyōkai Honbu (ed.) (1948–49)   *Osashizu* (8 vols) (in Japanese). Tenri: Tenrikyō Dōyūsha (Tenrikyō Church Headquarters).

Tenrikyō Overseas Mission Department (ed.) (1966)   *Tenrikyō: Its History and Teachings*. Tenri: Tenri Jihōsha.

Umehara, Masaki (1977)   *Tenkeisha no Shūkyō Honmichi (The Religion of the Revealed: Honmichi)*. Tokyo: Kōdansha.

van Straelen, Henry (1957)   *The Religion of Divine Wisdom: Japan's Most Powerful Religious Movement*. Kyoto: Veritas Shoin.

Yasumaru, Yoshio and Masaki Hirota (1966)   'Yonaoshi no Ronri no Keifu: Maruyamakyō o Chūshin ni' ('A Genealogy of the Logic of "Yonaoshi" (world-renewal): Mainly on Marayamakyō', *Nihonshi Kenkyū*, Vols 85–6.

4

Social change and movements of revitalization in contemporary Islam

Saïd Amir Arjomand*

Movements of revitalization, renewal and orthodox reform are periodically found in the history of Islam since its very beginning in the seventh century. In the more recent past, continuous social change has set in motion a variety of movements of religious revitalization in Muslim lands, as it has in the rest of the world. Perhaps the most remarkable fact about these more recent movements is the degree to which they replicate the historical patterns of spread and revitalization of Islam. Time and again, religious and sectarian movements in the history of medieval Islam have advocated a return to the Book of God and to the pristine Islam of the Prophet and his disciples — the Qur'an and this Golden Age thus being conceived as the source of the eternally valid normative model for worldly life and of guidance to other-worldly salvation. Similarly, most Islamic movements in modern history have conceived of their tasks as renewal (*tajdid*) of the teaching of the Prophet and a return to the Qur'an. What has been said of the participants in one nineteenth-century movement of renewal equally applies to others: 'To them their attitudes and orientation were not different from a traditional past, for they did not view history as a road to modernity, but rather as a setting for periodic occasions (as they hoped this was) when humans emulated the great historic peak which is the period of revelation itself' (Metcalf, 1982: 360).

Let us begin by identifying the processes of social change which are likely to strengthen disciplined religiosity and, under favourable conditions, to give rise to movements for orthodox reform and renewal of Islam. Broadly speaking, five such processes can be identified in the modern period. These are often interrelated and chronologically overlapping: (1) integration into the international system (Western colonialism and colonial and imperialist encroachments, advent of Christian missionary activities); (2) development of transport, communication and the mass media; (3) urbanization; (4) the spread of literacy and education; and (5) the incorporation of the masses into the political society. Of these processes, the first is the oldest and the last the newest; their examination — attempted

* I am grateful to Professor Binnaz Toprak for her comments on this paper and for kindly supplying me with additional statistics.

elsewhere (Arjomand, 1984b) — would take us either too far back into history or too much into the midst of an unsettled current turmoil. The remaining three processes, however, can be conveniently treated within the scope of this chapter. The last process will be touched upon only indirectly or at the end; nevertheless, I hope our perspective on it will be enriched by the consideration of the preceding processes.

What has currently struck those who subscribe to some variant of theories of modernization is that urbanization and the spread of literacy and the expansion of higher education in the Islamic world have been accompanied by an *increase*, rather than a lowering, of religious propensity on the part of the majority of the population. In other words, with the development of media of communication, urbanization and the spread of literacy and higher education, religion has flourished: it has not declined. In the context of national integration, this general increase in religious propensity has been a crucial precondition of the contemporary resurgence and politicization of Islam which has set in motion many movements for the revitalization of Islam, this time through the establishment of Islamic theocratic government.

To be understood at all, this recent phenomenon must be put in the historical perspective of the expansion and intensive consolidation of Islam. To convey the sense both of the geographical extent and the historical depth of the ongoing process of intensive Islamization which has tended to accompany the above-mentioned processes of social change, I will present my evidence in the form of a mosaic covering different countries and different historical periods, rather than confining myself to a single country and a more limited period. This method seems most suited to the purpose of illustrating the connection between specific kinds of social change and the movements of revival in Islam.

Development of the media of communication and transportation
The advent of books, periodicals and newspapers creates a public sphere in which the literate members of society can participate. The institution of public debates and lectures adds to the vitality of activity in this public sphere while perhaps also extending its boundaries to include some of the semi-literate. That the creation and enlargement of the public sphere provides the conditions for the rise of socio-political movements has long been taken for granted. However, it is just as possible for the arrival of the media of communication to give rise to and sustain a *religious* movement.

This was the case with the Islamic revival in British India, especially under the leadership of the *'ulama* of Deoband in the last four decades of the nineteenth century. With the powerful catalyst of the threat to Islam posed by British colonial rule and the accompanying Christian missionary activity in early nineteenth century, the newly available printing presses were put to good use by the reformist Muslim leaders of northern India. They were used to disseminate the injunctions (singular, *fatwa*) of Shah 'Abdu'l-'Aziz (d. 1824), the son and heir of the great Renewer (*mujaddid*) Shah Waliu'llah of Delhi (d. 1762), as an important tool for teaching the Sacred Law which was ceasing to be enforced in the law courts, being transformed in British India to the hybrid Anglo-Muhammadan Law (Metcalf, 1982: 49, 52). In the 1820s and 1830s, the followers of the ageing Shah 'Abdu'l-'Aziz launched a movement for the orthodox reform of Islam combined with political action. Under the leadership of Sayyid Ahmad Barelwi, the Martyr (d. 1830), the movement culminated in an abortive *jihad* (holy war) in the tribal areas of the North-Western Province (Mujeeb, 1976: 391–7, 445–7; Lapidus, 1980: 92–3). Two reformist works of Sayyid Ahmad, *The Strait Path* (*Siratu'l-Mustaqim*) and *The Strengthening of Faith* (*Taqwiyatu'l-Iman*), were printed on the new lithographic press of the day and were reissued in numerous subsequent editions throughout the nineteenth century. A translation of the Qur'an with commentary was another notable publication of the reform movement, which, according to Metcalf, had a substantial role in shaping the Urdu language as a medium of communication with a popular audience. The extensive use of the press by the missionary reformers to disseminate the fundamental tenets of Islam was noted by an observer in Calcutta in 1832, who was impressed by this 'new feature in the history of the efforts for the propagation of Mohammedanism, or for the reform of its corruptions . . .' (Metcalf, 1982: 67).

Some three decades later, the same motive of the eradication of corruptions, alteration of non-Islamic customs and more strict adherence to the written tradition of Islam was behind the foundation of the seminary of Deoband in 1867. The *'ulama* who founded the seminary had a clear and coherent image of the world to which such set notions of the anglicized elite as progress, constitutional government and the superiority of European civilization were irrelevancies (Metcalf, 1982: 15). They were convinced of the superiority of Islam as the final Revelation and the youngest world-religion, and saw their task as its spread and the purification of customs according to its written tenets. 'They did, however, find a new popular basis of support, and assimilated to their own ends the modern organizational style of the new educational institutions. In so doing they adhered to a single goal: the rigorous training in religious classics of *'ulama* who would spread instruction in Islamic norms and beliefs' (Metcalf, 1982: 136–7).

To finance its activities, the seminary of Deoband developed a network of donors most of whom also acted as disseminators of its ideas. Its organizational innovations included the printing of an annual report. Almost immediately (1867–80) there spread a network of Deobandi schools in the region around Deoband and through northern/north-eastern India by the end of the nineteenth century. The expansion continued throughout the present century. In 1967, a hundred years after the foundation of the seminary of Deoband, there were 1,934 schools of Deobandi orientation. This expansion was led by Deoband's graduates. Between 1867 and 1967 the seminary of Deoband itself produced 5,888 teachers, 4,288 preachers and missionaries, 1,540 debators and over 4,000 graduates in other professions. The seminary also established a department of injunctions (*daru'l-ifta'*) to circumvent British courts and the Anglo-Muhammadan Law, and had issued 269,000 injunctions by 1967 (Metcalf, 1982: 94, 111, 127–46).

Like those of the earlier decades, the Deobandi orthodox reformists of the last decades of the nineteenth century were to avail themselves of printing and other media of communication. The seminary of Deoband made effective use of mail, money order services and above all cheap methods of printing. Thus, in India, 'indigenous leaders welcomed cheap publications and public preaching not as a source of a new world-view but as a way of spreading their own new formulations of self-statement and identity' (Metcalf, 1982: 198). Here even a good historian like Metcalf is constrained by the prejudices of secularized social scientists and fudges her observation, using such pleasantly vague terms as 'self-statement' and 'identity' instead of the much more accurate, albeit tabooed, term 'religion'. The truth, admirably shown by Metcalf herself, is that the orthodox reformists of Deoband were engaged in using new technology for public formulation of their religion, of Islam.

The new technology of communication gave unprecedented publicity to the missionary, reformist activity of the Deobandis. The fundamentals of Islam were expounded, often in simple Urdu, and disseminated among a large audience, an audience far larger than the number of books sold and the number of those who were themselves literate, as new books would be passed from hand to hand and read aloud in public. In addition, classical religious works, particularly of *Hadith (Traditions of the Prophet)*, usually with Urdu translation, were being published. Predictably, tracts against Hindus (especially the revivalist Arya Samajis) and Christians also made their appearance. Some religious books were written for women and typically were given as gifts to new brides (Metcalf, 1982: 198–211). As the quantity of published books dramatically increased in the second half of the nineteenth century, the proportion of religious works remained substantial — so much so that in 1877 the Director of Public Instruction for the North-Western Provinces considered the copious religious publications the sign of 'a marked tendency to religious revival among the Mahomedans', and in 1902 a Christian missionary would remark: 'The Mahomedans are certainly learning the power of the press' (cited in Metcalf, 1982: 203).

Another interesting feature of the publicistic activity of the Deobandis was public preaching and pamphlet controversy. Oral debates with Hindu revivalists, Christian missionaries and rival Muslim revivalist groups attracted large audiences. Deoband even established a separate department of debate to prepare the seminarians for lectures and oral debates (Metcalf, 1982: 232–3).

Better known than the Deobandi movement is the movement of orthodox reform in the Middle East and North Africa designated the Salafiyya, a movement whose purpose was the revival of the ways of the Pious Ancestors or the first generations of Muslims (Merad, 1971: 141–63). Like the political pan-Islamism of Afghani (d. 1897) (Keddie, 1969) and the reformism of Muhammad 'Abaduh (d. 1906) from which it originated (Kerr, 1966), the Salafiyya movement was closely bound to the spread of publicistic activity and journalism in the Muslim world. A thorough study of this movement in Algeria during the interwar period (Merad, 1967) underscores the role of journalism and publicistic activity in its inception and expansion. Here again, the French colonial rule and the menace of cultural 'Frenchization' acted as a powerful factor in initiating a movement in defence of the Islamic tradition. Its founder, 'Abd al-Hamid ibn Badis (d. 1941), was a religious scholar and a journalist whose collaborators in the journal *Shihab* formed the leading nucleus of the orthodox reformism in Algeria. The *Shihab* naturally became the organ of the orthodox reformist movement whose cause was also taken up by more than a dozen other journals in Arabic and French (Merad, 1967: 89 ff. and the photographs between pp. 184–5). An article in the *Shihab* which Merad (1967: 293) considers the doctrinal manifesto of the movement throws an interesting light on its self-conception: 'the attempt at renewal (*tajdid*) and at reformation (which is the primary ambition of the orthodox reformists) has nothing in common with modernism, nor, *a fortiori*, with the extremist tendencies of the latter.'

The geography of Islamic reformism in Algeria also brings out the importance of the channels of physical communication, such as roads, for the spread of the movement. The non-existence of good roads constituted an important constraint on the expansion of orthodox reformism: 'In the period when the use of motorcars was restricted and expensive, the reformist penetration was a function of the facility of the means of transport. The reformist agents preferred to follow the great railway routes.' This pattern of expansion is particularly evident in the case of the spread of the reformist movement along the national route, no. 1, from Alger to Laghouat (Merad, 1967: 195–6).

A study of an orthodox reform movement known as the Wahhabiyya in French Africa in the postwar period reveals a similar pattern of expansion. Kaba (1974: 65) regards the improvement of transport as the main economic change in West Africa since the second world war. The Wahhabiyya considered itself a movement of orthodox reform distinct from and opposed to modernism which was condemned for leading to syncretism (Kaba, 1974: 22–3). The Wahhabi missionaries spread along the newly built or improved roads. Of some 20 Wahhabi centres in French West Africa, all except three or possibly four were on 'major roads' and/or 'rail-roads' (of the latter, two were located less than 50 km from a major road) (Kaba, 1974: xvi, map).

Having finally reached the infrastructure of national integration, I must also stress the crucial importance of the international integration resulting from the continuous improvement in international transport since the eighteenth century. Safer and cheaper sea transport brought many of the leaders of the Indian revitalization movement to Mecca (Voll, 1982; Metcalf, 1982). Facilitation of the pilgrimage to Mecca and of visits to the centre of Islamic learning at al-Azhar was similarly an important factor in the spread of Islam in Africa (Martin, 1976). Since the second world war, the declining cost of air transport and economic prosperity have greatly increased the number of pilgrims to Mecca, which has in turn contributed to the spread of movements such as the Wahhabiyya in West Africa (Kaba, 1974: 72).

Urbanization
In view of the incontestable historical association between urban strata and congregational religiosity, especially of the ethical type (Weber, 1968: 481–4), the neglect of religion in the studies on urbanization in the Third World is somewhat surprising. What is even more surprising is that those writers who have recently countered the *Gemeinschaft–Gesellschaft*-inspired views on urbanism by assertions of the absence of anomie, marginality and atomization have paid little (Perlman, 1976) or no attention to religion (Portes, 1972; Portes and Walton, 1976; Germani, 1980). The fact remains, however, that

cities throughout history have been the seats of Christian, Jewish and Islamic piety. Furthermore, there is evidence from the recent past and the contemporary period that social dislocation — migration from villages to towns — is accompanied by increased religious practice which could, under favourable conditions, sustain movements of religious revival. The Methodist revival spread hand in hand with the growth of industrial cities in England (Hobsbawm, 1959; Thompson, 1963). For the three-quarters of a century after 1750, Semmel (1973: 9) finds that 'a religious awakening appeared, district by district, to accompany industrial growth'. Similarly, many nominally Catholic Irish immigrants who had scant prior knowledge of the Catholic doctrine became practising believers in the course of Catholic revivalism in New York in the second half of the nineteenth century (Dolan, 1975: 57; 1978: 133–4). Moving to the present century, Lewis (1973: 129) tells us that his research on Mexico City in 1951 led him to the conclusion that 'religious life became more Catholic and disciplined, indicating the reverse of the anticipated secularization process'. Fry (1978: 178) draws a parallel between the present-day growth of Pentecostalism in São Paolo and of Methodism in nineteenth-century Manchester as hierarchically organized evangelizing movements which stress rigorous moral discipline, and proceeds to juxtapose it with the growth of the Afro-Brazilian Umbanda movement as an alternative channel for religion in urban Brazil. Finally, to complete our selective examples, we can refer to Roberts' (1968) work on the growth of Protestant groups in Guatemala City.

The historical connection between congregational religion and urban life is at least as firm in Islam as in Christianity — if not even firmer (Planhol, 1959). In its classic pattern, cities with their mosques and *madrasas* (seminaries) constitute centres of Islamic orthodoxy, while tribal areas form the periphery which comprises those who are 'most stubborn in their unbelief and hypocrisy' (Qur'an, VI. 98). Movement from the tribal — and by extension rural — periphery into urban centres has thus been historically associated with increasing religious orthodoxy and a more rigorous adherence to the central tradition of Islam. It would be interesting to see whether this historical relationship holds for the recent decades of rapid urbanization in the Middle East.

What enables us to answer this question in the affirmative at the outset is the unmistakable impression of the striking decline of popular Sufism (Maraboutism in North and West Africa) throughout the Islamic world. The decline of this peripheral variant of Islam[1] has gone hand in hand with the growth in the urban centres of what Geertz (1971) has termed 'scripturalism' and what I refer to as

'orthodoxy' or 'orthodox reformism', depending on the context.
A survey in 1976 of a sample of 105 men, most of whom had lived in
the Medina of Dakar for more than ten years, nicely illustrates the
gradual decline of peripheral Islam and the spread of orthodoxy as a
consequence of urbanization. Maraboutic orders have historically
been instrumental in the conversion of Senegal to Islam, and they still
remain influential in Senegalese society and politics. Nevertheless,
the survey showed a weakening of the marabouts' influence among
the Medina inhabitants. By contrast, 'virtually all Muslims [who
constituted 90 percent of the sample] prayed five times a day every
day and went to the mosque on Friday regularly. Over 80 percent sent
their children to Qur'anic schools as well. Yet in regard to the
marabouts they exhibited a rather tolerant or disengaged view'
(Creevey, 1980: 219). Furthermore, some 13 percent of these men
had joined new religious associations (Creevey, 1980: 220).

Let us now take a macrosociological perspective and look at two
countries in the Middle East which were dominated by two of the
most aggressively secularizing states in the interwar period: Iran and
Turkey. Both countries have experienced over three decades of rapid
urban growth since the second world war, and in both there has been
a renewed vitality of religious activities in the 1960s and 1970s.

Table 1 shows an increase of 10 million in the urban population of
Iran in two decades. In this period, the urban population nearly
trebled while the rural population increased by just over one-third.[2]
As Tables 2 and 3 show, internal migration accounts for a substantial
proportion of this growth in urban population. (Note that the
offspring of the migrants born in the cities are *not* included in these
figures.) Furthermore, it is worth noting that the percentage of rural–
urban internal migrants is considerably higher for the most
developed and urbanized Central Province (capital, Tehran), being
46.6 percent in 1972 (Kazemi, 1980: 31).

TABLE 1
Urban population of Iran

Year	(Islamic year)	Urban population ('000)	% of total population
1956	(1335)	5,954	31.4
1966	(1345)	9,794	38.0
1971	(1350)	12,398	41.3
1976	(1355)	15,854	47.0

Sources: The Iranian National Censuses of 1956, 1966 and 1976 and the *Statistical
Yearbook of 1974–5 (Salnameh-ye Amari-ye 1353)*. Tehran: Sazeman-e Barnameh va
Budgeh, 1976.

TABLE 2
Internal migration in Iran

Year	(Islamic year)	Total population ('000)	Migrants	Migrants as % of total population
1956	(1335)	18,955	2,081	11.0
1966	(1345)	25,079	3,224	12.9
1972	(1351)	29,526	4,275	14.5
1976	(1355)	33,709	5,056	15.0

Sources: as for Table 1.

TABLE 3
Increase in urban population in Iran, 1966–1976

	Total population ('000)	As % of total increase
Natural population increase	2,621	43.7
Population in expanded city boundaries	380	6.3
Population in new urban centres	891	14.8
Rural to urban migration	2,111	35.2
Total	6,003	100.0

Source: Kazemi (1980: 14, Table 2.2).

In the late 1960s and 1970s, these expanding urban centres of Iran witnessed an increasing vitality in religious activities of a variety of kinds. Table 4 reflects some of these for the period preceding the Islamic revolution. As it shows, there were almost twice as many mosques per capita in Tehran in 1975 as compared with 1961[3] (meanwhile, Tehran's population had more than doubled), and religious activities such as pilgrimages to Mecca and donations to the shrines had greatly increased with economic growth and prosperity. Furthermore, a large number of religious associations had mushroomed among laymen. Brotherhoods and religious associations of the laity have always constituted an important feature of popular religion, whether in England on the eve of the Reformation (Scarisbrick, 1982), in eighteenth-century Catholic Europe (Chadwick, 1981: esp. 40) or in contemporary Egypt (where they accounted for the majority of registered voluntary associations in the mid-1950s) (Berger, 1970: 99–100). From 1965 onwards, there was an astonishing growth in the number of religious associations in Iran. These were often associated with the groupings of humbler occupations or in poorer city quarters.

TABLE 4
Selected indicators of religious activity in Iran in the 1970s

Year	(Islamic year)	Mosques in Tehran	Per 10,000 buildings	Per 10,000 persons*	Pilgrims to Mecca ('000)	Index	Cash donations to shrine in Mashhad Millions of rials	Index	National income Billions of rials	Index
1961–62	(1340)	293	—	14.6	—	—	—	—	—	—
1970–71	(1349)	—	—	—	27	100	—	—	684.9	100
1971–72	(1350)	—	—	—	34.5	128	19.9***	100	829.9	121
1972–73	(1351)	700	14.7	19.2	45	167	24.4	123	1,041.1	152
1973–74	(1352)	909	18.6	23.7	57	211**	34.5	174	1,581.2	231
1974–75	(1353)	—	—	—	51	189**	79.4	400	2,814.9	411
1975–76	(1354)	1,140	22.6	22.6	72	267**	105.5	531	—	—

Sources: Arjomand (1984b: Tables 2, 3 and 4) and those used for Table 1 above.

* Estimated from projections of the population of Tehran on the basis of the censuses of 1956, 1966 and 1976.

** The number of applicants for pilgrimage to Mecca may have exceeded the government quota by as much as six to eight times.

*** Average for Islamic years 1347, 1348 and 1349.

They met mostly during the religious months of Muharram and Ramadan but occasionally also at other times. By 1974 there were 322 Hosayniyyeh-type centres in Tehran, 305 in Khuzestan and 731 in Azerbaijan.

In addition, there were over 12,300 'religious associations' in Tehran alone, most of which were formed after 1965. Of these, 1,821 designated themselves formally by a title. These titles typically refer either to the guild or profession of the members, to their geographical town or region of origin, or to their aspirations. As such, they are highly revealing of the social background of their members, and of the type of religious sentiment motivating them to form these associations. The unmistakable impression given by the titles is that their members fall into two quite possibly overlapping social groups: lower-middle-class guilds and professions associated with the bazaar economy, and recent migrants from the provinces. Furthermore, there can be no mistake that their religious practice is solidly traditional. Here are some typical examples: Religious Associations of Shoemakers, of Workers at Public Baths, of the Guild of Fruit-Juicers (on street-corners), of Tailors, of the Natives of Natanz Resident in Tehran, of the Natives of Semnan, of the Desperates (*bicharehha*) of [Imam] Husayn, of the Abjects (*Zalilha*) of [Imam] Musa ibn Ja'ifar (Najafi, 1976: 161, 162). A survey of the immigrant poor in Tehran in the 1970s (Kazemi, 1980: 63) found these religious groups to be the only secondary voluntary associations of significance among them. As one young squatter told the researcher, 'Nothing brings us together more than the love for Imam Husayn. My personal view is that these *hey'ats* (associations) have a positive aspect in uniting us and keeping us informed about each other's affairs.'

As I have tried to show elsewhere (Arjomand, 1981a), the increased vitality of religion in expanding cities and the organizational network provided by these religious associations were harnessed to support Khomeini's movement for the establishment of Islamic theocracy which led to the overthrow of the Shah in 1979.

In the recent decades, the pattern of urbanization and internal migration in Turkey has been somewhat similar to that in Iran. Urban population as a percentage of the total population of Turkey rose from 30 percent in 1960 to 34.4 percent in 1965 and 41.8 percent in 1975 (the Iranian and Turkish figures are not strictly comparable[4]) (OECD, 1978; Clarke, 1981). Similarly to Iran, internal migrants accounted for 15.7 percent of the total population of 31.4 million (Dewdney, 1972: 63), and, with the number of migrants rising from 1.7 million in 1950 to 4 million in 1965, internal migration accounted for much of urban growth (Karpat, 1976: 59). The spread of *gecekondus* (shanty towns), which house the bulk of the internal migrants, is the foremost feature of this urban growth. The Turkish government estimated the total number of squatter dwellings in Turkey at 500,000 in 1969, 700,000 in 1972; by 1974 an estimated 3.5–4.5 million people inhabited the *gecekondus* (Karpat, 1976: 62). A number of interesting findings support the correlation between urbanization and increased vitality of religious activities. Yücekök (1971) has found that religious organizations and schools for Qur'an courses are concentrated in the more developed and urbanized regions of Turkey, and that the growth of guild associations in provincial towns goes hand in hand with their increased support for religious activities (cited in Mardin, 1977, and Heper, 1981: 359, n. 72). Scott (1971) similarly reports that Qur'an courses (either official — found in larger settlements, towns and cities, frequently attached to a mosque — or private — given by teachers supported by voluntary contributions from students) are offered at the lowest per capita rate in the least developed and predominantly rural eastern or south-eastern provinces, while the most developed and urbanized western and north-western provinces have the highest rate. There has also been a notable increase in the activities of the officially banned Sufi orders, especially of the Naksibendi order, in Turkish towns and their adjoining villages (Vergin, 1973). The Nurcu movement, a Sufi movement founded by Bediuzzeman Said-i Nursi (d. 1961), is flourishing; and one occasionally hears of such groups as the Suleymanci, whose aim is 'to establish the army of Islam instead of the Republic and to restore the Caliphate' (Vergin, 1973: 317; cited in Mardin, 1977).

The above findings on the increasing interest and participation in religious activities accompanying urban development can be supplemented by an analysis of the revealing electoral data on the Turkish general election of 1973, in which the nascent Islamic party, the National Salvation Party (NSP) (Milli Selamat Partisi), polled a surprising 11.8 percent of the national vote and saw 48 of its candidates elected to the Turkish parliament. To my knowledge, the full significance of these data has been obscure to Turkish social scientists (Toprak, 1981; Heper, 1981), who seem too much in awe of the modernization theory to push the analysis of the data far enough.

Two markedly different patterns of NSP vote emerge from the 1973 data. The dominant pattern, it is true, confirms the impression gained from the fact that the strongholds of the NSP were the least developed and least urbanized regions of Turkey: eastern and central Anatolia. However, far more interesting is the second crucially important pattern revealed by our analysis. Table 5 indicates the dominant pattern of NSP support in predominantly rural areas, divided in turn into changing and stagnant regions. Twelve other

TABLE 5
The ten administrative districts with the highest percentage* of NSP vote

	% rural vote	No. of deputies elected	Rate of development**	Gecekondu***
Pattern I (i) (Changing rural)				
Elazig	68.2	2	+ +	—
Kahraman Maras	68.2	2	+	†
Sivas	70.0	3	+	+
Rize†	81.0	1	+ +	—
Corum	76.6	2	+	—
Pattern I (ii) (Stagnant rural)				
Erzurum†	74.2	3	—	+
Bingol	87.5	1	—	—
Adiyaman	70.3	1	—	—
Gumushane	92.2	1	—	—
Yozgat	87.3	1	—	+

Sources: Karpat (1976: esp. Tables 2.1, 2.2, pp. 59–60); Toprak (1981: esp. Tables 9, 14, pp. 111–12, 116); Türkiye Cumhuriyeti Başbakanlık Devlet Planlama Teşkilatı, Türkiye'de İller İtibarıyla Sosyo–Ekonomik Gelişmişlik Endeksi (1963–1967), Ankara, 1970; Clark (1972: 62–3) (additional information on economic development).

* From 21.5 to 29.5 percent against the national average of 11.8 percent.
** Below average for Turkey (—), above average (+) and high (+ +) on the basis of national ranking.
*** Negligible (—), sizeable (+) and very large (+ +) on the basis of the absolute number of dwellings.
† Centre of Islamic traditionalist opposition to Ataturk.

cases, administrative districts where one NSP deputy was returned, fit this dominant Pattern I (i or ii), altogether accounting for 29, or over a half, of the 48 NSP elected deputies (Toprak, 1981: 111-12). It is worth noting that, even in this predominantly rural pattern, the actual percentage of NSP vote in towns in most cases exceeded, by a considerable margin, what one would expect on the basis of the relative weight of urban population in the respective administrative district. Only in two cases out of these ten does the actual percentage of urban vote fall slightly below the expected level.[5]

The last note prepares us for the examination of the appeal of, and support for, the NSP among the urban population of Turkey. Table 6 shows the remarkable fact that 14 of the 48 NSP deputies were elected in areas of high concentration of urban vote, comprising growing cities with large migrant populations living in shanty towns.

For the sake of completion, let us examine the remaining five cases of NSP success in the 1973 elections. In Table 7, note the remarkable

TABLE 6

Administrative districts of NSP strength with urban concentration (over 40 percent*) of the vote

Administrative district	% urban vote	No. of deputies elected	Level of development**	Size of *gecekondu****
Pattern II (i) (Changing)				
Adana	51.5	1	+ +	+ +
Ankara	66.0	2	+ +	+ +
Bursa†	43.3	1	+	+ +
Istanbul	77.1	3	+ +	+ +
Pattern II (ii) (Stagnant)				
Konya†	47.0	3	—	+ +
Gaziantep	46.0	1	—	+ +
Malatya	41.2	1	—	+ +
Urfa	43.6	1	—	+ +
Kaysari	46.7	1	—	

Sources: as for Table 5.
* The national average of the NSP urban vote being 32.8 percent.
** Below average (—), above average (+) and high (+ +). The level of development seems a better indicator of the situation in the large cities than its rate. For the 'stagnant' districts, both the level and the rate of development are negative.
*** Negligible (—), sizeable (+) and very large (+ +).
† Centre of Islamic traditionalist opposition to Ataturk.

TABLE 7

Intermediate cases: above-average* urban vote and size of shanty towns

Administrative district	% of urban vote	No. of deputies elected	Rate of development**	Size of *gecekondu****
Pattern III (i) (Changing)				
Kocaeli	38.2	1	+	+ +
Diyarbakir†	35.6	1	+	+ +
Zonguldak	36.0	1	+	+ +
Pattern III (ii) (Stagnant)				
Afyon	35.2	1	—	—
Tokart	37.1	1	—	+ +

Sources: as for Table 5.
* 32.8 percent.
** Below average (—) and above average (+).
*** Negligible (—), sizeable (+) and very large (+ +).
† Centre of Islamic traditionalist opposition to Ataturk.

fact that Patterns II and III of the NSP vote include almost all Turkish towns with very large (+ +), or sizeable (+) migrant populations. Only two cities with a very large migrant population failed to elect an NSP candidate. Even here, in one of them — Izmir — over 50 percent of the NSP votes were nevertheless urban, including those cast in the *gecekondu*.) Similarly in only four cities with sizeable (+) *gecekondus* was the NSP not successful. (Here again, in Eskisehir — a city with a high rate of industrialization — many migrants voted for the NSP, which polled over half of its vote in the urban areas.) Furthermore, the greater propensity of the migrants to vote for the NSP, which is strongly implied by Tables 6 and 7, finds direct confirmation as regards the inhabitants of the *gecekondus* of Ankara in a survey cited by Toprak (1981: 110).

We may conclude from the evidence presented above that the rapid urbanization of Iran and Turkey over the past decades has been accompanied by an increase in the level and intensity of religious activities and a multifaceted revival of Islam which has included its spectacular entry into the political arena. This correlation conforms remarkably well to the classic pattern of intensive Islamicization consequent upon the movement from the pastoralist and rural peripheries to the urban centres of Islamic orthodoxy.

This conclusion is hardly surprising. A world religion with some form of organized clergy is at least as capable of providing the dislocated migrant masses with a cognitive and moral map of the universe as are secular movements or political ideologies and parties, be they populist, nationalist, fascist or socialist. Furthermore, a world religion· can hold forth a much more appealing promise of redemption than can political movements and thus has a distinct advantage. Let us not forget that, from the classical perspective of the sociology of religion, secular socio-political movements appear to be 'functional equivalents' of religion, and not vice versa.

The spread of literacy and higher education
In Turkey, Iran and many other Muslim countries, the considerable spread of literacy occurred at the same time as rapid urbanization. The increase in literacy seems to increase the interest in religion independently of urbanization. Scott (1971: 250) found that those provinces of Turkey with above-average rural literacy had above-average rates (of enrolment and instruction) for Qur'an courses. The two phenomena, however, are closely interrelated. Kazemi (1980: 30), for instance, found a significantly greater propensity to migrate to towns among literate as compared with illiterate rural individuals.

The spread of literacy has usually gone hand in hand with the

expansion of higher education in the Islamic world. The figures for
Iran, given in Tables 8 and 9, tell a familiar tale and exemplify a
pattern similar to what can be found in Egypt, Malaysia, Indonesia
and elsewhere. To this second process of social change corresponds
the increasing circulation of religious books and periodicals, and the
activities of Islamic associations in the universities. Table 10 shows
the increased popularity of religious books relative to other
categories.

Islamic societies of students have existed on the margin of university
political activities in Iran since the first such society was founded in
the University of Tehran by Mehdi Bazargan, who was then a

TABLE 8
Literacy and higher education in Iran

| | Literate persons over 10 yrs as % of total population | | | Persons with higher education | |
	Total for country	Urban	Total	Last 3 yrs of secondary & vocational schools	University & professional schools
1956 (1335)	15	33	—	—	—
1966 (1345)	28	49	247,717	176,586	71,131
1976 (1355)	43	60	1,134,432	851,584	282,848

Sources: Iranian National Censuses of 1956, 1966 and 1976: *National Census of Population and Housing, Aban 1345/November 1966* (Tehran: Sazeman-e Barnameh, 1968, Vol. 168, Tables B and 14); *National Census of Population and Housing, Aban 1355/November 1976* (Tehran: Sazeman-e Barnameh va Budgeh, 1981, Vol. 186, Tables 2.2, 2.3, 2.4, 2.5 and 10, pp. xviii–xix, 29–33).

TABLE 9
Enrolment in universities and professional schools in Iran

Academic year	
1969–70	67,268
1970–71	74,708
1971–72	97,338
1972–73	115,311
1973–74	123,114
1974–75	135,354

Source: *Statistical Yearbook* (*Salnameh-ye Amari*, 1353) (Tehran: Sazeman-e Barnameh va Budgeh, 1976, Table 51, p. 99).

TABLE 10
Religious books published in Iran, 1954–1975

Year	No. of religious titles per yr	As % of total titles of published books	Ordinal rank (among categories of titles) (Highest = 1)
From 1954 to 1963–64 (ave.) (1333–1342)	56.7	10.1	4
From 1964 to 1967–68 (ave.) (1342–1346)	153	—	—
From 1969–70 to 1971–72 (ave.) (1348–1350)	251.7	—	—
1972–73 (1351)	578	25.8	1
1973–74 (1352)	576 (a: 516)*	24.8 (a:22.3)*	1 (a:2 [literature, 25.7%])*
1974–75 (1353)	541 (a:438)*	33.d5d (a:23.4)*	1 (a:1)*

Source: Najafi (1976: 51–2); *Statistical Yearbook (Salnameh-ye Amari, 1353)* (Tehran: Sazeman-e Barnameh va Budgeh, 1976, p. 171) for additional classifications (a).
* a = additional classifications

professor of engineering, in 1942 (Haydari, 1954: 120–3). With the Islamic revival of the late 1960s and the 1970s, their number of members and level of activity increased dramatically (Arjomand, 1981a). Islamic societies were formed among Iranian students abroad and flourished under the guidance of such future revolutionary figures as Dr Ibrahim Yazdi (in the United States) and Dr Abu'l-Hasan Bani-Sadr (in France). These societies drew their membership largely from students of engineering, medicine and the natural sciences. Since the Islamic revolution, and especially after the ouster of Bani-Sadr in 1981, the militants of these Islamic student associations in Iran and abroad have come to constitute the 'second stratum' of Khomeini's regime and occupy the highest echelons of its non-clerical cadre.

If the striking growth of Islamic associations in Iranian universities and among Iranian students abroad in the 1970s does not offer us conclusive evidence of their preponderance over other kinds of student associations and organizations, evidence of the preponderance of Islamic activism over other forms of militancy can be found in Egypt, where the landslide victories of Muslim groups in university student unions during 1975–79 prompted Sadat to dissolve these unions (Ibrahim, 1980: 425). Similar evidence can be found in other countries. In Malaysia, according to van der Mehden (1980: 169, 173; also Tasker, 1979: 23) some 80 percent of the Malay university students are members of one of the many Dakwah organizations (*da'wa*: [Islamic] mission). The inclination towards Islamic activism is particularly strong among the Malay students in foreign countries, especially Britain, discovering their Islam in alien lands and away from home. A close connection between higher education and Islamic activism, especially among university students abroad, has also been observed in Nigeria (Muhammad, 1980: 197) and other Muslim parts of West Africa (Kaba, 1974). In fact, there is hardly a country which has not been affected by the phenomenon of Islamic student militancy. Islamic student militants from a number of Muslim countries were strongly represented in the group who occupied the Holy Mosque in Mecca in November 1979 under the leadership of Juhaiman al-'Utaiba (22 out of the 63 executed were from Muslim countries other than Saudi Arabia). Juhaiman, who proclaimed a friend the Mahdi, is now claimed by Islamic militant students of Riyadh University as 'our martyr' (Mortimer, 1982: 181–2; Dessouki, 1982: 15). In Egypt an estimated half a million persons in the intelligentsia (out of a total population of 40 million) are sympathizers of the Islamic movement, while the percentage of sympathizers is put at 30 percent among the students in Tunisia and at 10 percent in Morocco (Clément, 1983: 98).

As in Iran, it is university students and graduates in technical fields and the sciences who predominate in the Islamic associations, open and clandestine. In Egypt, for instance, it is estimated that Islamic activists constitute 25 percent of the students in the faculty of letters as compared with 60–80 percent in medicine and the faculty of sciences (Clément, 1983: 98). Furthermore, the leadership of Islamic movements, which comprise and often extend beyond these associations, are invariably highly educated. Whether in Morocco, Algeria, Tunisia, Egypt, Turkey, Iran or Afghanistan, doctors, university professors, lawyers and engineers figure prominently among the leaders of the Islamic groups (Ibrahim, 1980: 437; Étienne and Tozy, 1981: 246–7; Clément 1983; Toprak, 1981). The Islamic militants tend to be academically highly motivated and achieving; and they tend to be socially upwardly mobile, entering the professions upon graduation (Ibrahim, 1980: 439–40). Finally, female university students and young women employed in the modern sector of the economy play a noteworthy — and certainly a conspicuous — role in Islamic associations (Williams, 1980; Belhassen, 1981).

A most interesting aspect of the phenomenon of Islamic activism among the intelligentsia created by the recent expansion of higher education is its connection with our previous process: urbanization and migration into towns. Some two-thirds of the sample of Islamic militants interviewed by Ibrahim (1980: 438–9) were from rural or small-town backgrounds, and fully one-half lived in the city, with or without their parents. Davis (1984) stresses the importance of the Egyptian militants' continued ties and attachment to their parents in the countryside or small town, which can be presumed to have alienated them from the impersonal and anonymous life of the metropolis. Belhassen's study of Islamic women activists presents a similar picture; one-half of her sample of interviewees were immigrants into the capital[6] (Belhassen, 1981: 78).

It seems convenient at this point to construct a composite idealtype of the young Islamic militant out of two careful profiles drawn by Ibrahim and Clément, the former capturing the sociological elements, the latter, the psychological–ideological aspects:

> The typical member of the militant Islamic groups could therefore be described as young (early twenties), of rural or small-town background, from the middle or lower middle class, with high achievement and motivation, upwardly mobile, with science or engineering educations, and from a normally cohesive family. (Ibrahim, 1980: 440)

> The Islamic militants are Muslim men or women who, generally after a brutal conversion, decide to observe rigorously what they consider the principles of the [Sacred] Law. But this individual project, which creates a positive self-image, is also accompanied by a social project: the realization of what they believe to be an Islamic state . . . the individual must deny him or herself, renounce his or her free choice and freedom of conscience as all totalitarian militants. (Clément, 1981: 60, 63)

The fact that the leaders, cadres and active members of the contemporary Islamic groups are well-educated persons with actual or prospective professional and middle-class occupations is most surprising to those who have accepted theories of modernization or secularization and have forgotten that many engineers adhered to a variety of twentieth-century mass movements, including Stalinism, nazism and fascism. Physicians, pharmacists, engineers, university students, schoolteachers and government clerks were assumed to be secular types and are now shown to be the backbone of Islamic fundamentalism. The rural and small-town backgrounds of the educated Islamic militants may go some way towards explaining this apparently anomalous phenomenon. So does the middle and lower middle-class background of many of the activists (Ibrahim, 1980; Belhassen, 1981; Souriau, 1981: 11; Ahmad, 1981) which makes for their strong attachment to the Islamic tradition. But the phenomenon, inextricably connected with the sharp political edge of the contemporary Islamic movement, cannot be adequately understood except with reference to our last process of social change, to which we must now turn, however briefly.

National political integration

'In traditional societies religion is a mass phenomenon, politics is not; in transitional societies, religion can serve as the means by which the masses become politicized.' With this simple idea, D. E. Smith (1970: 124) seemed to have found an ingenious way of reconciling the increased visibility of religion in the contemporary political arena with theories of political modernization. The idea is undoubtedly not without merit. It can explain a number of facts: the conspicuousness of the religious factor and the prominence of the men of religion in the elected assemblies in Iran and Turkey before the autocratic centralization of the mid-1920s;[7] the consistently high percentage of the vote received by the Islamic parties in Indonesia in general elections since 1955 (between 17 and 43.5 percent: Tasker, 1979: 25); and the dominant pattern of the National Salvation Party vote in Turkey as presented in Table 5. But it cannot explain the Islamic activism of the intelligentsia and the advent of a comprehensive and militant Islamic ideology whose novel feature is the insistent advocacy of Islamic theocratic government (Zubaida, 1982; Étienne and Tozy, 1981: 256).

A complete explanation of this last phenomenon is beyond the scope of this chapter, which focuses on social change. Our last process of social change, national political integration, can help us understand the political awareness and mobilization of the intelligentsia. It can further help us understand how a politicized Islamic movement, once spearheaded by ideologues drawn from the intelligentsia, is likely to appeal to *another* important social group, the vitality of whose religion has perhaps not increased but has continued. This latter group, which may now be tempted to state its political demands in terms of an Islamic ideology, is no other than the age-old stronghold of Islam: the traditional middle and lower-middle class consisting of the merchants, craftsmen and distributive traders of the bazaar economy.

But national political integration per se cannot explain our phenomenon any further. It cannot explain why a substantial proportion of the intelligentsia would turn to the Islamic movement in the late 1960s and 1970s, whereas their counterparts had turned in the early part of the century to nationalism (Khalidi, 1984) or to varieties of socialism with a strong nationalistic tinge, or in the middle part of the century to communism (Batatu, 1978; Abrahamian, 1981). In other words, it cannot explain why the Islamic ideology is presently more popular than other panaceas. I have tried to deal with the question elsewhere (Arjomand, 1984a). Perhaps the shortest answer is supplied by the Algerian Minister of Religious Affairs: 'Neither nationalism nor Arabization has solved [the crisis of identity] since independence' (*Le Monde*, 4 September 1980; cited in Clément, 1983). This answer, however, is too short. Let me conclude by adding parliamentary democracy, socialism and communism to the list of panaceas which are currently presumed to have failed in the Muslim world. The general presumption of their failure leaves the arena of mass politics to the Islamic ideology as the uncontested panacea which, furthermore, can claim 'authenticity' in contrast to the 'imported' ideologies of the preceding decades.

Conclusion

We have examined four broad processes of social change which are generally associated with secularization, only to discover that they have in fact fostered a variety of movements of revitalization in the Islamic world. Our evidence demonstrates that these processes of social change have facilitated the rise and spread of Islamic revitalization movements. It would however be both unnecessary and simple-minded to consider them the effective causes of the revitalization of Islam. As the latter's preconditions, the vitality of the Islamic tradition — which has on occasion been incidentally touched upon above — and certain specific aspects of the socio-political orientation of Islam — which have not been discussed — are at least as important, if not more essential.

The one inescapable conclusion suggested by our analysis is that the secularization of culture must be recognized as an independent factor and separated from other processes of social change and modernization with which it has been associated in the Western historical experience. The association between the secularization of Western culture and the processes of urbanization, national integration and the spread of literacy would then appear as a result of historical contingency rather than inherent necessity. Once we consider secularization of culture an analytically distinct phenomenon and note its absence as regards large sections of the population of the Muslim world, the association of the contemporary revitalization of Islam with rapid social change ceases to be a puzzle and can be seen as consistent with comparative sociological evidence.

Notes

1. It is necessary to disclaim categorical inevitability for this process. I have cited with approval Fry's (1978) presentation of ethical Pentecostalism and magico-therapeutic Umbanda as *alternative* religious orientations in the Brazilian urban environment. There can be no doubt that a similar option is in principle open to the

recently urbanized population of the Middle East: orthodox Islam and magico-therapeutic popular cults are alternatives into which their religious energies can be channelled. In fact, Étienne has found a parallel flourishing of orthodox Islam and the cults of maraboutic saints in Casablanca (Étienne, 1981: 26–84). However, the building of mosques — in this respect Casablanca badly lags behind most cities (Étienne and Tozy, 1981: 236–9) — the creation of lay religious organizations and other religious activities to be described presently tend to make orthodox Islam the more attractive and the more typically adopted alternative.

2. From 13 million to 17.85 million.

3. It is interesting to note a similar growth of mosques in Jakarta, for which we are given (Tasker, 1979: 27):

1965	460
1974	907
1978 or early 1979	1,186

4. The definitions of urban population used for compiling the Iranian and Turkish statistics differ. For Iran, all places of 5,000 or more inhabitants are defined as towns. For Turkey, the urban population of localities within the municipality limits of administrative centres of provinces and districts are defined as urban (Clarke, 1981: 160).

5. The actual breakdown of the total vote within each administrative district between urban and rural is unfortunately not available. However, on the basis of the degree of urbanization in respective districts, a table can be constructed (Toprak, 1981: Tables 9, 10). Only in two cases does the actual percentage of urban vote fall slightly below the expected, while in the other eight cases it is considerably higher.

Percentage of NSP urban vote in its predominantly rural strongholds

Administrative district	% of vote expected	Actual % of vote	Excess over expected value
Erzurum	19.0	25.8	6.8
Elazig	32.8	31.8	–1
Kauraman-Maras	18.6	31.8	13.2
Sivas	16.0	30.0	14
Bingol	8.1	12.5	4.4
Gumushane	9.4	7.8	–1.6
Adiyaman	14.2	29.7	15.5
Rize	15.4	19.0	4.6
Corum	13.7	23.4	9.7
Yozgat	9.5	12.7	3.2

6. The size of Ibrahim's sample is 34, that of Belhassen, 20.

7. In both countries vigorous Islamic traditionalist opposition to parliamentarianism set in shortly after the introduction of parliamentary democracy (Arjomand, 1981b; Lewis, 1964: 105–6). On the other hand, many men of religion participated in the parliamentary assemblies: 22 out of 163 deputies of the first Iranian National Consultative Assembly (the Majlis) convened in 1906 were professional men of religion; and their proportion increased to about one-fifth in the subsequent three Majilses (Shaji'i, 1965). As regards Turkey, about one-fifth of the deputies (73 of the 361) of the Grand National Assembly convened in 1920 were professional men of religion (Lewis, 1964: 107–8; Toprak, 1981: 64–6).

References

Abrahamian, E. (1981)   *Iran between the Two Revolutions*. Princeton: Princeton University Press.

Ahmad, M. (1981) 'Class, Power and Religion: Some Aspects of Islamic Fundamentalism in Pakistan', paper presented at the annual convention of the American Sociological Association in Toronto.

Arjomand, S. A. (1981a) 'Shi'ite Iran and the Revolution in Iran', *Government and Opposition. A Journal of Comparative Politics*, 16(3).

—— (1981b) 'The *Ulama's* Traditionalist Opposition to Parliamentarianism; 1907–1909', *Middle Eastern Studies*, 17(2).

—— (1984a) 'Introduction: Social Movements in the Contemporary Middle and Near East', in *From Nationalism to Revolutionary Islam*. London: Macmillan/ Albany, NY: SUNY Press.

—— (1984b) 'Traditionalism in Twentieth Century Iran', in *From Nationalism to Revolutionary Islam*. London: Macmillan/Albany, NY: SUNY Press.

Batatu, H. (1978)   *The Old Social Classes and the Revolutionary Movement of Iraq*. Princeton: Princeton University Press.

Belhassen, S. (1981) 'Femmes tunisiennes islamistes', in Ch. Souriau (ed.), *Le Maghreb musulman en 1979*. Paris: Editions du CNRS (reprinted from *L'Annuaire de l'Afrique du Nord*, 1979).

Berger, M. (1970)   *Islam in Egypt Today*. Cambridge: Cambridge University Press.

Chadwick, O. (1981)   *The Popes and the European Revolution*. Oxford: Clarendon Press.

Clark, B. D. (1972) 'Iran: Changing Population Patterns', in J. I. Clarke and W. B. Fisher (eds), *Populations of the Middle East and North Africa*. London: University of London Press.

Clarke, J. I. (1981) 'Contemporary Urban Growth in the Middle East', in J. I. Clarke and H. Bowen Jones (eds), *Change and Development in the Middle East*. London and New York: Methuen.

Clément, J. F. (1981) 'Mouvements islamiques et représentation de l'Islam dans la Tensift', in E. Gellner and J. C. Vatin (eds), *Islam et politique au Maghreb*. Paris: Editions du CNRS.

—— (1983) 'Journalistes et chercheurs des sciences sociales face aux mouvements islamistes', *Archives des Sciences Sociales des Religions*, 55(1).

Creevey, L. (1980) 'Religion and Modernization in Senegal', in J. L. Esposito (ed.), *Islam and Development. Religion and Sociopolitical Change*. Syracuse, NY: Syracuse University Press.

Davis, E. (1984) 'Islamic Radicalism in Egypt', in S. A. Arjomand (ed.), *From Nationalism to Revolutionary Islam*. London: Macmillan/Albany, NY: SUNY Press.

Dessouki, A. E. H. (1982) 'The Islamic Resurgence: Sources, Dynamics, and Implications', in *Islamic Resurgence in the Arab World*. New York: Praeger.

Dewdney, J. C. (1972) 'Turkey: Recent Population Trends', in J. I. Clarke and W. B. Fisher (eds), *Populations of the Middle East and North Africa*. London: University of London Press.

Dolan, J. P. (1975)   *The Immigrant Church: New York's Irish and German Catholics, 1815–1865*. Baltimore and London: Johns Hopkins University Press.

—— (1978)   *Catholic Revivalism: The American Experience 1830–1900*. Notre Dame and London: University of Notre Dame Press.

Étienne, B. (1981) 'Magie et Thérapie à Casablanca', in Ch. Souriau (ed.), *Le*

110   Saïd Amir Arjomand

Maghreb musulman en 1979. Paris: Editions du CNRS (reprinted from *l'Annuaire de l'Afrique du Nord*, 1979).

—— and M. Tozy (1981) 'Le Glissement des obligations islamiques vers le phénomène associatif à Casablanca', in Ch. Souriau (ed.), *Le Maghreb musulman en 1979.* Paris: Editions du CNRS (reprinted from *L'Annuaire de l'Afrique du Nord*, 1979).

Fry, P. (1978) 'Two Religious Movements: Protestantism and Umbanda', in J. D. Wirth and R. L. Jones (eds), *Manchester and São Paolo: Problems of Rapid Urban Growth.* Stanford: Stanford University Press.

Geertz, C. (1971) *Islam Observed.* Chicago: University of Chicago Press.

Germani, G. (1980) *Marginality.* New Brunswick, NJ: Transaction Books.

Haydari, A. (1954) 'Some Aspects of Islamic Modernism in Iran', unpublished MA thesis, McGill University.

Heper, M. (1981) 'Islam, Polity and Society in Turkey: A Middle Eastern Perspective', *Middle East Journal*, 35.

Hobsbawm, E. J. (1959) *Primitive Rebels: Studies in Archaic Forms of Social Movements in the 19th and 20th Centuries.* New York: W. W. Norton.

Ibrahim, S. (1980) 'Anatomy of Egypt's Militant Islamic Groups: Methodological Note and Preliminary Findings', *International Journal of Middle East Studies*, 12(4).

Kaba, L. (1974) *The Wahhabiyya: Islamic Reform and Politics in French West Africa.* Evanston, Illinois: Northwestern University Press.

Karpat, K. H. (1976) *The Gecekondu: Rural Migration and Urbanization.* Cambridge: Cambridge University Press.

Kazemi, F. (1980) *Poverty and Revolution in Iran: The Migrant Poor, Urban Marginality and Politics.* New York: New York University Press.

Keddie, N. R. (1969) 'Pan-Islam as Proto-Nationalism', *Journal of Modern History*, 41.

Kerr, M. (1966) *Islamic Reform.* Berkeley and Los Angeles: University of California Press.

Khalidi, R. (1984) 'Rise of the Arab National Movement in Syria', in S. A. Arjomand, *From Nationalism to Revolutionary Islam.* London: Macmillan/ Albany, NY: SUNY Press.

Lapidus, I. (1980) 'Islam and the Historical Experience of Muslim Peoples', in M. H. Kerr (ed.), *Islamic Studies: A Tradition and Its Problems.* Malibu, California: Undena Publications.

Lewis, B. (1964) *The Middle East and the West.* New York: Harper & Row.

Lewis, O. (1973) 'Some Perspectives on Urbanization with Special Reference to Mexico City', in A. Southall (ed.), *Urban Anthropology: Cross-cultural Studies of Urbanization.* Oxford and New York: Oxford University Press.

Mardin, Ş. (1977) 'Religion in Modern Turkey', *International Social Science Journal*, 29.

Martin, B. (1976) *Muslim Brotherhoods in 19th Century Africa.* Cambridge and New York: Cambridge University Press.

Merad, A. (1967) *Le réformisme musulman en Algérie de 1925–1940.* Paris and The Hague: Mouton.

—— (1971) 'ISLAH', *Encyclopedia of Islam* (2nd edn), Vol. 4.

Metcalf, B. D. (1982) *Islamic Revival in British India: Deoband, 1860–1900.* Princeton: Princeton University Press.

Mortimer, E. (1982) *Faith and Power: The Politics of Islam.* New York: Random House.

Muhammad, A. (1980) 'Islam and National Integration through Education in Nigeria', in J. L. Esposito (ed.), *Islam and Development. Religion and Sociopolitical Change*. Syracuse, NY: Syracuse University Press.

Mujeeb, M. (1976) *The Muslims of India*. London: Allen and Unwin.

Najafi, S. M. B. (1976) 'Appendix (*Peyvast*) on Religious Media, Centers and Organizations', in A. Asadi and M. Mehrdad (eds), *Naqsh-e Rasanehha dar Poshtibani-ye Tause'a-ye Farhangi*. Tehran: Iran Communications and Development Institute.

Organization for Economic Cooperation and Development (1978) *Economic Survey: Turkey*. Paris: OECD.

Perlman, J. (1976) *The Myth of Marginality: Urban Poverty in Rio de Janeiro*. Berkeley: University of California Press.

Planhol, X. (1959) *The World of Islam*. Ithaca, NY: Cornell University Press.

Portes, A. (1972) 'Rationality in the Slum: An Essay on Interpretive Sociology', *Comparative Studies in Society and History*, 14.

—— and J. Walton (1976) *Urban Latin America: The Political Condition from Above and Below*. Austin: University of Texas Press.

Roberts, B.R. (1968) 'Protestant Groups and Coping with Urban Life in Guatemala City', *American Journal of Sociology*, 73(6).

Sazeman-e Barnameh va Budgeh (1968) *National Census of Population and Housing, Aban 1345/November 1966*, Vol. 168. Tehran.

—— (1976) *Salnameh-ye Amari-ye Keshvar, 1353*. Tehran.

—— (1981) *National Census of Population and Housing, Aban 1355/November 1976*, Vol. 186. Tehran.

Scarisbrick, J. J. (1982) 'Lay Confraternities in the Early Sixteenth Century', lecture delivered at Oxford University.

Scott, R. B. (1971) 'Qur'an Courses in Turkey', *Muslim World*, 61(4).

Semmel, B. (1973) *The Methodist Revolution*. New York: Basic Books.

Shaji'i, Z. (1965) *Nemayandegan-e Majles-e Shura-ye Melli dar 21 Dawreh-ye Qanun-gozari*. Tehran: Tehran University Press.

Smith, D. E. (1970) *Religion and Political Development*. Boston: Little, Brown.

Souriau, Ch. (1981) 'Introduction', in *Le Maghreb Musulman en 1979*. Paris: Editions du CNRS (reprinted from *l'Annuaire de l'Afrique du Nord*, 1979).

Tasker, R. (1979) 'The Explosive Mix of Muhammad and Modernity', *Far Eastern Economic Review*, 9 February.

Thompson, E. P. (1963) *The Making of the English Working Class*. Harmondsworth: Penguin Books.

Toprak, B. (1981) *Islam and Political Development in Turkey*. Leiden: E. J. Brill.

van der Mehden, F. R. (1980) 'Islamic Resurgence in Malaysia', in J. L. Esposito (ed.), *Islam and Development. Religion and Sociopolitical Change*. Syracuse, NY: Syracuse University Press.

Vergin, N. (1973) 'Industrialisation et changement social, étude comparée dans trois villages d'Eregli', unpublished doctoral thesis, Université René-Descartes, Paris.

Voll, J. O. (1982) *Islam, Continuity and Change in the Modern World*. Boulder, Colorado: Westview Press.

Weber, M. (1968) *Economy and Society*, ed. G. Roth and C. Wittich. Berkeley: University of California Press.

Williams, J.A. (1980) 'Veiling in Egypt as a Political and Social Phenomenon', in J. L. Esposito (ed.), *Islam and Development. Religion and Sociopolitical Change*. Syracuse, NY; Syracuse University Press.

112   Saïd Amir Arjomand

Yücekök, A. H. (1971) *Turkiye'de Dinin Sosyo-Ekonomik Tabani 1946–1968*. Ankara: Ankara Universitesi Siyasal Bilgiler Fakultesi.

Zubaida, S. (1982) 'The Ideological Conditions for Khomeini's Doctrine of Government', *Economy and Society*, 11(2).

5

A comparative study of two new religious movements in the Republic of Korea: the Unification Church and the Full Gospel Central Church

Syn-Duk Choi

Introduction

The rise of new religions in Korea
There were only a few kinds of faith in Korea before the end of the eighteenth century; there was shamanism, a traditional folk belief, or Confucianism and Buddhism, which were accepted as foreign religions. In the middle of the nineteenth century, however, new ethnocentric religions, namely, Donghak, Namhak, Dangun and Jeungsan, came on the scene. At the end of that century, Catholicism was introduced into Korea as well. Various new sects, with forms and doctrines very different from those of original Confucianism and Buddhism, also arose. Subsequently, these sects gave birth, in turn, to even more sects. Prior to the Liberation from Japan in 1945, there were 67 new religious bodies in Korea, according to the report of the Government-General of Korea. But immediately after the Liberation a great number of new religions sprang up rapidly, like mushrooms after a shower of rain. Today, about 300 kinds of new religions, including new foreign religions, are being propagated.

This brief historical sketch illustrates the general point that, as religious organizations become more highly institutionalized, they inevitably begin to become estranged from the dominant theme emphasized by their founder, or to face protests from those who are dissatisfied with any form of established church. Separation from the original organization usually brings changes in either doctrines or rituals. Thus, when the religious system loses some of its ability to satisfy various individual and group needs, it gives rise to sectarianism or new religious movements.

Classifications of the new religions
All the new religious bodies in Korea may be placed in 13 categories as in Table 1.

New religions may be classified as four types on the basis of their developmental process and the form in which they were founded:

TABLE 1
New religious bodies in Korea

Original religious body	No. of new religious branches
Those with Korean founders	
(1) Dong-hak gyo (Soo-un gyo)	17
(2) Dan-gun gyo	27
(3) Nam-hak gyo (Yeon-dam gyo)	8
(4) Jeung-san gyo (U-da gyo)	59
(5) Bong-nam gyo	16
(6) Sin-gye gyo	10
Others	
(7) Buddhism	49
(8) Christianity	40
(9) Shamanism	27
(10) United (miscellaneous religions)	5
(11) (Unidentified)	24
(12) Il-gwan do (from China)	5
(13) New foreign religions	16
	303

Source: Cultural Research Centre (1982: 610–11)

there are creative, sectarian, reformative and fabricated types. The creative type is a new religious body created by a (Korean) founder. The sectarian type is a group separated from an already established religion as a result of differences of opinion on doctrines, rites, leadership, management, etc. The reformative type is established as a modification of a conventional religion by means of the reformer's innovative interpretation of doctrines. The fabricated type is deliberately created by religious opportunists in order to satisfy their personal needs or to secure their livelihood.

The conditions providing for new religions
The occurrence of the new religions, in general, may be attributed to the following conditions.

1. *The precarious politico-social and economic conditions.* Uncertainty in political, economic and social conditions, confusion of thought, and deterioration of morality and ethics led people to feel hopeless and uneasy. Towards the end of the nineteenth century, Koreans were in danger of losing their political sovereignty; their economy was in a state of panic, and thus the social climate was chaotic. Such a situation led people to look forward to the appearance of a leader who would reign over the whole country and

conquer oppressive foreign powers. Furthermore, they felt that they were in great need of a saviour whose arrival would also solve their spiritual problems.

2. *Opening the doors of religious freedom.* The rulers and ordinary Koreans of the nineteenth century firmly believed that Confucianism was the only norm for morality and religion, and that even within Confucianism the Chu orthodoxy was the only one to pursue. All the rest, including Buddhism (the 'spiritual prop for the lower classes'), were stubbornly rejected as heresy. There was hardly any room for other faiths throughout the 500 years of the Yi dynasty, but as a result of the political chaos and the decay of Confucianism, Chu orthodoxy came to lose the power to enforce ideological uniformity upon the people. Moreover, with the introduction and expansion of Catholicism ('western learning'), people came to realize that they could select a religion of their choice. This even led them to develop new religions.

3. *Rapid social change and mobility.* The liberation from Japan, the Korean war in 1950 and subsequent political revolutions were accompanied by drastic social changes and movements in both physical and spiritual terms. What is more, the rush of liberalism from the West claiming to stand for democracy, the national emphasis on progressive technology, industrialization, the corresponding urbanization and various institutional changes — all of these rapid and heterogeneous factors urged the people into cultural conflicts, alienation and emotional starvation.

4. *Failures of existing religious groups.* The functions of religion may be summarized as (a) to afford the individual emotional release and a sense of confidence in the throes of despair, hate and anxiety, and (b) to integrate the social order, and to facilitate societal reform by presenting a framework of fundamental and transcendental values. These functions were supposed to be carried out by religious bodies especially when the people were in a wretched state caused by national calamities. But religious groups were in chaos themselves around 1950 as a result of problems about their resettlement, ecclesiastical authority, disputes over doctrinal or biblical interpretations, etc. From 1960 on, Korean Christian groups made remarkable gains in the numbers of converts and leaders and in the construction of churches, which, wherever possible, were built on a massive scale. The churches today are becoming centred on their own organizational concerns. Although services of worship and church programmes are well conducted, the thirst of the masses for solutions to life's problems is hardly catered for. So these people have to go elsewhere for relief.

Among the many new religious movements in Korea, those of

Christian origin are attracting the lion's share of public attention, especially two movements represented by the Rev. Sun Myung Moon's Unification Church and the Rev. Yonggi Cho's Full Gospel Central Church. These two movements in particular have achieved phenomenal success since the 1960s. They share some basic similarities: their development has been rapid, and they have strong leaders. But they differ in many ways, particularly in the essence of their doctrines and in the areas where they have gained popularity.

This chapter will compare these two movements, which have both developed in Korea in the past two decades. The plan is first to examine the relationship between their success and charisma and then to locate them in the context of a rapidly changing Korean society. To explain the history of the two movements, I shall use a modified version of Max Weber's paradigm on charisma as a handy framework for the comparison. The paradigm has been summarized by Park (1981) as in Table 2.

TABLE 2
Max Weber's paradigm on charisma

Stages of development of charisma	Strategic actions taken by charismatic individual
Crisis situation	Symbolization
Appearance of charisma	Mobilization
Gathering of followers and formation of congregation	Routinization
Co-operative behaviour	Re-institutionalization

The Full Gospel Central Church
The life of the Reverend Yonggi Cho and his associate. The main pastor of the Full Gospel Central Church, Yonggi Cho, was born on 14 February 1936 in Kyungnam Province. He was a very bright student, and his English was particularly good, but in 1953, in his sophomore year in Pusan Technical High School, he caught tuberculosis of the lungs and had to face the fear of death. His family was not wealthy, and Korean medical technology after the war was not good enough to allow him to have proper surgery.

At this time he met the missionary Ken Tise and started doing missionary work with Tise as an interpreter. One day, in 1955, Cho saw Jesus wearing a white gown in the midst of a big fire and telling him, 'I will cure your illness. Will you be my servant for the rest of your life?' He was subsequently cured of tuberculosis and was able to engage in mission work with more confidence. As a result of this religious experience, Cho came to Seoul and entered the Full Gospel

Seminary in 1956.[1] With his energetic approach and fluent English, he was elected president of the students' association and was able to work as an interpreter in many of the revival services led by foreign missionaries. While he was in the seminary, Jasil Choi, who is now the associate pastor, helped him, and this led them to start a tent church together in 1958.

Rev. Choi, the associate pastor, was born on 15 August 1915. Her mother and eldest daughter both died in 1953, and her business proved to be a complete failure just at the time that she had her first experience of a revival service. She decided to enter the Full Gospel Seminary in 1956. It was while she was there that she met her fellow-student Cho, and after graduation they started the tent church. It was on 18 May 1958, in fact, that a small tent church was opened near a graveyard in the western part of Seoul by Jasil Choi, with her three children and with Yonggi Cho as the preacher of the evening service. This was the start of the Full Gospel Central Church.

The appearance of charisma — symbolization and mobilization. Although only five people attended the first service at the tent church, more people began to come after a person who had been paralysed by a stroke for seven years was cured, a shaman was converted and a person was freed from possession by an evil spirit. The scene at the revival service in the tent church in 1961 was described as follows: 'Hundreds of people came from all over the place to the revival service at the tent church. There were more than 200 patients alone, and many were cured within each hour. Cho prayed and preached with all his might of body and soul' (Yo, 1982: 49).

The grand revival service which started at the tent church on 1 September 1961 lasted for a month and was crucial to the growth of the membership. The membership already exceeded 300 and was expanding rapidly. As a result of the expansion, the Church was able to open the West Gate Full Gospel Revival Centre in November 1961. On 26 April 1962, when Cho was ordained as a minister, the Church's name was changed from the 'Full Gospel Revival Centre' to the 'Full Gospel Central Church'. In 1964 the membership reached 3,000, and the Rev. Cho was invited to the fiftieth anniversary of the Foundation of the Assemblies of God denomination in the United States and made his first missionary trip abroad.

The sermons of Rev. Cho became more powerful, and by 1968 the membership reached 8,000. The Sunday service was held three times a day to accommodate the increased membership. In 1969 Cho purchased the land for a new church in Yoeido, but since Yoeido was not developed at all at that time, many people were not in favour of building the new church there. Moreover, the Church possessed only

1 million won, and the estimated cost of building the new church was 800 billion won. (One US dollar was then worth 272 won.) Common sense seemed to be against building the new church, since a large budget deficit and technical problems in building would have to be confronted. Rev. Cho did not give in, however, and went to Yoeido every night and prayed with all his heart, embracing an unfinished pillar of the new church.

Routinization and the establishment of a permanent community. After the dome-style church at Yoeido, which could accommodate 10,000 people, was finished, the congregation experienced growth on an unprecedented scale: from 12,500 in 1973, to 61,214 in 1978, to 149,435 in 1981, and to 255,389 in January 1983. To keep pace with the increasing number of members, the Church built a 10-storey Educational Centre in January 1977. The Twentieth Anniversary Memorial Centre was completed in July of the same year, after their 13-storey International Missionary Centre had been built. In January 1983 there were 46 pastors, 222 missionaries and 220 employees, in all about 500 people, working for the Full Gospel Central Church.

The Rev. Cho's sermons are now broadcast on 12 radio stations and four television stations throughout Korea, and are broadcast to the United States and Japan as well. Less than 25 years after Cho started the tent church, his Full Gospel Church was holding seven services each Sunday in 1983. His sermons are broadcast by television to the Educational Centre and the International Missionary Centre where people who could not get into the main church can listen to him.

The Rev. Cho retains a firm charismatic leadership over the Full Gospel Church and was expected to increase the size of his congregation to half a million members by 1984.

The Unification Church
The life of the Reverend Moon. The Rev. Moon, the founder of the Holy Spirit Association for the Unification of World Christianity, was born in Jungjoo-gun in North Pyungan Province. He learned Chinese characters when he was young and thus learned about Confucianism. In 1934, when he was 15, he had a chance to go to Jungjoo to study modern science, and in March 1938 he graduated from the Jungjoo Public School. While he was studying, his family converted to Presbyterianism as a result of many sufferings.

His biography says that on Easter morning 1936, when he was 16, he received his calling from Jesus in his prayers, and was asked to save the world from misery and sin, and to bring about the world of God. He then studied for ten years how to build a firm foundation on which to base God's world.

He came to Seoul in 1938 and entered the Seoul Engineering High School. He was a follower of Yongdo Lee, a pastor who believed in mysticism, but he also studied the Bible on his own. From 1941 to 1943 he studied electrical engineering at the Associated Engineering High School of Waseda University in Japan. When he came back to Korea, he was put in gaol for engaging in anti-Japanese movements. After his release he married Sungil Choi in April 1945, but she allegedly did not understand her husband's mission and once even had him placed under arrest. Finally they were divorced.

In June 1946, he began to preach in Pyungyang, the 'Jerusalem of the East', but was arrested because of the ensuing agitation and was imprisoned. He was released from gaol at the beginning of the Korean war and was able to escape to Pusan on 14 October 1950 with the help of the UN forces.

In Pusan he wrote a book on the Principles of the Unification Church, and in August 1951 he built a small mud house in which to start his own church. Two evangelists, Hyunsil Kang and the Rev. Yohan Lee, who started working with the Rev. Moon in 1952, went to Taegu on a mission trip, and the Rev. Moon went to Seoul to work on the foundation of the future headquarters of his church. By that time he had met Hyowon Yu, who was also from Jungjoo and who was impressed with Moon's book. They started working on the foundation of the Church together.

The appearance of charisma — symbolization and mobilization. On 1 May 1954 the Holy Spirit Association for the Unification of World Christianity was founded in Seoul with the Rev. Moon as its leader. As the Principles of the Unification Church, regarded with suspicion by existing churches, spread rapidly among the young, strong opposition was heard from churches, families and schools. Five professors and 14 students of Ewha Women's University who allegedly supported the Unification Church, along with two students of Yonsei University, (both of which were Christian universities), were expelled from their universities because they were regarded as heretics. Rev. Moon was also charged with corrupting public morals, but was acquitted of the charge 100 days later. Young-oon Kim, one of the expelled professors, went on to develop a theological grounding for the Principles of the Unification Church.

Routinization and the establishment of a permanent community. On 11 April 1960 the Rev. Moon married Hakja Han, the 17-year-old daughter of Soonae Hong, in a marriage which has been called 'the wedding of the little lambs'. He commemorates this marriage as a new beginning in the history of the Unification Church. If the period before this marriage is considered as 'the individual evangelization period', the period after the marriage is considered as 'the period of evangelization based on the family'. Five days after the marriage, three families were formed, blessed, and named 'the four bases'. This made marriages among the members of the Church possible.

A mass wedding for 33 couples was performed in May 1961, and these, along with the three families above mentioned, are called the '36 basic families'. The three families, four bases, 33 families and 36 basic families all have a special meaning in the terms of the Principles of the Unification Church. The basic family is respected by the members of the Church, and the Unification Church performs mass weddings to make a unified world through marriages among members, thus creating a large family. Young members think it an honour to be married by the Rev. Moon, and their families are called 'the blessed families'.

Bongchun Choi was the Unification Church's first overseas missionary, and he managed, with much hardship, to build a basis for the Church in Japan. Young-oon Kim travelled to the United States as a student in January 1959 and inaugurated the mission work there. The Holy Spirit Association for the Unification of World Christianity was registered in May 1963 as a social organization by the Korean government. An organization was founded in the United States in March 1966, and the Rev. Moon soon started overseas mission work himself. In May 1976 the Church bought the New Yorker Hotel in New York, a 43-storey building with 2,000 rooms which is used as its International Missionary Headquarters.

More than 12,000 couples have been married in the many mass weddings celebrated by the Rev. Moon. In 1984 there were 835 churches and 416,756 members in Korea. The Church has sent missionaries to 138 countries, and there are churches in more than 300 cities in the United States.

The Church has never publicized its assets, but they are known to be about 80 trillion won in Korea. Their assets in the United States have been estimated by *Newsweek* to be $7.5 billion. They own about 150 companies around the world, including pharmaceuticals, shipbuilding, transport, exports, construction, press, publishing and so forth.

New religious movements and society: basic characteristics of the followers

The Full Gospel Central Church
Membership: aggregate numbers. The Full Gospel Church, which started with five members in 1958, had already acquired 300 when it moved to the West Gate church. By 1973, however, when the new church was built in Yoeido, there were 12,500 members. Since then

the number of members has increased geometrically. Between 1973 and 1975 the Church showed an 83 percent increase, and between 1975 and 1977 it showed a remarkable 121 percent increase in membership. In June 1978 there were 61,214 members and 92 religious workers; by 1981 the numbers had increased to 188,232 members and in January 1983 the total was 255,389 members (see Table 3).

Overseas membership has also grown rapidly. After the International Missionary Association of the Full Gospel Church was established on 1 April 1975, the North American branch, the South American branch, the European branch and the Asian branch were founded. In 1975, 22 missionaries were sent to three countries where the Church had 572 members; five years later, 83 missionaries were working in 14 countries among 7,336 members; by 1982 there were 116 missionaries working in 17 countries.

According to the figures in Table 4 the overseas growth rate has begun to slow down in recent years. It should be remembered, however, that there are very few churches in the world with 250,000 members. The Rev. Cho firmly believes that the growth of his Church is God's will, and he continues to work for the evangelization of the whole world. Another interesting characteristic of the Full Gospel Church is that it is more active than the wider denomination to which it belongs.

Analysis of the membership. There are not many sources of data

TABLE 3
Membership in Korea of the Full Gospel Church

	Large parishes	Small parishes	Districts	Households	Members	Religious workers
1973					12,500	
June 1978	8	66	3,063	23,643	61,214	92
July 1981	12	149	13,791	92,854	188,232	224
January 1983	14		17,696	125,447	255,389	325

TABLE 4
Membership overseas of the Full Gospel Church

	Missionaries	Churches	Members
1975	22	8	572
1980	83	66	7,336
August 1982	116	110	13,176

available on the Church's membership structure. Thus, my own study of the Church's structure in 1978 will be used (Choi, 1979), for which the data were gathered by questionnaires distributed to members of the eight largest parishes.

Among the 300 respondents, 84 were men (28 percent) and 216 were women (72 percent). The age structure shows that the age-group 36–45 was the largest, but the age-groups 26–35 and 46–55 were also quite large. A large proportion of the members are therefore women in the age group 36–55 which is the most energetic, working-age group.

Analysis of the educational level of the respondents (Table 5) reveals that college graduates form the second largest group. But when the whole of the Church's membership is considered, the majority have less than a high school education.

Small shop-owners, office workers and manual labourers form the largest occupational groups, as can be seen in Table 6. 'Housewife' was the most common occupation among women.

In terms of living conditions, almost half the members are of the middle and lower class. Categorization of living conditions was by occupation and education of the head of the household, condition of the house and ownership of certain household goods, such as a car, a refrigerator, a piano, a washing machine and the like. The results show that 22.3 percent belong to the upper class, 34.7 percent to the middle class and 41.7 percent to the lower class. The educational level, occupation and living conditions of the members of the Full Gospel Church show that it is a church of the middle and lower classes.

The organization and functions of the Church. According to the

TABLE 5
Educational level of members of the Full Gospel Church

	Respondents		Church members, 1978	
	No.	%	No.	%
No education	3	1.0	1,901	6.0
Less than completion of elementary school	34	11.3	7,382	23.2
Less than completion of junior high school	43	14.3	7,343	23.1
Less than completion of high school	118	39.3	10,223	32.2
More than college entrance	102	34.0	4,943	15.5
Total	300	99.9	31,792	100.0

rules of the organization and its official positions, the Church is composed of a common assembly, a religious workers' assembly and a church assembly. The head of the church assembly represents the Church and becomes the chairperson of the common assembly, the religious workers' assembly and the church assembly. The associate pastor helps the head of the church assembly and is involved in the management of the Church and its prayer house.

The organization and functions of the Full Gospel Church are shown in Figure 1, and the organization of its International Missionary Association in Figure 2. As the figures (Yo, 1982) show, the organization of the Full Gospel Church is massive but well structured. The organization chart indicates both its effectiveness and the administrative ability of the Rev. Cho. Although the organization looks as if it is centred on the church assembly, it is very decentralized in its actual functions.

One question that arises about this massive organization is whether the head of the church assembly can manage to handle the growth of each individual association. Another is whether it is possible to overcome the negative characteristics of large bureaucracies. Even with these difficulties, however, the Full Gospel Church continues to grow.

Motivation for attending this Church. One-half of my respondents said they attended the Full Gospel Church 'because of the persuasion of family members or friends'. About one-fifth of them said that the motive had been 'to recover from illness'. 'To experience the power of the Holy Spirit' was the next most frequently mentioned motive, but only 6.0 percent of respondents fell into this category (see Choi, 1979).

TABLE 6
Occupation of members of the Full Gospel Church

Occupation	No. of respondents	%
Professional and managerial workers	9	3.0
Office workers	44	14.7
Small shop-owners	28	9.3
Poor shop-owners	35	11.7
Unskilled manual workers	6	2.0
Soldiers, policemen	3	1.0
Students	13	4.3
Housewives	126	42.0
Others		
Unemployed	24	8.0
No response	12	4.0
Total	300	100.0

FIGURE 1
Organization and functions of the Full Gospel Church

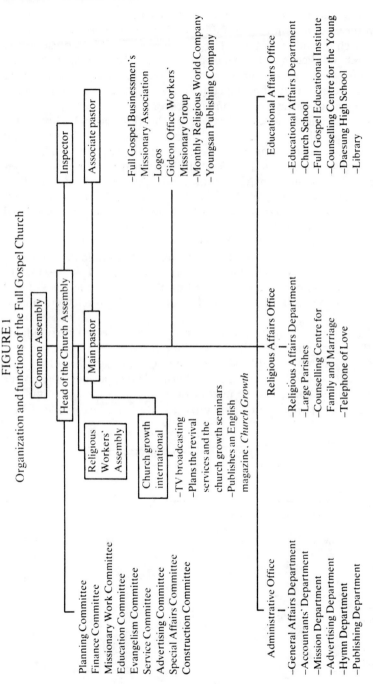

Source: Yo (1982: 275).

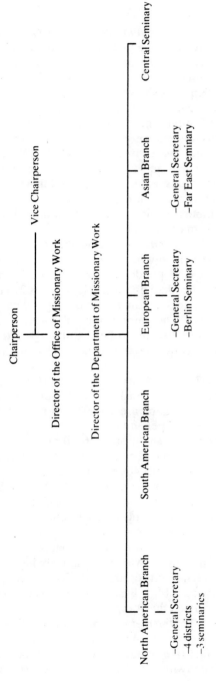

FIGURE 2
Organization chart of the International
Missionary Association of the Full Gospel Church

Chairperson

————— Vice Chairperson

Director of the Office of Missionary Work

Director of the Department of Missionary Work

North American Branch

–General Secretary
–4 districts
–3 seminaries

South American Branch

European Branch

–General Secretary
–Berlin Seminary

Asian Branch

–General Secretary
–Far East Seminary

Central Seminary

Source: Yo (1982: 278).

The Unification Church

Membership: aggregate numbers. Sontag (1977) argues that the Unification Church has one million associate members and 500,000 core members around the world. The Unification Church claims to have 416,756 members in 835 churches in Korea. A breakdown of the membership in Korea is shown in Table 7.

I conducted research on the characteristics of all the members of the Unification Church's headquarters at Chungpadong in February 1983. The items studied were: (1) religious status of the members (i.e., whether they were 'blessed' or not); (2) sex; (3) age; (4) education and occupation; (5) education and occupation of the head of each member's household; (6) year of joining the Church; and (7) reasons for joining the Church. We shall now examine the characteristics of members of the Unification Church on the basis of the data gathered from this research.

Analysis of the membership. One criterion for classifying the members is whether they have been 'blessed' by Rev. Moon. The number of blessed respondents was 209 (48.95 percent), and the number of those who had not been blessed was 218 (51.05 percent). There are 12,000 blessed families (about 24,000 people) among the church members. The proportion of blessed people in the Chungpadong church seems to be slightly higher than the national average, but this could be due to the fact that this church is the headquarters.

Among the 327 respondents, there were 207 men (48.48 percent), and 220 women (51.52 percent). As for the sex ratio for the Church as a whole (Table 7), there are 242,036 men (58.08 percent), and 174,720 women (41.92 percent).

The data show that age-groups 36–40 and 41–45 are the largest groups, both comprising 18.50 percent of the total. The next largest groups are the over-61s (15.46 percent), 31–35 (12.65 percent), 26–30 and 46–50. In all, 59.49 percent of the members belong to the 31–50 age-group, which is the most energetic working-age group.

In terms of the level of educational attainment, the largest group is of college graduates, who comprise 34.19 percent. It is interesting to note that 69.33 percent of the total are people with more than high school education, thus showing the relatively high educational level of church members. (Considering that 15.46 percent of the members are at least 61 years old, it is not very surprising that 11.01 percent report having had no education.)

The occupations of the members are shown in Table 8. 'Housewife' is the largest category (28.34 percent), but this is not very surprising in view of the fact that about half of the members are women and that, in accordance with Korean custom, they do not usually have any

TABLE 7
Total membership (by province) of the Unification Church

	Religious workers					Members				
No. of churches	Male Pastors	Missionaries	Female Pastors	Missionaries	Total	Male Baptized	Others	Female Baptized	Others	Total
433	435	160		125	720	12,191	30,118	12,910	19,205	74,424
12	12	3		54	69	1,623	3,369	2,019	3,794	10,805
8	8			36	44	532	859	708	967	3,066
42	42	8		12	62	945	1,545	512	799	3,801
79	79	43		42	164	12,950	28,949	10,020	20,040	71,959
38	38	26		47	111	2,015	6,053	2,201	7,107	17,376
17	17	24		24	65	2,110	6,613	1,015	4,450	14,188
37	37	31		41	109	9,952	11,225	3,062	5,006	29,245
56	56	24		36	116	12,455	20,254	7,086	10,686	50,481
43	43	55		42	140	3,670	22,009	2,908	13,120	41,707
36	36	46		54	136	12,256	18,254	8,508	18,526	57,544
30	30	37		58	125	6,219	12,460	6,116	12,410	37,205
4	4			12	16	910	2,500	520	1,025	4,955
835	837	457		583	1,877	77,828	164,208	57,585	117,135	416,756

TABLE 8
Occupation of members
of the Unification Church in Korea

Occupation	No. of respondents	%
Professional & managerial workers	44	10.30
Office workers	112	26.23
Shop-owners	10	2.34
Unskilled manual workers	2	0.47
Soldiers, policemen	4	0.94
Technical workers	9	2.11
Housewives	121	28.34
Others	48	11.24
Unemployed men and single women	77	18.03
Total	427	100.00

particular job outside the home. The 'Others' category includes employees of the Unification Church and two students. The 'Technical workers' category includes drivers, engineers, pressmen, designers and the like. In the Church at large students would come under the 'Others' category, and some would be under 'Professional and managerial workers'.

In order to assess the social class of the respondents, I utilized only the information on education and occupation. This includes the head of the household's education and occupation when he/she is not the same person as the respondent. With this information, I classified their social class as upper, middle and lower. The results show that 67.68 percent are middle-class, 16.86 percent are lower-class and 15.46 percent are upper-class.

Some people argue that, generally speaking, the social composition of the ordinary Christian churches shows: (1) more women than men, (2) a low level of education and (3) lower social class. However, the Unification Church displays: (1) more men than women, (2) more young people than elderly, (3) a high level of education and (4) more people from the middle class.

The institutions and organizations of the Church. The organizations, institutions and companies related to the Unification Church are shown in Figure 3. Limitations of space do not permit discussion of this feature here.

Motivation for attending this Church. Members gave the following as their main motives for attending:

(1) They believe the Divine Principle is superior and logical.
(2) This Church is the only road for the salvation of the Korean

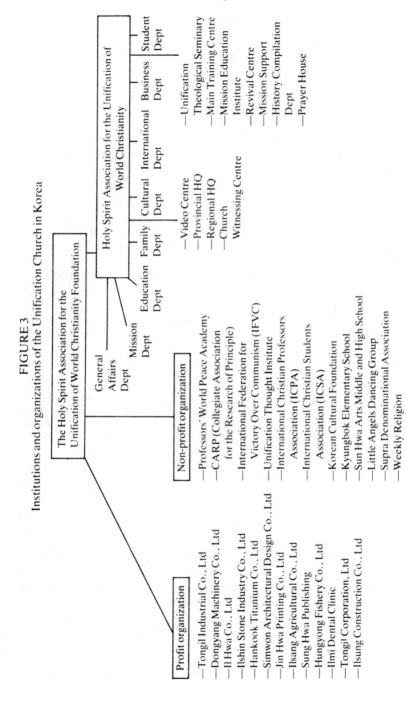

FIGURE 3
Institutions and organizations of the Unification Church in Korea

people who are suffering from misery.

(3) They are disgusted with the traditional churches because of their disputes, and because their doctrines are illogical (see Choi, 1965).

Comparison of the doctrines

The Full Gospel Central Church

The Full Gospel Church belongs to the Assemblies of God denomination, and it follows their doctrines. For example, they share the following teachings:

1. The Bible was written by the Holy Spirit and is thus believed to be the Word of God with the authority of infallibility.

2. God is everlasting and exists as One Body with the Father, the Son and the Holy Ghost. The doctrine of the Full Gospel Church is generally similar to that of most conservative churches, especially the fundamentalist ones. One particular difference, however, lies in the concept of holy baptism. The Full Gospel Church emphasizes glossolalia (speaking in tongues) as the first evidence of holy baptism, and it stresses healing by God as the special grace of God bestowed upon the saints whose sins were cleansed. These two aspects are emphasized above everything else. The belief system which is based on the emphases given to these doctrines can be summarized as follows:

> Before the Fall, man enjoyed the power to rule over the universe with eternal life, blessing and health, as he was created in the image of God. But when man fell, as the price paid for sin, there appeared death, curse, sickness and the fire of hell. Man consequently had to live under the enslavement of sin. But he could escape from curse, sickness and the fire of hell by the price paid on the cross by Jesus Christ. Through repentance and faith, man became free from the law of sin and in Jesus became a new being, enjoying the blessing of everlasting heaven and health, and was able to recover his power to rule over the universe. (Korea Christian Academy, 1982)

In a nutshell, the doctrine of the Full Gospel Church emphasizes the 'three-fold salvation' through the work of Jesus Christ on the cross, based on 3 John, 2: 'Beloved, I pray that all may go well with you and that you may be in health: I know that it is well with your soul.' This 'three-fold salvation' means that salvation is the union of spirit and body for new life and yearning for the better life.

According to the Rev. Cho,

> The salvation through Jesus Christ is not only the salvation of our soul, but it includes the changes of our life condition, curse into blessings, and of our body of death and sickness into life everlasting. It is the salvation of much wider significance than saving our soul only. (Cho, 1978: 29)

When we see salvation in its wider meaning, there are three basic elements: (1) salvation of soul, (2) salvation in the conditions of life, and (3) salvation from sickness. These three elements are called the 'three-fold salvation' (literally, three musical beats). The way to reach the three-fold salvation is to believe in God wholeheartedly. Then, the specific evidence of salvation is: with regard to the spiritual side, to experience glossolalia (speaking in tongues); with regard to the conditions of life, to experience the improvement of material life; and with regard to the physical side, to experience healing from sickness.

According to my research, the 'S Church' (Choi, 1979) respondents approached and experienced the evidence of three-fold salvation in the following fashion.

The salvation of soul. Salvation of the soul can be achieved by having one's desires of the flesh crucified on the cross through (1) water baptism, (2) baptism by fire (baptism of the Holy Ghost) and (3) fasting prayer.

About 90 percent of respondents had received water baptism within the previous ten years. More than 80 percent had received baptism by fire in the same period. This occurred mostly during fasting prayer at the prayer house. And more than 90 percent of the respondents had taken part in fasting prayer. Of them, more than 90 percent experienced baptism by fire.

Fasting prayer is practised more frequently by women, the less educated, the older people, and those with relatively high standards of living. More than 80 percent practised fasting prayer in the course of any given week. As shown in Table 9, the main objectives of fasting prayer were the solution of family problems, healing and job success. The revitalization of one's own faith, and 'for nation and society' accounted for only 20 percent of the respondents. What is surprising is that 82 percent of those who had practised fasting prayer claimed that their objectives had been achieved.

Glossolalia (speaking in tongues). Glossolalia is regarded as the first sign of the baptism of the Holy Spirit. Seventy-three percent of respondents stated that they had had such experiences. The grace of glossolalia was received mostly by older respondents with a low level of education. While 88.7 percent of those who had received the grace of glossolalia had also experienced baptism by fire, only 11.3 percent of those who had not received glossolalia had received the baptism of fire. This indicates a significant relationship between the grace of glossolalia and baptism by fire.

Salvation in the conditions of life. This means improvement in the specifically material conditions of life. As shown in Table 10, 83.7 percent of the respondents stated that their conditions of living had

TABLE 9
The objectives and results of fasting prayer

Objectives	%	Results	%
Healing	26.6	Not clear	16.4
Job success	20.0	Achieved as I wished	46.4
Solution of family	27.0	Achieved as I wished	
problems		and even with grace	35.8
For nation and society	1.4	Other	1.4
Revitalization of own faith	18.8		
Other	6.0		
	99.8		100.0

improved and only 1 percent claimed that their conditions had deteriorated after they became members of the Church. Those who are 25 years of age or below and with at least a college education tend to predominate among the 'don't knows'.

Of those who had 'received the baptism of fire', 91.2 percent indicated an improvement in their living conditions, while 7.5 percent indicated 'don't know yet', and 1.3 percent, 'deteriorated'. This means that there is significant association between perceived improvement in material life and the experience of baptism of fire.

Salvation of the body. This means that one is saved from bodily illness. Seventy-five percent of the respondents stated that they had been cured of internal diseases, neuralgia and skin disease; 80 percent of those who fasted said that they had been cured.

In summary, the Full Gospel Church consists of those who have actually experienced the work of the Holy Spirit and those who wish to receive such experiences, which include the cure of disease, improvement in the material conditions of life and baptism by fire. Since there are so many people in poverty and/or suffering physical or mental illness in Korea, it seems natural for them to have an interest in these experiences of the three-fold salvation.

In addition to the three-fold salvation, I must also mention another aspect of the Full Gospel Church, namely, the Rev. Cho's preaching at worship services. In answer to the question, 'What would be the most effective means towards a successful religious life?' the most frequently chosen items were 'Rev. Cho's preaching' (39.4 percent), 'the Bible' (22.3 percent), 'the moving power of the Holy Spirit' (18.0 percent), and 'prayers' (13 percent). In other words, the Rev. Cho's preaching was considered the most effective means by which the members could live a faithful religious life. Moreover, during my one year participant observation of the Full Gospel Church's worship services in 1978, the setting and the responses to the Rev. Cho's

TABLE 10
Perceived changes in the material conditions of life (%)

| | Sex | | Age | | | | | Educational level: completion of | | | |
	M	F	Below 25	26–35	36–45	46–55	Above 56	Primary school	Junior high school	High school	Above college
Don't know yet	17.9	14.4	37.1	10.0	13.2	12.3	14.8	13.5	9.3	13.6	20.6
Deteriorated	2.4	0.4	—	1.7	1.7	—	—	2.7	2.3	—	1.0
Improved	79.7	85.2	62.9	88.3	85.1	87.7	85.2	83.8	88.4	86.4	78.4
Total	100.0	100.0	100.0	100.0	100.0	100.0	100.0	100.0	100.0	100.0	100.0

preaching did make a strong impression.

When I revisited the Church more recently, however, phenomena such as hand-clapping and loud speaking in tongues had almost disappeared, and the service was rather solemn, as in other established churches. The peak moment at which cures used to be announced had been replaced with the Rev. Cho's earnest prayer for the sick. It will be interesting to see how things develop in the future.

The Unification Church

The doctrine of the Unification Church is precisely explained in the bulky volume, *The Divine Principle*. There is a strong likelihood that it has been polished and rationally and theologically systematized by various scholars. I shall summarize only a few extracts from the Declaration of Unification Theological Affirmations (at Barrytown, New York, 14 October 1976) to illustrate the worldview of the Unification Church.

God. There is one living, eternal and true God, a Person beyond space and time, who possesses perfect intellect, emotion and will, whose deepest nature is heart and love, who combines both masculinity and femininity, who is the source of all truth, beauty and goodness, and who is the creator and sustainer of man and the universe and of all things visible and invisible. Man and the universe reflect His personality, nature and purpose.

Jesus. Jesus of Nazareth came as the Christ, the Second Adam, the only begotten Son of God. He became one with God, speaking the words of God and doing the works of God, and revealing God to the people. The people, however, rejected and crucified him, thereby preventing him from building the Kingdom of God on earth. Jesus, however, was victorious over Satan in his crucifixion and resurrection, and thus made possible spiritual salvation for those who are reborn through him and the Holy Spirit. The restoration of the Kingdom of God on earth awaits the Second Coming of Christ.

Sin. The first man and woman (Adam and Eve), before they had become perfected, were tempted by the archangel Lucifer into illicit and forbidden love. Through this, Adam and Eve wilfully turned away from God's will and purpose for them, thus bringing themselves and the human race into spiritual death. As a result of this Fall, Satan usurped the position of mankind's true father so that, thereafter, all people were born in sin both physically and spiritually and have a sinful propensity. Human beings therefore tend to oppose God and His will, and live in ignorance of their true nature and parentage and of all that they have lost. God grieves for His lost children and lost world, and has had to struggle incessantly to restore them to Himself.

Creation groans in travail, waiting to be united through the true children of God.

Christology. Fallen mankind can be restored to God only through Christ (the Messiah), who comes as a new Adam to become the new head of the human race (replacing the sinful parents), through whom mankind can be reborn into God's family. In order for God to send the Messiah, mankind must fulfil certain conditions which restore what was lost through the Fall.

The Bible. The Old and New Testament Scriptures are the record of God's progressive revelation to mankind, and the purpose of the Bible is to bring us to Christ, and to reveal God's heart. Truth is unique, eternal and unchanging, so any new message from God will be in conformity with the Bible and will illuminate it more deeply. Yet in these last days, new truth must come from God if mankind is to be able to accomplish what is still to be done.

Second Coming and Eschatology. The Second Coming of Christ will occur in our age, an age much like that of the First Advent. Christ will come as before, as a man in the flesh; and he will establish a family through marriage to his Bride, a woman in the flesh, and they will become the True Parents of all mankind. Through our accepting the True Parents (the Second Coming of Christ), obeying them and following them, our original sin will be eliminated and we will eventually become perfect. True families fulfilling God's ideal will be started, and the Kingdom of God will be established both on earth and in heaven. That day is now at hand.

In commenting on *The Divine Principle*, some theologians have remarked that it bears the most scientific and up-to-date logic as well as visions of the new era; but many Korean professors did not want to accept it on the grounds that it distorted or interpreted the Bible allegorically.[2] It is clear that the doctrine of the Unification Church differs basically from that of most established churches.

Relationship with the established churches

The Full Gospel Central Church
A recent report from the Institute of Modern Society (1982) on 'The Relative Degree of Cordiality Shown by Protestants Toward Other Sects and Religions' clearly indicates the variable character of relations between Korean sects and religions. Tables 11 and 12 indicate that about half of the Protestant laypeople who were surveyed showed cordiality towards the Full Gospel Church, while the degree of cordiality shown by pastors was lower.

TABLE 11

The relative degree of cordiality shown by Protestant laypeople towards other sects and religions

Sects and religions	Cordiality	Less cordiality	Little cordiality	No cordiality	Hatred	Total	Cordiality rating
Presbyterian Church							
Tonghap	48.3	30.3	16.1	2.4	2.9	100.0	79.7
Haptong	50.5	27.3	15.4	3.3	3.4	100.0	79.5
Koshin	37.5	27.2	20.2	7.3	7.8	100.0	69.8
Kijang	27.8	27.0	21.0	11.7	12.4	100.0	61.5
Methodist Church	35.5	30.8	22.4	6.0	5.3	100.0	71.3
Baptist Church	34.4	28.7	22.4	8.0	6.5	100.0	69.1
Full Gospel Church	21.4	22.0	20.8	13.7	22.1	100.0	51.7
Unification Church	0.1	0.7	1.8	3.8	93.7	100.0	2.4
Jehovah's Witnesses	1.2	1.0	2.1	3.3	92.4	100.0	3.8
Catholic Church	15.6	18.2	20.7	17.0	28.5	100.0	43.8
Buddhism	2.8	5.3	9.1	14.2	68.6	100.0	14.9
Confucianism	2.3	3.5	11.2	18.3	64.8	100.0	15.0
Unbelievers	4.3	5.5	19.2	14.4	56.6	100.0	21.6

Source: Institute of Modern Society (1982: 106–91).

TABLE 12
The relative degree of cordiality shown by Protestant Pastors towards other sects and religions

Sects and religions	Cordiality	Less cordiality	Little cordiality	No cordiality	Hatred	Total	Cordiality rating
Presbyterian Church							
Tonghap	51.0	35.0	10.5	2.8	0.7	100.0	83.2
Haptong	36.2	26.2	19.9	9.2	8.5	100.0	68.0
Koshin	32.2	28.0	17.5	11.9	10.5	100.0	64.8
Kijang	28.5	27.8	15.3	15.3	13.9	100.0	60.2
Methodist Church	32.2	32.0	—	8.8	3.6	100.0	70.2
Baptist Church	27.3	31.7	30.9	8.6	1.4	100.0	68.7
Full Gospel Church	10.4	9.6	33.3	20.7	25.9	100.0	39.4
Unification Church	0.0	0.0	0.0	2.8	97.2	100.0	0.7
Jehovah's Witnesses	0.0	0.0	0.0	2.8	97.2	100.0	0.7
Catholic Church	8.6	15.7	20.0	26.4	29.3	100.0	37.0
Buddhism	1.4	2.8	7.1	15.6	73.0	100.0	11.0
Confucianism	0.0	2.9	10.0	22.1	65.0	100.0	12.0
Unbelievers	4.3	4.3	25.4	19.6	46.4	100.0	25.2

Source: Institute of Modern Society (1982: 152–94).

The Unification Church
The relationship with the established churches is clearly shown in Tables 11 and 12. The relative degrees of cordiality shown towards the Unification Church by Protestant laity and pastors alike are the lowest for all categories of religion. One way of putting this is to say that the Unification Church is regarded by many people as a heresy.[3]

Relationship to the family

The Full Gospel Central Church
The Rev. Cho's views on family life (Cho, 1982) are to the effect that the family is the basis of human life. A happy family not only lets you enjoy the happiness and values of life but is also a source of energy for daily living. There are not many matters in the world which require as much effort on the part of a person as family life. When a lot of patience and effort is put into the family, it becomes harmonious and beautiful. The basic factors of a happy family — husband and wife, and their ethical relationship — are said to be as follows.

The family and the wife. The head and the body are both parts of a human person, and they are equal; but their importance and duties are different. So it is with the relationship between husband and wife. The wife's first duty is to submit — 'wives, submit to your husbands as to the Lord' — but submission is different from obedience. Obedience means that you do something from your own will, while submission means that you have to do something even if you don't want to. 'Submit to your husbands as to the Lord' means that you should submit to your husband only when he is guiding you to the right and just way like God.

Second, the wife has a duty to respect her husband. Men are psychologically different from women. Women try to decorate their appearance, while men like to boast. God did not give men a prettier appearance, but they become prestigious by earning money and achieving high status and fame. Do you know whom a man first wants to talk to about his achievements? It is his wife. The husband wants his lovable wife to respect and praise him. Men who are praised by their wives will be pleased and will never leave them. Today's women, however, do not understand the psychology of men, and thus men lack vigour.

The word 'respect' has many meanings here. The first meaning is to pay attention: husbands will feel loved and cared for when their wives pay constant attention to them. Second, it means to honour: God tells us,'make the husband feel honourable'. Third, it means to treat the husband as the head of the house. Fourth, it means to revere: there should always be reverence between husband and wife. The husband will even try to use force when he feels that his wife does not revere him. It is important for the wife to revere the husband, because he will not be competent outside the home unless he is revered by his own family. Fifth, it means to praise, to compliment, for compliments help to smooth family relationships. Sixth, it means to admire with love: since God created men to boast, they need psychological encouragement as well as physical nutrition. The most important thing in family life is a warm, kind heart. As time goes by, a kind heart is more appreciated as the most important element in maintaining a happy family. The wife should also help her husband to overcome the difficulties that he has to face in the outside world.

The family and the husband. First, God told husbands to love their wives as God loves His Church. Husbands should love their wives with the same love that Christ had for us. Second, husbands should encourage their wives rather than find fault with them. Even if the wife lacks some qualities, it is the duty of the husband to help her find those qualities rather than to make a fool of her because she is not perfect. Third, husbands should protect their wives as they protect themselves. Husbands should protect and love their wives, and not merely demand love from them. Fourth, husbands should take care of, love and respect their wives, for wives need to be taken care of and loved by their husbands. Finally, husbands should make their wives feel secure. A woman feels insecure when she does not have a husband to depend on, and when the husband is not dependable and is always wavering, the wife feels very insecure. Thus, husbands should meet their responsibility and always try to make their wives feel secure.

The relationship between husband and wife. It is important to remember that blood is thicker than water. Even when a man and woman marry and form their own family, they both belong to their own families of origin. So, it is not good for either of them to put down the other's family of origin. The basic rules for a harmonious relationship are:

— Do not talk about things that one's partner has done wrong in the past.
— Do not talk about the partner's faults directly. It is always good to compliment the merits first, then ask for certain things to be changed in an indirect, gentle way.
— Do not talk about your marital life in public.
— Always show gratitude to each other.

But the most important requirement for a happy family is to have God's blessing and love. Whenever you feel like screaming at your spouse, or feel that nothing is going right, you should come before

God and humbly pray for His love and care. Then you will be freed from such sufferings and will be able to live a fuller life in God.

The Unification Church

The Rev. Moon himself described the importance of family in the Unification Church as follows:

> I emphasize that our movement has always been centered upon families as the basic unit of heavenly society . . . More blessings in marriage will be given, more children will be born, more families will be created. Then we will become elevated from the present communal type of centers to family-oriented homes. The family will always be the basic unit of happiness and cornerstone of the kingdom of God on earth and thereafter in heaven. (Quoted in Sontag, 1977: 155.)

The doctrine of marriage and the family in the Unification Church is the central concept of Unification thought and life-style. Marriage is called 'the Blessing' by the members of the Church. For Unificationists, the Blessing is a passport to heaven, and the Blessing ceremony has sacramental qualities. It has elements of the traditional Christian sacraments, as well as much that is new or different. During the ceremony, for example, holy water is used in a baptismal fashion, and holy wine in a eucharistic manner. In the course of the Blessing ceremony, according to Unification theology, one's sins are forgiven and new life is given. In Unification marriages, there is a deep sense of mission and of sharing God's love. The Unificationists regard their marriages as being beneficial for mankind, not merely for themselves. They are taught to sacrifice their comforts and desires (and even to leave their families, if necessary) in order to serve others first and best. The Rev. Moon inspires a willingness to sacrifice one's own good life for a higher purpose.

According to Unification theology, members of the Church are at the beginning of an era when they can all have truly God-centred families. Unificationists see themselves as helping to usher in a new age in which all men and women will reach spiritual perfection. Restored families, communities and nations — indeed, an ideal world — are ultimately possible.

Some Unificationists mention that they do not expect to find a perfect mate but, rather, they expect to *make* a perfect marriage. The Rev. Moon teaches them not to fear struggle, for through struggle people become better. A wife becomes the right person for the spouse and vice versa. He also teaches them to enter their marriages with the intention of considering more than just themselves and their own personal happiness: they should also develop some ability to extend themselves to others.

Regarding the future of families, the Rev. Moon often talks about creating trinities among the married couples. A trinity is made up of three couples from families that are especially responsible for helping one another. It is like an extended family, and they could be financially concerned for each other. At present, many of them live in a communal system, but that will not always be the case, although three couples could make up a small community.

They also conceive of home churches or services to the general public as part of the plan for the future. For Unificationists, this is a new providential era, and the Unification Church is developing a pattern of helping other families spiritually — of helping not only individuals but entire homes to become God-centred. They would serve in the capacity of pastors, but not necessarily with a church building.

The Rev. Moon encourages couples to have large families, but he does not talk of birth control as sinful. Much is left to the individual. He encourages them to go ahead and have many children. Their children are the only thing that they can attain in this world that is eternal, and Blessed children are regarded as a contribution to the world.

The Unificationists want to help their children to have a sense of respect and reverence for God and for other people. The Rev. Moon suggests that they should have a special place in their homes, no matter how small the homes are, for prayer — a spot that is a sanctuary. He also teaches that they should pray in front of the children. They are encouraged to let the children feel and learn the pattern of reverence and of being attentive to God by observing the parents' example. The parents should also try to instil in children a sense of dignity, self-warmth and confidence as children born after the Blessing. The children should develop character by learning to be selfless and sacrificial. The Rev. Moon's advice to parents is not to place too many limitations on their children, and to let them live a full and stimulating life. The highest goal for the children would be to pass on the values of unselfishness in the service of God and humanity (see Quebedeaux, 1982).

Conclusion
The results of the comparative examination of two of the new religious movements in Korea may be summarized as follows:

Both of them are under the guidance of charismatic leaders. But they differ in the following respect. The Rev. Cho is respected as charismatic by the followers, but he has never claimed to be charismatic himself, although he is aware of the fact that he is so regarded. The Rev. Moon is respected as the lord of the Second Advent by his followers, and they obey him as True Father. He also claims to be a 'prophet' entrusted with a great mission.

As to the basic characteristics of the followers, the Full Gospel Church members show: (1) a preponderance of women who outnumber the men by more than 2 to 1; (2) a preponderance of educational attainment at or below the level of high school; (3) a bipolar age distribution; (4) a preponderance of working and middle classes. The membership of the Unification Church, on the other hand, is composed of (1) more men than women; (2) people with college and high school levels of education; (3) a bipolar age distribution; (4) a majority of people from the middle class.

The most common motivation for attending the Full Gospel Church is 'to get healed', while people interested in the Unification Church are more ideologically oriented.

The leading feature of the Full Gospel Church's doctrines is the notion of three-fold salvation — physical, spiritual and material — with special emphasis on the power of the Holy Spirit. *The Divine Principle* of the Unification Church is basically different from the basic teachings of the established churches. It is revolutionary, and theoretically oriented.

The Full Gospel Church stresses the stability of the family and its role in society. Its conservative ideas about family structure and the role of family members may appear to go against the trend in the rapidly changing society of Korea, for the family is believed to function to stabilize the psyche of individuals in coping with their life and therefore to support the social and political status quo.

Emphasis on the family is also revealed in the Unification Church, but the method of incorporating the idea of the family is different. The Church is conceived as one large family, the ideal and blessed family in this world. Moreover, the doctrine emphasizes that the future world will become a family-centred, unified world. Both new religions emphasize that the family, which has become a smaller and more vulnerable institution in the modern world, is the real foundation of society.

The crucial problem for both movements, however, will be the problem of succession, which accords with Max Weber's expectations. In the Full Gospel Church, the Rev. Cho once claimed in a sermon that the Second Advent would occur before his hair turned grey. If this specific prophecy fails, what will happen to the unity of his huge organization and to its present ethos? In the Unification Church, which celebrates the birthdays of the Rev. Moon's children as sacred, will the position of leader become hereditary, as in royal families? And when Moon has gone, can *The Divine Principle* continue to make the believers bring about the Kingdom of God on earth?

Both of these religious movements have achieved successful growth in numbers of church members, but their patterns of growth are different. The Full Gospel Church had much faster growth at home than the Unification Church; while the Unification Church had wider growth abroad than in Korea. Why is the Unification Church spreading more rapidly abroad than at home? Why has it spread more slowly than the Full Gospel Church at home?

The reason may be found in the social and cultural conditions of Korean society. The basis of Korean social and cultural structure has been Confucian teachings, which laid down the basic behavioural norms for human relationships and social order, but without any conception of salvation for man or the world. They also inculcated in Koreans an attitude of allegiance to traditional values, so that they have a tendency to be reluctant to participate in anything very new or unconventional. By contrast, most Westerners have been oriented to the teachings of Christianity and are thus more progressive and tend continually to seek better values and the improvement of human life.

The doctrine of the Unification Church is basically different from that of the established Christian churches. *The Divine Principle*, with its message that the Kingdom of God is to be realized on earth and thereafter in heaven through True Parents, may sound attractive to Westerners. Furthermore, the family-like solidarity of the Unificationists offers a refuge for those alienated from the family and the urban community as well.

By contrast, the Full Gospel Church's doctrine is similar to that of the conservative churches, and it offers more visible and immediately perceived blessings, such as healing.

What social functions can we expect these new religious movements to fulfil?

1. They share some common functions. They put emphasis on this world as well as on the other world. And they lighten people's lives by releasing them from uneasiness and uncertainty about decisions affecting their future course of life. The Rev. Cho's view is that shouting about repentance and heaven to those who are in starvation and in despair is like talking in one's sleep. What is most needed is to give them the strength and the faith with which to live.

The Divine Principle claims that everybody should put their primary emphasis on this world rather than on the other world. It emphasizes that without real happiness of the flesh there is no spiritual bliss, because there cannot be a future separated from the present. It urges that active social reform should be accompanied by rooting out the structural contradictions of the present if a desirable world is to be achieved.

2. These new religious movements take on a prophet-like role by criticizing the contradictions and illogicalities of the established religions and the social structure.

The Rev. Cho says that many of the established church pastors are simply uttering monologues from the pulpits when they present their own philosophy and ideology. Members are therefore on the decrease, whereas he is trying to give answers to his followers' questions, and that is why his Church grows.

The Divine Principle says that conventional Christianity was almost lost in ecclesiasticism and got so embroiled in disputes over power or denominational schisms that it could not pay attention to the salvation of man and the world. The Unification Church insists that all the religions of modern times should be unified under its own religion based on a very new truth.

3.They express a strong desire to adhere to traditional Korean culture and to subjective ethnic identity.

The Rev. Cho believes that Christianity had previously acted as a catalyst for the modernization of Korea by assimilating Western civilization and modern technology. Now it is time for Christianity to work for a cultural metamorphosis by uniting with traditional Korean culture and to mature spiritually so that it can form the basis of the Korean people in the future.

According to *The Divine Principle*, believers crave for the Second Coming of the Messiah and are responsive to the idea that they are a chosen people, the founder of whose religion is the Messiah, and that Korea is the very place from which he will come in glory.

In summary, comparison between the Full Gospel Central Church and the Unification Church in the Republic of Korea shows that the religious responses to rapid social change in a single country can take various forms. Both movements have enjoyed considerable success; but they have achieved it in different ways among different 'constituencies'. Even their shared concern for the this-worldly benefits of religion, the sanctity of the family institution and the cultural integrity of Korean society cannot conceal the gulf which separates them in matters of basic doctrine, organization, rites and relations with the wider society. The scale of these differences should serve as a warning against facile arguments about the allegedly necessary concomitants of rapid social change. Only detailed empirical investigation can reveal the precise connections between social change and religious innovation.

Notes

1. The Full Gospel Central Church belongs to the Association of God denomination in the United States. This denomination was introduced into Korea in 1928 by Miss

Mary C. Rumsy, a missionary who introduced the gospel and opened the Full Gospel Seminary there.
  2. The Public Theological Discussion of the Auditorium of Seoul National University, 28 October 1970.
  3. In the words of the Rev. Moon, '. . . God needs man to have an absolutely new and totally fresh outlook. God needs a new vision of life to be instilled in the minds of the people . . . From the Christian church's point of view, my teaching, the new revelation, is not only extraordinary but revolutionary. I can understand why Christians call us heretics' (quoted in Sontag, 1977: 131–2, 135).

References

Bellah, Robert N. (1970)   *Beyond Belief*. New York: Harper & Row.
Byong, Jong-ho (1978)   *History of the Assembly of God Movement in Korea*. Seoul: Shin-saeng Gwan.
Cho, Yonggi (1978)   *Three-fold Salvation*. Seoul: Yungsan Publishing Co.
—— (1982)   *A Happy Person*. Seoul: Yungsan Publishing Co.
Choi, Ja-sil (1978)   *I was 'Hallelujah Ajumma'*. Seoul: Yungsan Publishing Co.
Choi, Syn Duk (1965)   *A Comparative Study of the New Religious Groups in Korea*. Seoul: Christian Seminary Press.
—— (1967)   'Korea's Tong-il Movement', in S. J. Palmer (ed.), *The New Religions of Korea. Transactions of the Korean Branch of the Royal Asiatic Society*, Vol. 53, pp. 167–80. Seoul: RAS.
—— (1979)   'A Sociological Study of the S-Church', *Journal of the Korean Sociological Association* (Seoul), 13, 49–77.
Cultural Research Centre (1982)   *Survey of Korean Folk Culture*. Seoul: Korea University Press.
Holy Spirit Association for the Unification of World Christianity (1982)   *Tong-il Kyo Hoi Sil Lok*. Seoul: SungWha Publishing.
—— (1983)   *Scenes of Suffering*. Seoul: SungWha Publishing.
Institute of Modern Society (1982)   *A Study of the Growth and Modes of Belief in Korean Churches*. Seoul: IMS.
Kim, Young-Oon (1980)   *Unification Theology*. New York: Unification Church.
Korea Christian Academy (1982)   *A Study of the Pentecostal Movement in Korea*. Seoul: KCA.
Park, Yong-Shin (1981)   'Max Weber's "Charisma": Its General Scheme for the Study of Social Movements', pp. 7–33 in Yong-Shin Park, *Modern Society and Social Theory*. Seoul: Il-chi-sa.
Quebedeaux, Richard (ed.) (1982)   *Lifestyle Conversations with Members of the Unification Church*. New York: Unification Theological Seminary.
Sontag, Frederick (1977)   *Sun Myung Moon and the Unification Church*. Nashville: Abingdon.
Suh, Nam Dong (1975)   *A Critical Study of the Divine Principle of the Unification Church*. Seoul: Tong-il Se Ge.
Weber, Max (1940)   *The Theory of Social and Economic Organization*. New York: Free Press.
Wilson, Bryan R. (ed.) (1981)   *The Social Impact of New Religious Movements*. New York: Rose of Sharon Press.
Yo, Woonhak (ed.) (1982)   *Lord, Your Will Be Done*. Seoul: Kyujang Moonwhasa.

6
New religious movements in the Caribbean

Laënnec Hurbon

Introduction

During the past twenty years or so, in other words since the beginning of the Castro regime, research on the Caribbean seems to have focused mainly on economics and politics. A real race to 'caribbeanization' is taking place, but it is determined largely by the worldly desire of powerful metropolitan areas which, from the fifteenth century until the present day, have used the Caribbean as a stage on which to act out their personal conflicts or their own whims in a whole series of genocides or ethnocides in accordance with the needs of economic exploitation or strategic use.

The study of the connection between religion and culture would, surely, bring to light an entirely different Caribbean, one more concerned perhaps with creating its own identity.

Although more significant in the British West Indies, research into religion is virtually unheard of elsewhere. The history of the way in which minority religious groups have been implanted is completely unknown, and the history of the established churches has been abandoned. In any case, even when there has been a certain amount of research into religions, there has been no attempt to examine the real Caribbean picture. One could mention Roger Bastide's studies of Afro-American religions, *Les Amériques noires* (1967), or G. Simpson's *Religious Cults of the Caribbean* (1970), but these are exceptions and have hardly aroused the interest that was hoped for; at best, the Afro-American religions have given rise to a quaint or exotic vision of what has been called the magic of the West Indies or the enchantment of the Caribbean. Marxist analysis tinged with scientism and positivism has undoubtedly brought to light an awareness of the role that religion has played in the history and development of the Caribbean, whereas the sociology of development has been preoccupied with the Caribbean's adaptation to the modern world and thus to patterns of Western culture. From this standpoint, religious practices in the Caribbean are considered in terms of their support for or rejection of external development influences.

There is, however, no disputing the fundamental importance of religion in the Caribbean. On the one hand, all modern religious sects descend on the Caribbean where they find an ideal breeding ground. Thus, for example, one finds several hundred religious denominations in Puerto Rico and Haiti, although we are talking about two countries which are diametrically opposed on both the economic and political levels: Puerto Rico, which is still under US rule, enjoys the highest standard of living in the Caribbean, whereas Haiti, the first country to gain independence, enjoys the lowest. On the other hand, Christianity as the official religion has played such an all-embracing role in this society dominated by slavery that in the end it has been bound up with the creation of a new cultural identity for each of the Caribbean nations. Slaves themselves have chosen churches as the battlegrounds on which to fight for recognition of their civil rights.[1] In fact, although it is accepted that in black Africa the new religious movements which have separated from the official Protestant, Anglican and Catholic Churches have played a leading role in the struggle towards independence and in the adoption of present-day values, investigations have barely begun into the effects that these same movements have had on the Caribbean.

This study will try to limit itself to examining new religious movements in the Caribbean, but it would seem that we are dealing with an entire continent. On every island, sects of the most varied hues have managed to prosper, making it difficult for one single investigator to cover the whole area of study. Here, I shall concentrate merely on a few of the more important movements which have had considerable influence on the socio-cultural and political problems in the Caribbean. But these movements arise from a religious background which we must examine first, in order to avoid certain misunderstandings.

Towards an archaeology of new religious movements
Sociological studies of Caribbean religion seem for the most part to consider only Afro-American religions — hybrids of Christianity and African religions — as contributory factors in the shaping of the Caribbean's unique culture. Thus, the works of Voodoo (in Haiti), of Santeria and the Ñanigos (in Cuba), of Shango (in Trinidad), of Obeahism (in Jamaica) and, further away, of Candomblé (in Brazil) are well known; but there has been little study of the Hindu-type religions which are still thriving in Guadeloupe, Martinique, Trinidad and Guyana. Likewise, the importance of Amerindian–Caribbean–type beliefs in the spiritist movements such as the Mesa Blanca in Puerto Rico is underestimated.

Even more serious is the confining of Afro-Americanism largely to the area of Haiti in the case of Voodoo and, to a smaller extent, to Jamaica and Trinidad with Rastafarianism and Shango. Elsewhere it is regarded as nothing more than little islands of persistence, doomed to disappear. I am personally amazed by the fanciful images surrounding the mere mention of Voodoo almost everywhere in the Caribbean. It is as if all the other islands see Haiti as the place where Negro culture has been maintained in a state of purity, so to speak, arousing both repulsion and fascination at the same time. Very few authors draw attention to this phenomenon, although it can both add to what we know about Voodoo and tell us more about the practice of exorcism, a remnant of African culture in the islands where Voodoo does not exist as such. The fact that sociologists can fall victim to common sense and limit their research to a rehash of received ideas, especially those concerning the Indian Caribbean – white mix on islands like the Dominican Republic or Puerto Rico, can be seen as a sign of the age-old practice of obscuring the real religious problematic of the Caribbean. Any purely empirical observation of Voodoo or Afro-American religious practices in the area merely underlines the prejudice and illusion which already surround Voodoo as an area of study. But in this context, the most deeply entrenched attitudes are those coloured by racism and xenophobia. All such reactions, well known and widespread since the nineteenth century, create an image of Voodoo as the focal point of magic, witchcraft and even cannibalism:[2] in Haiti, where the black population has been least contaminated since 1804 by Western civilization and where negritude first developed, Voodoo is considered reminiscent of a culture still close to a black Africa in the grip of savagery and barbarism. It is even blamed for sowing the seeds of the despotism recurrent in Haitian political life. The effort made by present-day Haitian writers and even by US anthropologists (such as Herskovits, 1937; Layburn, 1945; and, more recently, Courlander, 1960) to paint a different picture of Voodoo have not had the expected effect. These authors have probably done too little to attack the prejudice prominent among the ruling and middle classes in the Caribbean.

Now, if Voodoo has been able to develop in Haiti, it is not merely as a means of supporting anti-slavery,[3] the task of which is almost finished and is surviving on borrowed time owing to the lack of symbols of modernity in the Haitian countryside (schools, hospitals, electricity, television, etc.); it has also developed because it is in tune with an inventive, living culture, one capable of adapting to the most varied conditions. Thorough investigations have already shown that Voodoo is a cult dedicated to spirits according to various rites and in different families with responsibility for man's relationship with nature and with fellow-man. Moreover, it is clear that Voodoo is based on specifically African anthropological assumptions about the body and the person as a meeting-point of multiple forces. Finally, Voodoo is a careful interpretation of history and of the world which is no more and no less valid than the interpretations of Western culture. But what receives most attention in this kind of logical symbolism is the realm of magic and witchcraft. The current Caribbean understanding of Voodoo is that it amounts to a domain of savagery and barbarism. This represents a victory for colonial domination, to which Caribbean sociology pays eloquent homage by its very silence. Yet, the relationship between Voodoo and Christianity, from which it has borrowed symbols, the calendar, the liturgy and even a certain amount of theology, reveals in close-up a process identical to that which has taken place in other Caribbean countries, albeit in less spectacular ways. I am referring not to Shango or Santeria, but to magico-religious practices occurring within the framework of Catholicism in the French Antilles, where Voodoo is non-existent and where there is only the symbolic nucleus of African or Afro-American types of religion to keep these practices alive.

In Guadeloupe, for example, the system of 'gifts' is a body of beliefs and practices which rests on a heritage of spirits and saints of the Voodoo or African type which may appear to people in dreams, during illness, or at turning-points in their lives demanding a religious service supplied by the *gadèdzafé* (specialists in things sacred or interpreters for the spirits).[4] Even though they are no longer called by their African names, these hold the rank of presiding spirits, more influential than the dead (or relatives who have recently died), and they live in trees, in the sea, inside animals and even in sugar cane mills. Like the Orixa of Brazilian Candomblé, the Iwa of Haitian Voodoo or the saints of Santeria, they are protected by Catholic saints and give rise to various pilgrimages, to the taking over of sanctuaries and to the attachment to Catholic cultural traditions. They provide, as a last resort, an underground system of symbols and images which keeps a constant distance from the dominant Western culture and values.

This contact with the spirits involves a precise understanding of the individual person as a being controlled by various 'powers', one of which — the Good ·Angel — acts as a receptor of the spirit during trances and possessions by, and appearances of, the spirit. This 'power' resides in a person's head and is believed to be sent by God Himself. At the time of death it is usually slow to leave the body, so the whole ritual of death seems to be focused on trying to persuade the Good Angel to go away. The other 'power', which is found near the person's feet, is the place where bad luck gathers and makes it the favourite place for 'dead souls' or zombies, who can make life a misery.

In the Dominican Republic, Voodoo-type beliefs and practices are as important as they are in Haiti, even though common sense persists in seeing Dominican Voodoo as an essentially Haitian import. In Puerto Rico, Santeria, which has many followers, is thought of as a Cuban cult, as if African religions no longer had any presence in Puerto Rico.[5] Even within the framework of popular Catholicism, rather like the case of the French Antilles, and within the framework of Pentecostalisms and Spiritisms, African elements are alive and easily found.

Throughout the Caribbean, a powerful nucleus of symbols could be said to persist. It has been in operation since the introduction of slavery, and it has spread by very reason of the imposition of Christianity on slaves. This nucleus contains traces not only of African and Christian religions but also of Amerindian–Carib, Muslim and then Hindu religions. It has been possible to obscure the importance of the Hindu religions only by the tendency to represent the characteristics of Caribbean culture as fixed and as exclusively connected to the era of slavery; immigration from Asia began around 1852 — in other words, shortly after the abolition of slavery — and thus its influence upon the evolution of the Caribbean is seen as superficial. This ignorance of (East) Indian culture, which is as vital in the French Antilles as in Trinidad, Guyana or Surinam, is yet another way of denying the multi-ethnicity of the Caribbean. It is reinforced by the onslaughts of covetous external forces.

Like the black slaves, the Indians have had the religions of the colonial people thrust on them, but they have nevertheless clung to the basic tenets of their own faith. In all the villages with a large Indian population (Moule, in St François, and Capesterre, in Guadeloupe) temples have been built. The name given to the religious observance which generally brings the Indian community together is Maliémin.[6] There are two different practices, one within the family and the other for public gatherings. Priests conduct ceremonies which take the form of offerings to the goddess Maliémin. The name is a corruption of 'Mariamman' a goddess from South India known as the goddess of smallpox. Alongside her is another awe-inspiring demigod, Maldevilan, who acts as guardian of the temple, as well as many other secondary divinities. The highlight of the ceremonies is the sacrificial act when, facing the sun, the head of a young goat is chopped off with a single blow. As a general rule, animal sacrifices are offered to the goddess MadouraiViran, a carnivorous god, for Maliémin is thought to be vegetarian. Purificatory baths, prayers, fasting, singing and dancing to the rhythm of drums and cymbals all help to create an intensely religious atmosphere, with the final feast and the priest's blessings strengthening the bonds of solidarity among the faithful. Funeral rites are equally important, even though the Indian custom of cremation has disappeared from the West Indies. The practice of making offerings to the dead in cemeteries is, for example, an essential part of religious practices in the Indian community.

The similarities between Maliémin and the Voodoo-type beliefs and customs are obvious to the blacks: funeral rites, multiple gods, sacrificial feasts, seeking of favours in daily life and so on all lead the blacks to frequent the Indian temples which they see as an additional support for their own African-type beliefs. In this way, Indian religious practices are not enclaves within a Caribbean cultural pattern completely centred on Afro-Americanism or on a few traces of an Amerindian (Caribbean) culture which has, for the most part, disappeared.

We shall attempt here to understand how new religious movements in the Caribbean have emerged and how they function by referring to the basic religious situation on which the mixing of various different religious systems has left its mark. We are speaking not only of the dominant Afro-Americanism but also of the continuous influence of symbols, beliefs and practices borrowed from the official religions.

It will become clear that, throughout the whole Caribbean, there is a central, underlying nucleus of symbols which accounts for a Caribbean identity that is still questing for itself and is still being put together. Developing such an hypothesis, however, is not without its problems, for research is still at the stuttering stage. In this chapter I shall bring out the main trends by sketching an analysis of those religious movements which have so far been the least researched but which permit a more thorough investigation of the vitality of Caribbean culture.

Imported religious movements

In order to avoid certain common confusions, it is useful at this point to make a preliminary distinction between (a) older sects such as the Jehovah's Witnesses and the Adventists and (b) the modern sects, and then between (c) modern imported sects and (d) native sects. For our purposes, the modern imported sects in the Caribbean refer to those which appeared in many places around the 1960s, first in the United States and then in Europe. As a general rule, these sects are either a mixture of Christian doctrine and practices and Far Eastern technique and philosophy, or quite simply a mixture of Christianity and the popular religious traditions of a given area. To mention only the best known examples, we have the 'Moonies' (the Association for the Unification of World Christianity), the Mahikari from Japan,

Hare Krishna and the Children of God. Sects like Mita or Rastafarianism are native products from Puerto Rico and Jamaica. We shall begin with a review of four imported religious movements: the Jehovah's Witnesses, the Seventh-Day Adventists, the Mahikari and the Apostles of Infinite Love.

Jehovah's Witnesses
Since 1974 I have been able to observe the steady growth of the Witnesses in Guadeloupe at first hand. There were about 4,000 of them in congregations on the island in 1975; in 1979 more than 7,000 islanders took part in a convention at Pointe-à-Pitre. Several other religious movements enjoyed unexpected success during the period 1973–79, namely, the Mahikari, the Adventists, the Apostles of Infinite Love and Transcendental Meditation.[7]

The Witnesses have their strongest hold among craftsmen, small shop-keepers, minor government workers, small and medium businessmen, employees in private houses, shops and banks, and poor and struggling peasants who have left their lands or who are up against increasing economic problems. According to statistics, the years 1967–74 saw a rapid fall in the economically active population and at the same time an increase in the number of salaried people in the tertiary sector. In less than ten years, seven sugar refineries disappeared in a country where agriculture is based on the production of sugar cane. Ideological resources seem very inadequate ways of confronting the insecurity engendered by the economic situation. The influence of the Western consumer society increases daily at all levels of the population, so that social contradictions become more acute.

Moreover, the pressure for modifications in liturgy and doctrine introduced by the Vatican Council's *aggiornamento* has wrought havoc with the Catholic Church's traditional language for regulating social relations. In fact, the new sects are trying to gain a foothold in Guadeloupe and Martinique at precisely the moment when these islands are in the throes of both a socio-economic and an ideological crisis.

A clear conflict between Catholicism and the sects emerges from accounts of conversion. Converts to Jehovah's Witnesses thereafter blame all moral and social disorders mainly on Catholicism, the ultimate bastion of the Devil, evil and falsehood. This is because the confrontation between the Witnesses and the Catholic Church is actually an echo of the confrontations occurring throughout the whole social system. Because it used to ensure the working of this system, the Church is said to have become its symbol. But Witnesses claim that the Church could fill such a role only as long as the African-type practices of magic and anti-witchcraft were counterbalanced, or if the Church successfully controlled social conflicts. Today, however, the changes that have been brought about in the Church are believed to have rendered it no longer capable of maintaining this balance between powers. Magic is supposedly practised freely with none of the customary restraints, and the faithful are becoming more vulnerable than ever.

The legacy of the 'spirits' which used to grip the faithful through the system of 'gifts', surviving under cover of Catholic practices, is said by Witnesses to have become an intolerable burden. To be more exact, the 'spirits' now seem to be beyond control: they are now merely pathological and ultimately the tools of the Devil in Witnesses' eyes. Considered good or evil according to whether they are understood or misunderstood, the 'spirits' are said to have become portents of evil and of damnation itself. It is claimed by converts that the new order promised by Jehovah's Witnesses will therefore, once and for all, remove everybody from contact with the 'spirits' and therefore from contact with the Catholic Church, since it was the Church which made such contact possible in the first place. 'To be a Catholic is true damnation: anyone can join; they get away with anything,' a convert told us, referring to the impossibility of controlling 'wrongdoers', that is, those who manipulate 'the spirits' and wish 'evil' on their neighbour.

But such opposition to Catholicism, like opposition to witchcraft, has very many causes. The 'order of evil' in question is a metaphor for social situations governed by concubines, adultery, debauchery, alcoholism and delinquency. It is thought that, at the heart of Catholicism, nobody knows the difference between good or order and evil or disorder. Legitimate and illegitimate children are both put in the same bracket. This suggests that the traditional symbolic system, having lost its authority, is now thought to refer to an order of deformity, confusion, the state of nature or, better still, anti-nature and barbarism, in contrast to the world of culture and civilization.

Can it be said that joining the Witnesses brings social and economic advantages which would be otherwise difficult to acquire through the traditional system of symbols? Certainly, social mobility is made possible, but by indirect means. For having access to the Bible is considered tantamount to having access to the foundations of the ruling order. When one lacks social and economic advantages, one uses the symbols of these advantages. This is because the holy scriptures, transcending both the traditional and modern social systems, are believed to be the culmination of both and, as such, offer complete protection against 'evil'. In order to benefit from this protection it is said that one must avoid all conniving with traditional society: one must give up carnivals, dances, alcohol, gossiping and gambling; keep away from the margins of society; dedicate oneself to the discipline of work; mix with 'good' people; and try to go back to the nuclear family. It all seems, then, as if conversion to the Witnesses helps people to make the transition to dominant values of Western society, or alternatively, to make a more definite and more radical assimilation of these values.

However, this view represents a failure to go beyond an empirical level in understanding the Witnesses' success. The research that I have done in the past shows that there is a new confrontation between the Witnesses and the traditional magico-religious beliefs of the Antilles. If conversion provides a shelter from witchcraft, it also finds a new expedient for returning to the fundamental components of the traditional system of symbols and images. Indeed, from one point of view, illnesses are interpreted as the language of 'the spirits', the latter representing nothing but persecution in the eyes of the Jehovah's Witness, and thereby only increasing the necessity to turn to the Bible as the supreme authority and ultimate truth which frees the individual from illness and makes him or her invulnerable to persecution from the outside. The belief that the dead or their souls can return in a dream or in broad daylight to persecute the living still remains strong. By proclaiming that people die completely, the Witnesses' doctrine is thought to eliminate, in theory, all fear of the dead. But the Guadeloupan convert still has this fear, in spite of all the denials. The whole pattern of traditional beliefs, including that of dead souls and their ability to return during one's daily routine, is ascribed to the kingdom of Satan. Thus, repeating the pattern set by the conflict between God and Satan, the two systems of values are entering a more bitter and more violent confrontation. In fact, the Guadeloupan Witnesses have experienced 'manifestations', or trances, on the occasion of baptismal ceremonies, whereas elsewhere, in Europe and the United States, these are somewhat rare. On the other hand, the very stages of conversion take over where the stages of the system of 'gifts' left off: hallucination, receiving a 'supernatural' message either in a dream or when awake, and an illness itself, which the Bible is going to be able to heal, as the first sign of being chosen by God.

Seventh-Day Adventists
Conversion to the Seventh-Day Adventist Church promises liberation from witchcraft to an even greater degree than joining the Witnesses does. In 1979 there were some 4,000 Adventists in Guadeloupe, whereas numbers had reached 7,000 in Martinique. Beginning in 1965, there was frantic building of churches and schools

on both islands. By 1978 there were 10,500 baptized and non-baptized Adventists on Martinique. The majority of converts are people on low salaries in the private sector: domestic staff, errand boys, masons, mechanics, craftsmen — all with seasonal, unreliable jobs. The surveys that we have carried out in Guadeloupe come to the same conclusions as those of Raymond Massé in his study (1978) of the Adventists in Martinique.[8] As with the Witnesses, the Adventist membership comes entirely from the Catholic Church, thenceforth an object of anathema. For the convert, the Church represents the source of all moral and social disorder because it tolerates magic and witchcraft in its own midst in an uncontrollable form. To break away from the Church, then, opens up the way to 'peace' and 'relief' from witchcraft. Accounts of the conversion of witches are very often used by Adventist pastors and believers as proof of the power of their Church. Some converts take pleasure in relating how they have been made immune from the bad spells cast on them by their neighbours. It would appear that the Adventist convert is even more obsessed with witchcraft than the Jehovah's Witness, because the latter is less ready to admit his previous links with the practice of magic and witchcraft. The Devil's power is said by Adventists to be directly related to these practices, whereas, according to the Witness, this power refers to many more situations of conflict of all kinds throughout the world.

Raymond Massé writes of exorcisms commonly performed by Adventist pastors to deliver the faithful from feeling persecuted in the middle of the night by evil 'spirits', bad spells or 'haunted' houses. In the same way, pastors are called to sick beds to arrange prayer meetings for the purpose of bringing about a rapid return to health. The battle against witchcraft occupies such an important position in the movement that the believers are urged strictly to obey a certain number of prohibitions. In relation to food and the body, there are prohibitions against ingesting blood, pork and crustaceans. Prohibitions relating to social behaviour include adultery, concubinage and collective gatherings like carnivals, cockfights, the cinema, etc.

As with the Witnesses, therefore, conversion breaks the link between the individual and the system of traditional religious symbols which is considered to be nothing but the Devil's handiwork. But through the expedient of this break, the convert undergoes a process of assimilation to present-day values, or, more precisely, tries to gain possession of those very symbols which open the door to social mobility. In so doing he or she continues to interpret social relationships in the same traditional manner, that is, on a magico-religious basis. The rejection of the 'spirits' who were worshipped for 'good' or 'evil' in the heart of the Catholic Church is achieved so violently that it actually strengthens belief in them. No longer able to solve the problems of daily life, the spirits are seen as powerless and defeated. It is believed that the Bible, as the supreme authority, will in the end nail them to the ground, eliminate them once and for all and make 'life' possible again.

Far from being completely assimilated to the dominant Western culture, the new convert joins a group of 'saved' and 'chosen' believers, a closed society where he fights a continuous battle against the traditional system. Does the effect of his conversion enable him actually to carry the burden of all social evil on his shoulders? It would seem that the interiorization of personal guilt which would indicate his transfer to modernity is still rejected. The realm of the persecuting spirits persists in the mind of the individual as the objective point of reference for interpretations of evil. The magical power attributed to the Bible is clear proof that this is a matter of the transfer of the 'spirits'' power. It is precisely this transfer which is responsible for bringing about a new classification of people in society. Attachment to the traditional system has made this reclassification difficult.

Massé talks of conversion as a 'cultural tool' and of religious movements as 'new culture' (1978: 67). In fact, it is exactly on this level that the converts express their desires: although indifferent to trades union and political strife, they do not shun rebellion and social demands. From the very beginning they have been preoccupied by something else: by the problematic of the traditional system of symbols and images which defined their place in the world, in history and in society. The precarious economic situation merely gives new life to this problematic, but alone it could not account for the massive surge in conversions.

The Mahikari

If the basic alternative for the Witnesses and the Adventists is either to reject the 'spirits' altogether or to reject links with them, the reverse is true for the Mahikarians and the Apostles of Infinite Love. Here we see a *strengthening* of members' relationship with the 'spirits'. This structural situation is most revealing. It means that henceforth any monograph written about a sect which does not include comparisons with other religious movements in a given society will be treated with suspicion.

The Mahikari movement was founded in 1959 in Japan by a man called Sukui Nushi Sama, who claims to be God's latest envoy to earth after the Buddha and Christ. It had spread to several European countries (France, Switzerland and Belgium), then into black Africa (especially the Ivory Coast), before reaching the French Caribbean islands. In Martinique, where it was introduced in 1975–76, it has almost 10,000 followers (or *kumites*) today, and in Guadeloupe there are about 7,000 members. But on both islands the Mahikari movement is experiencing growth. There are already centres, or *dojo*, in all the important towns. In Martinique, a huge Mahikari temple has been built at Fort-de-France entirely from members' donations. This temple can hold many more followers than even the city's cathedral. While it does not consider itself a separate religion in its own right, the movement claims to bring all religions together and offers a certain number of religious practices which take over the individual's whole life.

The movement's doctrine, set out in the book of Revelations or *Goseigen* (the sacred writ of the founder prophet), is simple in spite of appearing to be a mixture of Far Eastern religious philosophy and elements of Judaeo-Christianity. First, there is God's (or *Su's*) act of creation; then there is Adam and Eve's sin, then the prophets' atonement, and finally the return to the Garden of Eden. In their everyday life, members prepare for this return as for a millennium. Man is said to be composed of three elements: physical, astral and spiritual (the last one being found in ancestral spirits). Unawareness of the third element is allegedly the source of troubles, disorder and conflicts, which attack the environment in the form of 'pollution'. The new convert is required to receive or to give the 'light' which he has within himself but which is really a fragment of God's light. You give 'light' by raising your hand about 30 cm away from another person and moving it towards the part of the person's body where the pain is located. The body consists of a certain number of 'points' which relate to different organs.

The demands made of the Mahikarians are far from excessive. Immediately after first experiencing the reception of 'light', the would-be initiate has to follow an initiation course to learn the different 'points' of the body and the essential elements of the doctrine. Various other initiation sessions are planned, depending on the interest shown by the new member. As a general rule, the meeting places or *dojo* are filled all day long with the sick who come to receive the 'light' and thereby to be healed.

The meetings themselves revolve around different prayers to the Creator, usually spoken in Japanese, and accounts of the sick being miraculously healed by the force of 'light'. In the centres, as well as in the larger assemblies, believers can experience what are known as 'manifestations'. These are really in the form of a trance or possession by the spirits of ancestors which remain in the person's body and cause his troubles because they have been forgotten. It is these ancestral 'spirits' which in fact receive the 'light', find peace and thus cease their persecution.

At the time of initiation, the member receives a medal, called *omitama*, which has to be worn all the time. It contains a fragment of divine 'light' and will have the power to protect against all accidents, mishaps and problems in everyday life. In seeking such protection, several members have been persuaded to set up a small altar to their ancestors in their own house or apartment, on which they place symbols of God *(Su)*. Like the medals, this altar acts as a link between man and the divine world, with the believer's awareness of his participation in the divine world being the essential factor. All true science is divine science, and the Mahikarian believes that he scatters the 'seeds' of spiritual and divine civilization on the world through the transmission of 'light'. One gains salvation by opening oneself up to this light, that is, to God's 'desire' or *sonen*, which is acquired by obeying God's laws. Everything outside the realm of the spiritual is considered superstition: science and technology are relegated to the level of superstition in the eyes of the new recruit whenever they are not spiritually orientated.

In concrete terms, Mahikari urges its members to be highly critical of modern medicine even to the point of refusing surgery. Every physical or mental problem, every social problem, every catastrophe in the natural world has its *raison d'être* in misinterpretations of the spiritual world. Mahikari is true therapy: the proof of its power is in the numerous healings brought about by the receiving of 'light'. Moreover, it subsumes all science in so far as it takes over the power of both modern medical knowledge and the traditional specialists in supernatural powers (*gadèdzafé, manti-mantè, kenbwa*, etc.). The act of giving 'light' results in pacifying and taming the ancestral spirits whose symptoms are ailments and mishaps of all sorts. The many testimonies available to us speak of Mahikari as a way of finally putting an end to persecution by the 'spirits'.

Thus, Mahikari in Guadeloupe and Martinique has taken root, like the sects described earlier, in a problematic of personal crises, the effect of which is felt first and foremost on the level of traditional symbolic and cultural logics. But, unlike the Witnesses and the Adventists, Mahikari provides new legitimation for the legacy of the ancestral spirits from African and slave societies. The link with such a heritage is therefore reinforced and loses its precariousness. The typical convert admitted that he was incapable of communicating with the spiritual world or the realm of the ancestors before conversion to Mahikari. The 'spirits' were therefore believed to be scattered all over the country, adrift with no attachments, ready to persecute whoever crossed their path.

In sum, Mahikari is a way of renewing links with the traditional cultural heritage; but at the same time it is an instrument for criticizing modernity, and it can rid the individual of his inferiority complexes. It also provides him with a reassuring explanation of all global problems and conflicts.

The Apostles of Infinite Love

The same problematic applies to the Apostles of Infinite Love. But this religious movement no longer conducts itself like a sect: it presents itself to the mass of Catholics as the only true Catholic Church, anxious to preserve all its traditions and indifferent to social changes.

The movement was founded in Canada in 1952 by Father Jean Grégoire as a Catholic religious association with the support of Cardinal Léger, but it quickly became the object of severe condemnation from Rome. The eccentricities of the founder, who considered himself to be 'the object of extraordinary manifestations', were suspicious in the eyes of the Canadian clergy. But Father Grégoire, a self-ordained new pope, blamed the Church for 'breaking away from its past' and for having set up the Second Vatican Council (Vatican II) with a view to rewriting the doctrine and liturgy in worldly terms.

For about ten years the movement had just three priests, who settled in the rural area of St Jovitte in Quebec doing manual work and praying. A sanctuary dedicated to the Virgin Mary succeeded in attracting several thousand Canadian pilgrims faithful to the traditions of the Church and dissatisfied with the changes brought about by Vatican II. Then, when they became the object of various lawsuits in Quebec for allegedly kidnapping young girls, fraud and issuing threats against members, the Apostles of Infinite Love tried to set up a new centre for their activities in the Caribbean. Their first choice was Haiti, but the 'concordat' between church and state there did nothing to help their cause. So they crossed to Guadeloupe, existed for several years in silence, then finally worked out a way of expanding. First, they opened a convent and a monastery which welcomed the laity and their families, one in the hills above Deshaies and the other near the Pointe-Noire waterfalls. A small place in Pointe-à-Pitre, consecrated as the 'Oratory of Our Lady of Bethlehem', every evening attracted small groups of Catholic believers in search of the old form of worship.

It was in 1976 and 1977 that the Apostles of Infinite Love had their most spectacular success. Several thousand Catholics from all over Guadeloupe flocked to the huge centre at Deshaies, keen to take part in the ceremonies organized by the new sect: the Stations of the Cross in the open air, Latin mass, and pilgrimages to the Virgin Mary.

The research that I carried out among many pilgrims, priests and social educators has shown that the clue to the sect's rapid development is the revival of the traditional magico-religious system which had been endangered by the Catholic Church as a result of the changes that it had undergone. Two aspects of the sect's activities deserve special attention.

1. If the recruitment of laypeople to the convent is carried out on the basis of threats ('You will cause fatal accidents'; 'you will have all sorts of bad luck if you don't obey the Virgin Mary's call'), the Apostles' job must have been to find those who were at risk or already undergoing some psychological crisis.

2. As far as group activity is concerned, it is clear that the sect's shrines are frequented by members who are keen on attending 'masses' and performing rituals recommended by the *gadèdzafé* and who attend all the religious ceremonies organized by the Apostles of Infinite Love. Similarly, there is a network of 'penitent' members who dress in white or brown and who hope to receive 'gifts' from the 'saints' or 'spirits' who choose them. They are the most likely to become proselytes, and in some cases they live in the convent. Trances and 'possessions' are witnessed in various centres of pilgrimage, as if the traditional magico-religious rites performed under cover of the Catholic Church were now emerging from their hiding place, thanks to the freedom offered by the sect.

It is the lower classes, both rural inhabitants and urban dwellers who have recently left the land, who make up the largest part of the Apostles' membership. Of course, as magico-religious practices and beliefs are found among all social groups, it is no exaggeration to talk about the implantation of the sect on a virtually nationwide scale. It seems at first that the obsession with rites which date from the time of slavery and from the nineteenth century (such as processions, Stations of the Cross, masses devoted to the Holy Spirit, various saints and the dead, and the worship of the Virgin Mary) represents a search for the apparatus of symbols and images of the (African-style) religions which had hitherto been supported by the framework of the Catholic Church. Paradoxically, in Puerto Rico the Apostles of Infinite Love, who have already set up two convents in the past few years, prowl around the old shrines and places of pilgrimage (like the Montana Santa near the village of Patillas in the south of the island) which have been deserted by the Catholic Church and are now the favourite haunt of believers in search of traditional forms of worship. The way has already been prepared for this strategy in the Caribbean, for it was laid down by the way in which Catholicism forced itself on the people on the basis of the traditional network of symbols and imagery whose effects were felt in the formation of the individual personality. To give up these old forms of worship would be to a certain extent running the risk of losing one's identity. The Apostles' success reveals not only the special way in which Catholicism beleaguered the populace from the days of slavery until the present in the Caribbean, but also the cardinal importance of the popular cultural heritage which was built up in the nineteenth century but had already existed in the fiery test of slavery. Confronting such a heritage was inevitable, given the present-day economic crisis. But the crisis was initially experienced as a painful shift in, or a failure of, the underground system of symbols and images which the faithful had either to revive or to remove once and for all as a source of pathology or as a Satanic realm.

Native religious movements
Rastafarianism
Among the new movements which have had the greatest impact on the Caribbean society, we must give pride of place to Rastafarianism.[9] The movement was founded in the 1920s and 1930s at the height of the Great Depression, and was based on the ideas and catch-phrases of Marcus Garvey: 'Africa for the Africans at home and abroad.'

As early as August 1914, Garvey launched the Universal Negro Improvement Association in Jamaica and then, both in this country and in the United States, tried to persuade the blacks to return to their own ancestral culture and to their history of servitude. Prophesying the importance for all the world's blacks of Haile Selassie's accession to the throne of Ethiopia as Ras Tafari (Ras means 'Prince' and Tafari, 'Creator'), he began to proclaim everywhere: 'Look towards Africa when a black king is crowned; the day of deliverance will be nigh.' In fact, various Ethiopian Churches were founded around the 1930s, and associations for the support of Ethiopia, already regarded as a symbol for the whole of black Africa, were formed. Nurtured in these Churches, some of which leant towards Baptism and others towards Methodism, several black leaders eagerly adopted an interpretation of the Bible in the light of the contemporary situation of the blacks. They were already reading into certain passages the announcement of the arrival of their own messiah and redeemer who would deliver them from white enslavement, as the Israelites had been delivered from Egypt.

In 1953 there were at least a dozen religious and secular associations supporting either the Emperor Haile Selassie or the movement for the redemption of the world's black population: the African Methodist Episcopal Church, the Ethiopian World Federation (which had raised money for Ethiopia in the struggle against Italian fascism), the Ethiopian Coptic Faith, the United Ethiopian Body, the Ethiopian Youth Cosmic Faith and the Fraternal Solidarity of United Ethiopians, to name only a few. At that time, the essential elements of the Rastafarian doctrine arose from a reinterpretation of the Bible which proclaimed Haile Selassie as the black Saviour. The blacks were the reincarnation of the ancient Israelites who had been exiled and enslaved in the West Indies. It was to them that the biblical Revelation was addressed, but this truth was distorted by the whites. The blacks would reign on earth one day, and the white man would be punished. The Day of Deliverance was already near at hand in the form of Haile Selassie the Messiah, the incarnation of God on earth, God Himself who would lead His black people out of the Hell of the West Indies and into the Paradise of Ethiopia.

The great majority of Rastafarians are young men between the ages of 17 and 35 who live in the Kingston area of Jamaica. They are all from the working class, are unemployed, often illiterate and living on their wits. Some are low-paid workers in the private sector without permanent jobs, or domestic staff and street vendors. The drift from the land, which has accelerated ever since the beginning of the century, had produced a concentration of 27 percent of the total island's population in the area around Kingston and Saint Andrew in 1970. By 1972 agriculture represented only 9 percent of the gross national product. Rastafarianism therefore concentrated its electoral campaign among the young unemployed urban youth who were at a loose end, had no future and were, moreover, despised by the ruling classes. The movement snatched them up at an opportune moment, speaking to them in their own language and talking of the restoration of their dignity.

As an anti-colonial and anti-racist movement, Rastafarianism's starting-point is that the abolition of slavery has not brought an end to the blacks' position of servitude in the world. Rastafarian meetings led by prophetic leaders are occasions of high emotional intensity during which the individual is encouraged to express his social frustrations freely, to live in the here-and-now, and to seek deliverance in Baptist-inspired hymns, in the reinterpretation of the Bible as the history of black slaves, in reggae music, and in 'ganja' or marijuana 'communion' services called 'taking the chalice'. What Rastafarianism does most of all for its devotees is to give them a feeling of pride and power, as well as access to the 'the truth', to a definitive explanation of all the world's problems and conflicts and all 'misfortunes' on both a personal and a collective level.

The interpretations put forward by certain sociologists and anthropologists tend for the most part towards a functionalist approach,[10] and they fail to grasp the true significance of

Rastafarianism in Jamaica and the Caribbean. To think of the movement in terms of an escape from social and political strife is to miss the essence of Rastafarian aims. As it happens, the political struggle for Jamaican independence owes a great deal to the 'awakening' aroused throughout the population by the 'Back to Africa' slogan. The majority of the campaigns for independence in black Africa began as politico-religious movements with millenarian or messianic tendencies. It is hardly surprising, then, given the apartheid conditions in which the poorer blacks had lived since the abolition of slavery, that politico-religious movements in Jamaica have been the only channels of expression for rebellion and, moreover, the only ones which spoke the same language as the black people. The frequent harassment of the Rastafarians by the police, together with the fear that they arouse in those 'middle-class' Jamaicans clinging to a British cultural background, is evidence of the social and political impact of the movement.

But to examine the movement more closely, its emergence and activities cannot be understood without reference to what could be called the archaeology of religious practices in Jamaica. As in Haiti, the rebirth of African religions took place in the shelter of the official churches which were established during colonization. As early as 1784, the Baptists and Methodists had tried to exert a certain amount of influence over the slaves. George Liele, a black preacher in an Ethiopian Baptist church, supported the anti-slavery campaigns. In 1831, before abolition, the spread of egalitarian ideas in the Baptist churches stirred up a revolt among the black people. But during the nineteenth century, African-type religious practices were thriving at the very heart of Protestantism, Anglicanism and Catholicism. Myalism and Obeahism are, like Haitian Voodoo, beliefs and practices centred on magic and witchcraft based on the worship of different 'spirits' which can appear before devotees during trances and possessions or can be embodied in the different natural elements. *Pukuma*, or the practice of possession, and 'catch the power' are rituals which have been able to develop freely within some Baptist churches under the guidance of a growing number of black leaders. Prophets have emerged among these leaders, announced themselves as the new Moses and reinterpreted the Bible in the light of black people's aspirations. Revivalism appears to be a fairly recurrent phenomenon in Jamaica's religious history, but could one go as far as to say that a movement like Rastafarianism is nothing more than the re-emergence on the social and political scene of a suppressed form of African culture?

In the first place, we are struck by the similarities between Rastafarianism and religious movements such as Kimbanguism,

N'gunzism and Matsouanism in Bakongo or Harrisism in the Ivory Coast.[11] They are all separatist movements, yet they insist that their members abandon their traditional worship of the 'spirits' and witchcraft once and for all. They are also all agreed on criticizing the fact that these practices represent a diversion from, or an obstacle to, the mission that men of the black 'race' have acquired by means of the Bible. Now, what this conveys at the same time is an interpretation of the world and of history which accords well with black African culture. The basic symbols of this culture have even been refurbished in order to emphasize the distinction between it and the culture of the white Western world. The smoking of 'ganja' or 'sacred grass', for example, which Rastafarianism authorizes and even encourages, is a new way of relating to the world and 'the other'. It allows the individual to get back into trance and to be possessed by the 'spirits', although the latter are rejected and criticized. The 'sacred grass' is thought to induce visions, increase powers of communication and suppress fear and guilt. It represents the supreme moment of intense and sacred sharing: individuals become brothers; they take off their hats as in the celebration of the eucharist, read passages from the Bible together and emit cries like 'Jah Rastafari'. (Jah, or Jehovah, is sometimes confused with Ras, or Redeeming Emperor.)

Similarly, there is no doubt that the values of the patriarchal community (subjection of women to men; refusal to accept the bonds of marriage or of Western-style relationships; rejection of birth control) remain the values of black Africa, but they are also those which were pursued in the very midst of the period of slavery that did its best to break up African tribes and lineages. Many other examples could be cited — reggae music itself, for example, which, together with the rhythm 'n blues tradition, picks up the musical and instrumental threads originating in *kumina*: drums, scraper boards and rhythm; a pattern of repetition or improvisation which evokes the language of the 'ancestors'. Suffice it to emphasize at this point that, as well as being a revival of the basic core of the slave and nineteenth-century cultures, Rastafarianism is also a symptom of the mobilization of the working classes to build a new identity not only for Jamaica but for other Caribbean islands as well.[12]

Mita

The Mita sect, which was founded in Puerto Rico in 1940 and is much less aggressive than Rastafarianism, is experiencing great success in several countries. It has established two temples and 60 congregations in the Dominican Republic since 1964, and 65 congregations with 14,000 followers in Colombia; more recent growth has taken place in Venezuela, Mexico and Haiti. From its humble origins in the countryside at Arecibo in Puerto Rico, it has now expanded to build a huge temple in San Juan which can hold about 5,000 people. Today it owns several businesses, a large school, a clinic, some extensive properties and a retreat for both men and women who wish to dedicate their whole lives to the sect.

The movement's present-day prosperity is in sharp contrast to its modest beginnings, and especially to its original millenarian prophecies which announced the end of the world and the salvation of only a small group of 'chosen' people. A well-structured organization, with priests, deacons, guards and groups of musicians under the direction of a leader who is proclaimed to be the new incarnation of the Holy Spirit, Mita has the appearance of being a better established church than any other in Puerto Rico.

What particularly surprised me during my first contact with the movement's leader, Teofile Vargas Sein, known as Aaron, and with several priests and members, was the almost total lack of interest in doctrines or theology. As far as Mita is concerned, God did not teach at all, and Jesus himself was an illiterate prophet. For the believer, the main thing is to feel the presence of the spirit within himself. There seems to be nothing to distinguish Mita from Pentecostalist denominations. The sect was founded by Juanita Garcia Peraza, a Pentecostalist who had assiduously attended her Church's meetings for a long time and had finally broken away from it with a small group of devotees. After a long illness which lasted eight years, she claimed that she had had a certain number of revelations. She finally believed that she was the incarnation of the Holy Spirit in Puerto Rico and that it was her task to reinstate the principles of primitive Christianity and to offer redemption to all who followed her. God is believed to have produced three revelations: that of the Old Testament, that of Jesus, and finally that of Juanita Garcia, known as 'Mita', which means the 'Word of Life' that is bestowed upon the chosen and is vouched for by visions, dreams and healings. Prayer meetings follow the Pentecostalist pattern: public confessions by believers, preaching, hymns and orchestras intended to evoke an intensely emotional atmosphere during which devotees feel the presence of the Holy Spirit within themselves.

After the foundress's death in 1970, the Holy Spirit, according to the sect's members, entered the body of the new leader, Aaron, and is continuing to issue revelations to the whole world.

Without going into the details of the sect's deviance from Pentecostalism, some remarks on the importance of popular cults are required at this point. With the establishment of Protestant denominations in Puerto Rico at the beginning of the century, thanks to the US occupation of the island from 1898, the Catholic Church, which was modelled on the Spanish pattern, withdrew into a position of strict conservatism in order to maintain its hegemony. This attitude allowed the mass of Catholics, few of whom had yet moved to the towns, to cling to, and at the same time to freely develop, the popular traditions which were linked with (Caribbean) Indian religions and with African cults inherited from the time of slavery. These traditions were also linked with the Spiritism which had been enjoying outstanding success in the country since the nineteenth century. A creeping resistance to deculturation took the form of the appearance of cults such as the one dedicated to Santa Elenita (of the Montana Santa), a Puerto Rican who, at the beginning of the century, had claimed to have visions of the Virgin Mary and was said to believe that she was the incarnation of the Virgin. The year 1953 saw the foundation of the 'Cecilia Temple', a deviant group of fundamentalist Protestants who follow the teachings of a prophetess, Cecilia Temple, in whom the Holy Spirit was incarnated in order to establish a community of the 'saved'.

All the signs are that Mita is an underground movement which is oblivious of opposition to modernity or of the increasing amount of control that the United States has over Puerto Rico. The following observations alone will confirm this theory. On the one hand, a compulsive preference for Caribbean–Indian and African-type inherited practices is evident from the very manner in which the prophets make an appearance: an illness, a vision, a revelation or an incarnation of the Holy Spirit within the prophet who is taken to be a real 'medium'. These, then, are the first steps that the native sects take towards establishing themselves. Their healing sessions act as proof of the movement's sincerity; but in an indirect way they lead the new recruit back to the traditional means of contact with ancestral 'spirits', which the present-day cultural crisis has made more difficult. On the other hand, the announcement of a new place of salvation (a temple or a tent at a specific spot on the map) from the evil which is spreading everywhere is the sign of an indirect challenge to the ruling system. Thus, these prophets or new messiahs strive to track down the 'demons', called *enemigos* or *huestes* (in Mita), who haunt individuals or enter their soul and body. They then strive to organize a community of chosen people who are protected from the 'world' where evil thrives today unchecked. In this way the members of Mita have managed to set up their own businesses, mark out their own residential areas and create their own space, basically in order to make contact easier among the 'chosen', those saved from present and future disasters.

La Palma Sola[13]

Once again we shall do no more than draw attention to another sect, this time in the Dominican Republic, which has had a considerable political impact.

The Palma Sola is a movement which was founded between 1961 and 1962 and in a short time recruited several thousand members in the mountains near the Haitian border. Its origins date from the period between 1910 and 1922 when a certain Liborio Mateo claimed to be God's messenger on earth. Because he was a healer, he attracted several thousand peasants during the time of the US occupation. Owing to persecution, he took refuge in the mountains at the beginning of Trujillo's dictatorship. He was killed in 1922, but in the eyes of his followers he remains alive and will return to complete his mission. The rebirth of his movement was thought to take place in 1961 under the leadership of a certain Plinio Ventura Rodriguez, who claimed that God had appeared to him to give him the task of forming the Union Christiana Mundial in a place called Palma Sola. About 5,000 people, drawn mainly from the rural peasantry, assembled in a huge community outside a wooden church, organized Stations of the Cross, and sang traditional Catholic hymns as well as some hymns composed by Liborio. Large crucifixes were erected, in front of which the believers had to confess all their sins; miracle healing took place; and the traditional worship of saints was re-established. But at the same time, all the Voodoo-type symbols, beliefs and practices (animal sacrifices, healing baths, worship of spirits living in trees, rivers and streams, soothsaying and so forth) were openly accepted within the community.

On the social and political level, the refusal to work for wages or vote in elections caused the public authorities to be highly suspicious of the movement. An even greater cause for concern were rumours of the re-introduction of Haitian Voodoo. Against the volatile political background of 1962, interrogations proceeded apace concerning the return of former supporters of Trujillo across the Haitian frontier, helped by the dictator Duvalier, or else an invasion of barbarism or Voodoo-witchcraft from Haiti. Finally, the government ('State Council') decided to attack the new community on 28 December 1962. The result was a real massacre: 200 dead according to some reports, 400–500 according to others. And so the Palma Sola came to a temporary end.

It is not possible, within the context of this chapter, to account for all the complex factors which contributed towards the appearance of this syncretic–messianic movement and the genocide chosen as a solution to the problem by the authorities in power at that time. Not only did the ignorance of the ruling class and even the press of popular religious practices appear to be great, but indeed, there is still such prejudice against Voodoo as being nothing more than the religion of 'black Haitians' that any attempt at a scientific investigation into Palma Sola runs into severe problems.

At the time of writing, charismatic movements which have come to light under cover of a now tolerant Catholic Church (like the Protestant denominations) are flourishing from Guadeloupe to Santo Domingo, in Haiti and in Puerto Rico. They attract several thousand people on each island and are led by Catholic priests or nuns. They encourage public confessions, healing and trances — all as manifestations of the Holy Spirit.

It is thus clear that, as was pointed out at the beginning of this study, there has been a return to the old beliefs and practices, which is a confirmation of the presence of a central nucleus, or focal point, of symbols that have been in operation since the time of slavery in the popular religious and cultural customs of the Caribbean. In the absence of spirit worship, the charismatic movement, as an experience of the Holy Spirit, enables trances and possessions to take place in urban areas and in fact amounts to a more legitimate renewal of beliefs considered to be characteristic of the lower classes in general.

Some theoretical thoughts in outline

As I have been able to give only a brief summary of some of the new religious movements in the Caribbean, it is still not possible to draw any firm conclusions. In spite of the astonishing revival of the most varied religious movements, the amount of documentation available in the Caribbean region is slight. Existing studies are still fragmentary and rarely have a true Caribbean perspective.

The problems raised by the movements to which I have drawn attention here are numerous and complex. First, in order to answer an initial misgiving, it is doubtful whether the simple theory of an economic and social crisis could provide the key to understanding how these sects or religious movements, imported or native, actually work. Certainly, all sects are conceived in a crisis situation in a given society. But this theory, however correct it may be, is too general and cannot take into account the symbolism and cultural system peculiar to each society. Analyses of Jehovah's Witnesses and Seventh-Day Adventists in Europe and the United States, for example, cannot be made to fit Guadeloupe and Martinique.

These movements can be seen to work differently, especially in respect of their failure to mesh with official doctrine and with widely accepted practices. The same problem is to be found in the case of the Apostles of Infinite Love and the Mahikari. On the other hand, it is equally doubtful whether one could consider the sects as false and illusory solutions to the so-called economic and social crises. This is the most common standpoint, widely adopted in analyses tending towards a functionalist or scientistic outlook. It is the dominant point of view not only in certain Marxist schools of thought, but even among non-Marxists. Using the supernatural as a means of escape from the current social and political struggles (according to functionalist theory), these sects have a therapeutic value or are more or less successful adaptations to modernity.[14] This is the position adopted by G. E. Simpson (1965) in his analysis of Rastafarianism, in which he can see a search for an 'escape route' but 'no attempt to alter the economic structure'. Thus, the functionalist theory is pre-occupied with establishing the activities and dysfunctions of the sects but not with grasping the hidden mechanisms or the underground logic which controls their emergence and their mode of operation.

Last but not least of the obstacles to a theoretical approach to new religious movements is the interpretation of them as business ventures and impostures. Here again we are faced with prejudices which are based on general observations but which are superficial since they avoid the question of the readiness of the vast majority of followers to rise to the bait. But look at how many established churches used to have weapons at their disposal in the form of dubious practices, fraud, extortion and coercion. It is not difficult to establish the fact that numerous modern sects are prosperous business enterprises. The fact that they show clear signs of totalitarianism has also been underlined.[15] This explains cases where members have been more or less forcibly separated from their families and their social background; where property has been seized; where the lives of prospective defectors have been threatened; where manipulation of a 'programming' type has been employed; and where members have been encouraged to take drugs or turn to prostitution. But it is rarely pointed out that modern sects often revive old practices drawn from Catholic religious congregations, so that it becomes difficult to confine totalitarianism exclusively to those sects which show obvious signs of it.

Nevertheless, the hypothesis about the sects' use of totalitarian methods deserves to be studied in more depth because it raises the unfathomable question of voluntary enslavement. The holocaust in Guyana, for example, which ought to arouse greater anxiety about Caribbean hospitality in the matter of the establishment of religion, has been analysed by a small number of researchers including Gordon Lewis (1979). But his study does not appear to have provoked the discussion that he was proposing. This is because people think that they already possess the theory of sects. Yet, the problem of the relationship between state and religion in the Caribbean, and more simply the problem of human rights in a modern sect, have hardly been studied. The cries of alarm are not enough, nor are they a substitute for analysis and investigations. One could even go as far as to say that the rise in popularity of these sects is due partly to the lack of attention shown to them by sociologists. In my opinion, it is the attempt to hide or obscure the religious phenomenon which leads many studies of economics and politics in the Caribbean into an impasse.

Above all, it is essential to grasp the importance of the underground work of systems of symbols and images in producing a culture in the Caribbean which is irreducible to Western culture. Studies of Voodoo in Haiti lead me to view it as a distinct language with the capacity to adapt to the most diverse conditions, as well as a source of inspiration for the arts in Haiti. But it was even more clearly apparent that, in spite of the attempts at manipulation and control on the part of the ruling powers, there existed a link between Voodoo and social conflicts which did not exhaust the significance of Voodoo. A non-reductionist analysis of the religious problem which would carefully and critically reconsider religion's utopian aspects has proved to be indispensable. The first task is to acknowledge the dual operation of sects in the Caribbean in so far as they rely on what we call a system of traditional symbols and images which they either revive or with which they provoke a radical confrontation. The success of the Apostles of Infinite Love in Guadeloupe, for example, is inexplicable in any other way. The same goes for Rastafarianism in Jamaica or Mita in Puerto Rico. It seems that the apocalyptic themes of these religious movements have been somewhat weakened, and this has favoured challenges to a popular cultural heritage which has been shredded or embarrassed by the invasion of the ruling cultural values of the West.

The economic and social crisis, which is the first gateway leading to the implantation or the emergence of new religious movements, is felt first of all on the cultural level, since it destroys or at least disturbs the apparatus of symbols and images which has traditionally been the starting-point of the individual's search for identity. In the case of the Caribbean, religious beliefs and practices forged in the crucible of slavery have always been the source of a continuous cultural vitality at the popular level as well as on the level of the intellectual stratum. Not only do these beliefs and practices serve as a way of interpreting history, as archives, as a source of medical knowledge and wisdom, but at the same time they also inspire poetry, drama, painting, music, dancing — in other words, the arts in general. The discovery of reggae music and of Haitian painting in the naïve style owes a lot to this central apparatus of symbols and images which acts as a focus for the culture. This is why a purely ideological analysis of the new religious movements as a mode of reproducing social relationships is insufficient because the problematic of symbolism and imagery at issue in the operation of conversion to the sects is more complex and possibly more basic than the ideological aspect.

We have proof that the economic and social crisis is not the fundamental reason for the success of the sects in the dual process of emigration and immigration which conversion has brought about. Puerto Ricans who have emigrated to the United States and been converted to the Mita sect have returned to settle in Puerto Rico; Haitian converts to Seventh-Day Adventism and Evangelicalism try to use the new sect indirectly as a way of escaping from Haiti; Mahikarians from the Antilles who live in Paris are now returning to their country of origin. Thus, the fact that sects obviously offer social mobility to their members is not enough to explain their success, in the same way that the pathological or therapeutic effects of joining the Seventh-Day Adventists in Martinique could not entirely account for the movement's popularity there. As James Beckford (1985) has pointed out, the Utopia offered by a sect does not remove the believer from all involvement in the world and society. It is essential to recognize and to reconsider the creative powers of symbolism operating in the new life-style experienced by those who join a sect. But to talk of symbolism is to talk of distinctly different ways of interpreting the success of the sects in the light of each particular culture. Thus, for example, while the Adventists in Guadeloupe and Martinique are obsessed with their struggle against the 'persecuting spirits', the Haitian Adventists who have emigrated to Guadeloupe seem to be more preoccupied with social mobility and with opportunities for contacting and meeting the host population; however, escape from the witchcraft, which is occupying an ever more important place in the sphere of Voodoo, remains the chief factor in conversion to sects, even in Haiti itself.

Of course, one must not be fooled by the total refusal of Witnesses and Adventists to participate in trades union and political struggles. Conversion indirectly offers a social advantage. Not only does the new sect offer bonds of friendship with the existing members of the sect who become the new extended family, replacing the one destroyed by present-day economic development, but it also opens up new possibilities for contacts even outside the member's own country, on an international level. This fits in particularly well with the requirements of migrants. In the case of Haitian refugees who have settled all over the Caribbean, the new religions are sought as a means of gaining insertion into the host society. And Rastafarianism promotes new forms of solidarity-in-conflict for blacks in Britain as well as in the Caribbean regardless of national differences. Setting aside the empirical aspects of conversion to new sects, we need to theorize from a starting-point in the problematic of symbolism as such. Since it actually supplies the constitutive ingredients of individual personality and collective identity, the apparatus of symbols and images opens the way to a procedure for producing meaning — in other words, a distinct language with which things social and the world are grasped. This involves going beyond a pre-Saussurian interpretation of symbolism, which is often the key to functionalist analyses. The latter are like scientistic, positivistic analyses which see religious beliefs and practices as being determined entirely by the level of development of the forces of production and by insufficient scientific knowledge of the world and society. The fact that certain sects, whether they enjoy government protection or not, actually bring about dangerous levels of deculturation or develop into totalitarian institutions is a phenomenon which demands attention and which must be exposed through analysis. Resorting, as we do here, to the concept of *creative symbolism* does not mean that we are turning a blind eye to the harmful aspects of these religious movements. Nor, however, are we setting out on a search for their purely positive aspects. The point is to account for, and to unearth, the hidden ways in which sects develop and operate in the Caribbean: not to make value-judgements.

In my view, everything points to the idea that the success of both the imported and the native sects stems from the fact that they provide the lower classes with a transitional culture in the face of both traditional and modern values. Thus, the new converts would appear to be real *bricoleurs*, leaving no stone unturned in their efforts to create for themselves a new context for life and a new language. Whether by legitimation or by rejection of the nucleus of traditional symbolism and imagery, the convert engages in a process of distancing himself from the dominant values. Even if the latter are adopted, they are then directly or indirectly reinterpreted on the basis of the old cultural system. By offering him a new collectivity, the sect shelters the individual from society, and this is undoubtedly the source of its powers of seduction.

Even when the Bible, that sacred text upon which all others are based, is taken for the whole of culture or for the culture par excellence, it is enveloped in a magical aura from which it derives the power of traditional as well as modern culture. By contrast, the favours bestowed on the individual by the Holy Spirit's visitation (as with Mita, Pentecostalisms and modern charismatic movements) indicate an indirect but henceforward legitimate renewal of links with the legacy of the 'spirits' ('saints', 'gifts' or 'mysteries') which had become too heavy a burden to bear as such. For their part, the Adventists and Witnesses, in their headlong flight from this heritage, do in fact run into it again in the very manner of their conversion: they receive the Bible in dreams, and it is through illness that God chooses them to enter the Kingdom of the Saved.

It is evident, therefore, that, while trying to flee his past, the individual is continually pursued by it. One could go as far as to say that the traces of his own past activate the new convert. The advantage of being converted appears to be a subconscious resistance to the destruction of one's identity. Yet in conversion one can still see the glow of the last embers of the traditional cultural heritage, doomed to be destroyed by modernity. The heritage burns out in its own brilliance. In its revitalization, no less than in its most violent rejection, it speaks of its own destruction and impotence. Like the *peau de chagrin*, it shrinks all the faster, the more feverish are the attempts to get it back. The followers of the Apostles of Infinite Love in Guadeloupe, the Palma Sola in the Dominican Republic or the Rastafarians are doing their utmost to win back the sacred trees, grottos, shrines, places of pilgrimage and mountains; utopian communities are reappearing; food farming, which had been seriously neglected, is being started again; there are new trends in music; patterns of eating are being reviewed; and the whole medical system is being questioned. In fact, in every sector of daily life, a continuous process of creation and a search for new identity are evident. Slaves who had escaped from their captive environment (Maroons) had already attempted to bring about a movement like this. The Caribbean, which was subject to the covetousness and whims of the great powers from the sixteenth century to the present day, is still moving towards the conquest of its own space. The new sects seem to indicate that Caribbean culture is still searching for its origins and is still in the process of developing.

Notes

1. See, for example, the point of view of Genovese (1972: 161 ff. and 280 ff.).

2. See the reactions of the Dominican press on the topic of the Palma Sola sect, of which we shall have more to say below. The newspaper *La Nacion*, for example, refers to Haiti as 'The Rome of black magic in America' (quoted in Martinez, 1981, p. 106). For Dominican Voodoo, see Esteban Deive (1975) and Davis (1981: 22–4). These recent research findings are evidence of attempts to accept African cultural components such as Voodoo as an integral part of Dominican national culture.

3. On the patterns of resistance among slaves in the Caribbean and in the United States in general, as well as the Maroons, the indispensable references are to works such as those of Debien (1974), Fouchard (1972), Bastide (1967), Herskovits (1941), Patterson (1967), Price (1973) and Buijtenhuijs (1971). I should probably have shown more traces of the Maroons in certain native religious sects in the Caribbean, such as

Palma Sola in the Dominican Republic. There is scope for a more intensive study of the topic.

4. See my analyses of religion in the French Antilles in Hurbon (1980a; 1981b).

5. Scott Cook's (1971: 577) view, for example, is that 'There is no published evidence of African survivals among existent Puerto Rican folk religious groups. The similarities are purely structural and functional, not historical'.

6. See Sangaravelou (1975) for fuller information about Maliémin.

7. I have given a more detailed analysis of the operations of Jehovah's Witnesses and Mahikari in Guadeloupe in Hurbon (1980b; 1981b).

8. Massé (1978: 39–44) examines numerous examples to show the magical character of conversion to Adventism and the seeking for exorcism from 'evil spirits' that is practised by converts on Martinique. I have been able to make the same observations on Guadeloupe.

9. On the history of Rastafarianism see, in particular, Clarke (1980), Cashmore (1981), Simpson (1965), Smith et al. (1967), Barrett (1968) and Williams (1981).

10. See, in particular, Simpson (1965). There is a discussion of functionalist and neo-Marxist tendencies in Cashmore (1981: 33–6). Even Bastide (1967: 173) seems to have misunderstood the meaning of Rastafarianism when he speaks of 'the change of the flight into mysticism to social opposition'. In fact, Rastafarianism has been neither pure mysticism nor pure social opposition: on the contrary, it has been strictly a politico-religious messianic movement. The interpretation put forward here is close to that offered by Cashmore, who is one of the few authors to emphasize the importance of symbolism in the operation of the Rastafarian movement.

11. Comparisons between African religious movements and those of the Caribbean are rarely drawn but would be highly instructive. Lack of space prevents me from expanding on the point here. Readers are referred to the following studies, for example, of African prophetisms: Sinda (1972), Auge (1975), Dozon (1974) and Balandier (1967).

12. One could apparently compare the connection made by Bob Marley (and his music) between Jamaica and black migrants to England with what happens in the French Antilles. Moreover, the figure of Bob Marley is that of a prophet and of a model, almost on a parallel with Marcus Garvey, who was also able to direct blacks towards questions of cultural identity (cf. Cashmore, 1981: 107–22).

13. On Palma Sola, see Martinez (1981).

14. Raymond Massé concludes: 'Adventism becomes an important factor in mental disturbance and hence in mental illness in so far as it destroys the traditional mechanisms of psychological adaptation as well as creating new sources of frustration by imposing a puritanism and an asceticism which is completely unsuited to the Caribbean context . . . We must not forget, however, that in other cases we have shown that conversion had the effect of a genuine therapy . . . .' (Massé, 1978: 68–9). These two possible effects of conversion prove that we must definitely adopt a perspective other than functionalist in order to grasp the causes of sectarian success.

15. See the work of Yves Lecerf (1975), who analysed the strategy of the Three Holy Hearts sect in Europe. No doubt the same strategy could be discovered in numerous other modern sects.

References

Auge, M. (1975) *Théorie des pouvoirs et idéologie. Etude de cas en Côte d'Ivoire.* Paris: Hermann.

Balandier, G. (1967) *Sociologie actuelle de l'Afrique noire.* Paris: Presses Universitaires de France.

Barrett, L. (1968)   *The Rastafarians. A Study in Messianic Cultism in Jamaica.* Puerto Rico: Institute of Caribbean Studies, University of Puerto Rico.

Bastide, R. (1967)   *Les Amériques noires.* Paris: Payot.

Beckford, J. (1985)   *Cult Controversies. The Societal Reaction to New Religious Movements.* London: Tavistock Publications.

Buijtenhuijs, R. (1971)   *Le Mouvement 'Mau Mau'. Une révolte paysanne et anticoloniale en Afrique noire.* Paris: Mouton.

Cashmore, E. (1981)   *Rastaman. The Rastafarian Movement in England.* London: Allen & Unwin.

Clarke, S. (1980)   *Jah Music.* London: Heinemann.

Cook, S. (1971)   'The Prophets: A Revivalistic Folk Religious Movement in Puerto Rico', pp. 560–79 in M. Horovitz (ed.), *Peoples and Cultures of the Caribbean.* New York: Natural History Press.

Courlander, H. (1960)   *The Drum and the Hoe.* Berkeley: University of California Press.

Davis, M. (1981)   *Voces del purgatorio. Estudio de la salve dominicana.* Santo-Domingo: Museo del Hombre Dominicano.

Debien, G. (1974)   *Les Esclaves aux Antilles françaises (XVIIe et XVIIIe siècles).* Fort-de-France: Société d'histoire de la Guadeloupe et de la Martinique.

Dozon, J. (1974)   'Les Mouvements politico-religieux: syncrétismes, messianismes, néo-traditionalismes', pp. 75–111 in M. Auge (ed.), *La Construction du monde.* Paris: Maspéro.

Esteban Deive, C. (1975)   *Vodu y Magia en Santo-Domingo.* Santo-Domingo: Museo del Hombre Dominicano.

Fouchard, J. (1972)   *Les Marrons de la liberté.* Paris: Editions de l'Ecole.

Genovese, E. (1972)   *Roll, Jordan, Roll: The World the Slaves Made.* New York: Pantheon Books.

Herskovits, M. (1937)   *Life in a Haitian Valley.* New York: Knopf.

—— (1941)   *The Myth of the Negro Past.* New York: Harper.

Horovitz, M. (1971)   *Peoples and Cultures of the Caribbean.* New York: Natural History Press.

Hurbon, L. (1972)   *Dieu dans le vaudou haitien.* Paris: Payot.

—— (1974)   *Ernst Bloch: utopie et espérance.* Paris: Cerf.

—— (1975)   *Cultures et pouvoirs dans la Caraïbe: langue créole, vaudou, sectes religieuses en Guadeloupe et en Haiti.* Paris: Harmattan.

—— (1979)   *Culture et dictature en Haiti: l'imaginaire sous contrôle.* Paris: Harmattan for CNRS.

—— (1980a)   'Le poids des pratiques magico-religieuses dans la culture antillaise', pp. 196–211 in *Actes du 1er Seminaire Inter-Caraïbe sur l'Inadaptation Juvénile.* Pointe-à-Pitre, Guadeloupe: Services et Clubs de Prévention.

—— (1980b)   'Le double fonctionnement des sectes aux Antilles: le cas du Mahikari en Guadeloupe', *Archives de sciences sociales des religions* (Paris), 50(1), 59–75.

—— (1981a)   'Sectes religieuses, loi et transgression aux Antilles, *Le CARE* (Centre antillais de recherches et d'etudes, Pointe-à-Pitre), May, 79–107.

—— (1981b)   'Le Nom du père et le recours aux esprits aux Antilles', pp. 89–106 in *Actes du 2e Seminaire Inter-Caraïbe sur l'inadaptation juvénile – La question du père.* Pointe-à-Pitre, Guadeloupe: Services et clubs de prévention.

Lecerf, Y. (1975)   *Les Marchands de Dieu. Analyse socio-politique de l'affaire Melchior.* Paris: Complexe.

Lewis, G. (1979)   *Gather with the Saints at the River: the Jonestown Guyana Holocaust 1978.* Puerto Rico: Institute of Caribbean Studies.

176   Laënnec Hurbon

Leyburn, J. (1945)   *The Haitian People*. New Haven, Conn.: Yale University Press.

Martinez, L.   (1981)   'Un Estudio preliminar acerca del movimiento de Palma Sola como movimiento messianico y social campesino', *Revista Dominicana de Antropologia e historia*, 10 (19–20), 83–209.

Massé, R.   (1978)   *Les Adventistes du septième jour aux Antilles françaises. Anthropologie d'une espérance millénariste*. Montréal: Centre de recherches caraïbes / Ste Marie, Martinique: Fonds Saint Jacques.

Mintz, S.   (1960)   *Papers in Caribbean Anthropology*. New Haven, Conn.: Yale University Press.

Patterson, O.   (1967)   *The Sociology of Slavery*. London: MacGibbon & Kee.

Price, R.   (1973)   *Maroon Society*. New York: Doubleday.

Sahlins, M.   (1976)   *Au coeur des sociétés. Raison utilitaire et raison culturelle*. Paris: Gallimard (1st English edn, *Culture and Practical Reason*, 1976).

Sangaravelou (1975)   'Les Indiens de la Guadeloupe: étude de géographie humaine'. Unpublished paper.

Séguy, J.   (1980) 'La socialisation utopique aux valeurs', *Archives de sciences sociales des religions*, 50(1), 7–21.

Simpson, G. E.   (1965)   *The Religious Cults of the Caribbean: Trinidad, Jamaica and Haiti*. Puerto Rico: Institute of Caribbean Studies (new edition 1970).

Sinda, M.   (1972)   *Le Messianisme congolais et ses incidences politiques*. Paris: Payot.

Smith, M. et al.   (1967)   'The Ras Tafari Movement in Kingston, Jamaica', *Caribbean Quarterly* 13(3), 3–29; 13(4), 3–14.

Williams, K. (1981)   *The Rastafarians*. London: Wardbeck Educational.

Wilson, B. (ed.) (1967)   *Patterns of Sectarianism*. London: Heinemann.

—— (1970)   *Religious Sects*. London: Weidenfeld & Nicolson.

7

The social impact of Nigeria's new religious movements

Friday M. Mbon

Introduction

One student of the phenomenon of new religious movements in Nigeria wrote a few years ago: 'The emergence of new religious movements in Nigeria seems to be a weekly affair especially among the Aladura[1] group of churches. You find new religious movements everywhere . . .'[2] The writer of these words may have exaggerated a bit about the frequency with which these movements arise, but most students of this phenomenon in Nigeria will readily agree that it is in this country that one witnesses the greatest proliferation of such movements in West Africa. For example, in any little town of about 2,000–3,000 inhabitants, one may easily count up to 50 or 60 different brands of religious movements. Within the small town of Calabar in the south-east of the country, with a population of approximately a million, one can spot literally hundreds of these movements (see Hackett, 1985: especially Ch. 7; Offiong, 1983: 60–3). These rough statistics should give some idea of the pullulation of new religious movements in Nigeria, particularly in the industrially undeveloped areas of the south-east (see Barrett, 1968: 121, 291; Ifeka-Moller, 1974: 63, 65), a region to which a politician from another part of the country some time ago referred, rather untactfully, as having only churches as its main industry. He was of course referring to the excessive money-making business and commercialization that go on in the new religious movements in that part of the country; but such money-making and commercialization cannot be said to be peculiar to that area.

My aim in this chapter is mainly to show in what ways Nigeria's new religious movements in general have influenced the political, economic and social life of Nigerians. It will be obvious from the following discussion that it is because of their impact on Nigerian society that the new religious movements emerge and continue to wax from strength to strength in terms of increases in the numbers of their church buildings, programmes and projects, and adherents. In other words, it should be clear that their social impact is the reason not only for their emergence and continued existence in contemporary Nigeria, but also the reason why they continue to attract and hold large numbers of members at home and (for the Aladura and

Brotherhood of the Cross and Star) in black and non-black countries abroad.

Perhaps one should clarify *ab initio* what is meant here by the expression, 'Nigeria's new religious movements'. I mean by this expression those movements which have sprung up in Nigeria, founded by Nigerians or other Africans living in Nigeria, during the last six decades or so. In the words of Harold Turner, I am referring here to religious movements 'founded in Africa, by Africans, and primarily for Africans; a three-fold description that is intended in a factual and historical sense, and not as a slogan' (Turner, 1979: 92). However, I do not agree with Turner that these movements are, or for that matter were ever intended to be, 'primarily for Africans'. On the contrary, some of them, such as the two brands dealt with here, see the whole world as their 'mission field' and have, in fact, started to penetrate many non-African countries. The word 'new' is used here because these movements are seen to be radically different in many respects from African traditional religions and from the two dominant non-African religious traditions in Nigeria, namely, Christianity and Islam.

Some of the new religious movements in Nigeria began to bloom as far back as the second decade of this century; others came to fruition during Nigerian independence, and still others afterwards. But the emergence of these movements was not necessarily linked with the struggle for Nigerian independence. Nigeria's new religious movements did not come into existence first and foremost as protest movements concerned primarily with nationalism and political interests, as some religious movements in other parts of Africa have often been — for instance, Kimbanguism in the former Belgian Congo (now Zaire) and other similar movements in East and South Africa.

The two prominent brands of new religious movements in Nigeria which are picked out for special reference in this chapter are, chronologically, the Aladura group of movements referred to earlier, and the Brotherhood of the Cross and Star. They are the most influential in terms of the numbers of their votaries, and together they constitute the greatest percentage of followers of new religious movements in contemporary Nigeria. The well-known ones in the Aladura confederation include the Eternal Order of Cherubim and Seraphim, the Church of the Lord (Aladura), the Christ Apostolic Church and the Celestial Church of Christ. As of now, the Brotherhood of the Cross and Star (founded about 1956) has not yet fissioned into any distinct groups. The reason for this may be traced to the fact that, unlike its Aladura counterparts, the Brotherhood of the Cross and Star still has its charismatic founder and leader, on whom the movement is incredibly strongly centred.

The differences which exist among Nigeria's new religious movements and African traditional religions on the one hand, and Christianity and Islam on the other hand, are such that 'these movements are usually disowned by those who adhere either to the continuing African [traditional] systems, or to the invasive Islamic or Christian systems' (Turner, 1976: 14). Furthermore, like their counterparts in other parts of the world, Nigeria's new religious movements are usually characterized by 'congenial forms of worship, a new corporate life-style and ethic, healing and revelations for personal guidance and security . . . and are concerned with immediate healing and the solution of daily problems [and with] active search for spiritual power' (Turner, 1976: 16–17). These movements are further characterized by their confidence that they have spiritual treasures to give to the whole world, especially to the whites. Other characteristics of the movements, according to Bryan Wilson, include 'exotic provenance; new cultural life-style . . . charismatic leadership; a following predominantly young and drawn in disproportionate measure from the better-educated and middle-class sections of the society; social conspicuity; international operation . . . ' (Wilson, 1981: v). Although Wilson is referring here specifically to Western new religious movements, it is an interesting coincidence that these very features also characterize Nigeria's new religious movements in general. One can only conclude from such a coincidence that it is perhaps the same spirit that moves new religious movements all over the world!

Since we in Nigeria are more acquainted with the new religious movements that claim to be Christian than with those that would call themselves Islamic or African-traditional, my discussion here focuses on the Christian movements. They are movements which have, to all intents and purposes, emerged in the course of the interaction between the Nigerian traditional society and its religions and the obviously more powerful and more advanced (in many ways) Euro-Arabic cultures and their major religions, Christianity and Islam. It will be seen in what follows that as a consequence of this interaction a new religious movement usually departs substantially from the religious traditions of both the interacting cultures, by reworking or adapting elements of their religious traditions into a new, largely different religious system; hence the appropriateness of the designation 'new religious movement' (Turner, 1976: 14).

Incidentally, the other popular nomenclature used for these movements in Nigeria is 'independent churches', with the stress on 'independent', signifying the fact that these churches claim to be independent of foreign origin or domination. But in certain contexts in which the causal factors are multi-dimensional, the label 'new religious movements' may be preferable because the term 'movement' is more comprehensive in those contexts than the word 'church'. Another reason is that some movements (for example the Brotherhood of the Cross and Star),[3] refuse to be called 'churches' since they do not want to be associated or confused with the historical, mission-oriented churches. Yet another reason why the term 'church' is not preferred here is that there are many elements in the new religious movements which make it not quite appropriate to call them 'churches' in the sense in which the West conceives of a church. For example, the practice of spiritual and physical healing (and the modes thereof), which is central in the new religious movements, does not receive the same degree of emphasis in Western-style churches.

One must hasten to add, however, that not all the new religious movements in Nigeria share all the characteristic features mentioned above. In fact, there are obvious differences among them in such areas as leadership, ideology, relation to the larger society, ways of operation in different hermeneutical situations, doctrine and dogma, organizational structure, ethics, the demands made on their votaries and what each movement claims to offer them, and the rate of change within each movement. However, the task before us here is not to point out and analyse these areas of differences among the movements, but rather to try to show how these movements have had an impact on the political, economic and social life of Nigerians.

The new religious movements and Nigerian politics
The basic attitude of Nigeria's new religious movements towards politics is still conditioned, to a greater or lesser extent, by the theological teachings of the older churches. Among most of the movements there remains the idea that Christians should steer clear of politics, and that in this respect the things of Caesar and those of Christ must remain in separate camps; or that Rome and Jerusalem must remain separate. As a consequence of this theological position, the new religious movements, like their older counterparts, have generally failed to provide leadership facilities to their members in the political affairs of the country. Nor has the membership of these movements been well informed on how to criticize the government constructively, when necessary.

This does not mean that individual members or small groups within these movements do not participate in partisan politics. For instance, in 1964 John Edokpolor, then an Apostle of the Cherubim and Seraphim branch of the Aladura movement, contested and won a parliamentary seat in Benin, Bendel State of Nigeria; and in 1965,

Rev. Akinadewo, also of the Cherubim and Seraphim, contested the regional election in his Ondo Constituency (Omoyajowo, 1975: 133). Some key members of the Brotherhood of the Cross and Star are also reported to have sought political appointments by contesting elections.[4] In fact, Pastor Asuquo Ekanem of the Brotherhood recently stood as a candidate in the 1983 governorship elections in the Cross River State, although he withdrew for personal reasons in the early stages of the race. But these individual participations do not usually have any observable impact on the general political scene of the country.

However, the Aladura group of movements, some of which began to emerge in the western part of the country in the early 1920s, could sometimes be quite vocal in matters of politics.[5] Although some of these movements are known to have proved to be apolitical through most of their history, a majority of them have been quite active in politics. Historically, their founder, J. O. Oshitelu, is reported to have been held as a suspect and interrogated by the colonial adminis- trators as early as 1931; and his very close associate, Joseph Babalola, served six months in prison for the apparent political implications of the Aladura movements (Turner, 1979: 135).

Nigerian independence in 1960 was enthusiastically welcomed by the Aladura movements with thanksgiving services. When the political unrest in the then Western Region catapulted the entire country into a series of crises in the early 1960s, it was the Aladura movements that played the prophetic role in warning the people of Nigeria against the impending social and political catastrophes that would result from the injustices that were rampant in the political arena. While the older churches maintained their characteristically acquiescent, nonchalant and generally sit-on-the-fence attitude, and exercised the greatest restraint in making statements that had any transparent political implications, the Aladura movements became quite outspoken in condemning those politicians whom they felt to be corrupt, thereby making life difficult for the Nigerian people in general.

When on 15 January 1966 the first coup d'état took place in Nigeria, many Aladura prophets claimed that the event had been shown to them in vision several weeks before. One of these prophets in Kaduna actually claimed that he had foreseen the coup in the form of an open combat between Jesus Christ and the Prophet Muhammad. Jesus, he narrated, was armed with a sword while the Prophet Muhammad fought with a spear. The outcome of the combat, according to this prophet, was victory for Jesus, while the Prophet Muhammad was set ablaze. The prophet is reported to have wept publicly during a service that he was conducting, crying out:

'Look, Muhammad is burning! . . . ' This incident was said to have occurred on the eve of the coup (14 January 1966). The Aladura movement in the North of Nigeria, naturally, interpreted the vision as portending the victory of the Christian South over the Muslim North. Since the Sardauna of Sokoto, then Premier of the North, was regarded by the Aladura as the symbol of Muslim unity in the North, his death in the coup was seen by the Aladura as the triumph of Christianity — especially the Aladura brand of Christianity — over Islam. Following the coup, some leaders of the Aladura in the North claimed that hundreds of Muslims there had been converted by them, leading to the establishment of many branches of the Aladura movement there.

When the Nigerian civil war broke out in 1967, most of the Aladura pledged their support for national unity and openly condemned the activities of Odumegwu Ojukwu, the leader of the secession, for whose defeat they openly prayed. But they did not stop there. Towards the end of the war, they went on to donate substantially to the Troops Comfort Funds. The women's associations, led by 'Captain' Christianah Abiodun of the Cherubim and Seraphim group, donated various articles to the residence of the head of state, General Yakubu Gowon, at Dodan Barracks. They are reported to have been warmly received by General Gowon who posed with the delegation in a number of photographs.

Even to this day, the Aladura movements are known to be keenly interested in the social and political problems that face the country. One hears of this concern for the unity, well-being and political stability of the country on the lips of the praying Aladura all over the country. Occasionally, they even visit some rulers of the country to tell them about their visions and to pray for them, What is more, it is the Aladura movements, rather than the mission-seeded churches, that have been known intermittently to ask their members to observe days of prayer and fasting for rulers and people of the country.

During the Nigerian civil war, there were several stories in Biafra to the effect that prophecies played a crucial part, especially in the surrender of one Biafran army division. And one senior officer in the Biafran administration recalls that several prophets constantly came to instruct him ('by revelation') to take specific courses of action, such as to call a fast (Walls, 1978: 207).

The official position of the Brotherhood of the Cross and Star in matters of politics is one of non-involvement. For instance, the Secretary to the founder and leader of the movement, Pastor Offu Ebongo, is reported to have said, in reaction to an alleged political article credited to a member of the movement, 'Brotherhood of the Cross and Star is not a political organization but exclusively religious, purely devoted to the spiritual welfare of the world.'[6] But this is not to say that individual members of the movement have not occasionally voiced political opinions.

Furthermore, it might be instructive to recall the involvement of members of the Brotherhood of the Cross and Star in Nigerian politics, it might also be instructive to recall that one of the sons of the founder and leader of this movement owns a very high-quality and generally popular journal called *Inside Out*, printed by the Brotherhood Press in Calabar. This journal publishes serious and timely articles by intellectuals on current political, economic and social issues in Nigeria and the world at large. In fact, a University of Calabar teacher who was serving part-time as the journal's special correspondent, associate editor and political analyst resigned his appointment with the university in order to take up a full-time appointment with the publishers of *InsideOut*. Although it is owned by Leader Obu's son, its publishers say that the journal is administratively independent of the workings and ideologies of the Brotherhood movement. Be that as it may, considering the kind of articles published in it during the NPN days, it was not difficult for anyone to see that in orientation and sympathy the journal was definitely pro-NPN, as could be illustrated by two articles published then: 'NPN Can't Lose at the Polls . . . ' (November 1981, pp. 118–21) and 'The Power of Incumbency: The Power that Can Keep a Ruler in Power Indefinitely' (November 1982, pp. 110–11). In spite of these facts, the publishers as a body still lay claim to political neutrality.

Although the founder and leader of the Celestial Church of Christ, Pastor S. B. J. Oschoffa (died September 1985), said officially that he had 'no political dealings with anybody', he admitted that he had been sending messages received 'in vision' to the government of his country, the Republic of Benin (formerly Dahomey), warning it of 'the impending doom of the influx of mercenaries in the country' (Nigerian Television Authority, 1981: 6). If that concern with the presence of foreign mercenaries in the Prophet's country was not a political and economic concern, one wonders what else it could have been.

In general, it is difficult to determine the extent to which the political voices in Nigeria's new religious movements have influenced the country's present political scene, or the weight of their impact on the country's political future. One thing seems certain, however: if these apparently lonely voices keep speaking up, their words are likely to have some measure of observable impact not only on the membership of the new religious movements, but also on the general political arena of the country. And if that happens, then the official policy in these movements of non-involvement in political affairs may have to be reviewed in the not-too-distant future.

The new religious movements and the Nigerian economy
When one begins to consider in what ways the new religious movements
have contributed to the economic development of Nigeria, one may be
tempted to look only at the negative impact that some of them seem to
have had on the country's economy. One may, for instance, notice only
those things which could have detrimental effects on various economic
sectors — for example, prohibitions in some movements against
drinking and the eating of meat; the requirement that only white
soutanes, which are usually available more widely and cheaply than
expensive clothes such as three-piece suits and lace dresses, should be
worn in church services and sometimes elsewhere as well; and the
practice of going about without shoes. Just imagine what would happen
to these sectors of the economy if thousands of Nigerians adhered
strictly to these prohibitions. (We realize, however, that money saved
by not indulging in luxuries could be put to better use, which in turn
could help to promote the country's economy.)

On the positive side of the coin, however, and in the face of acute
shortages of essential social services, such as medical care, welfare
services, employment and educational opportunities at both state and
national levels, it is gratifying to see some of the new religious
movements, such as the Aladura group, the Brotherhood of the Cross
and Star and the Celestial Church of Christ, rising to the situation by
building their own schools, factories, grocery stores, health centres,
maternity services, publishing and printing houses, bookshops, stores
for religious musical albums, public transport services, guest houses and
the like.

For instance, the Aiyetoro socio-religious community, founded in
1947 in Western Nigeria by the Cherubim and Seraphim wing of the
Aladura group, had established, within the first 25 years of its existence,
hospitals, a fishing industry, a shoe factory, a textile factory, a bakery,
tailoring and laundry services, a cabinet workshop, an electrical department, an internal telephone system, pipe-borne water, a water and land
transport system, a technical school, a secondary school, a primary
school, a kindergarten school and an adult education programme
(Omoyajowo, 1975: 88; Barrett, 1977: 2–4). So successful has the
Aiyetoro community become in economic terms that it has been
described as 'Nigeria's most successful case of village-level development' and as having 'the highest standard of living of any village in the
country' (Barrett, 1977: 2). According to Barrett, the people of this
community 'contend that their economic success was a result of their
religious belief'; and part of this religious belief was that 'hard work and
economic prosperity reflected a person's faith, and hence were a means
to salvation and immortality' (Barrett, 1977: 2, 4).

Members working in the establishments of the new religious movements are not usually paid a full salary, and in some cases are not paid at all, because their services are seen as being 'for the Lord'. But those who are not paid salaries are nevertheless given small honoraria for their daily living — that is, if they do not live communally, as in the Aiyetoro community. [7] These workers themselves may never become rich, but their services are invaluable to the society. Money accrued from their work also helps to boost Nigeria's economy.

In Ibadan a new religious movement, the Cross of Christ World Mission, is building a maternity hospital, to be financed by the revenues from a supermarket and an office complex built next to the hospital (Hackett, 1981a: 17). This project will no doubt provide job opportunities for many Nigerians — doctors, nurses, clerks, attendants and so on — possibly including non-members of the Church.

In a Calabar-wide Sunday service held on 15 November 1981 to raise funds in aid of disabled persons, the Brotherhood of the Cross and Star donated more than 2,000 naira on the spot. [8] And in December 1981 this same movement announced a plan to build a centre for the disabled in the Cross River State at a cost of over 2 million naira, [9] in addition to their existing vocational centre for the handicapped at Ikot Ide, Ibesikpo LGA. Moreover, the Brotherhood of the Cross and Star operates large plantations of yam, cassava (tropical plant of genus *Manihot*), plantain, pineapple and other fruit trees in Ikom in the northern area of the Cross River State. These plantations not only contribute tremendously to the Green Revolution programme which has been the subject of much discussion in Nigeria, but they also offer job opportunities to many Nigerians, both members and non-members of the movement. Also, the Brotherhood has a large company of buying and selling contractors called 'Globemaster', branches of which can be seen in many parts of the country.

Such projects will obviously be a positive note on Nigeria's keyboard of economic development. Similar projects and the many healing homes built by these religious movements will certainly supplement and complement existing inadequate medical and health care services in the country.

The founder of the Celestial Church of Christ explained how his members become quite rich: 'The money some of them may have used in drinking beer, adultery, fornication, smoking and visiting native doctors could become useful and may be used for other tangible things. That is why the members have money' (Nigerian Television Authority, 1981: 7). One of our informants in the Brotherhood of the Cross and Star gave almost the same reasons why their members who work for the movement are not financially poor even though they do not receive full salaries but merely allowances for their daily living. Among other things, he said that merely working for the movement was in itself a source of divine blessing: 'Although our workers are not paid full salaries, they nevertheless gain in many other ways.' Then he continued:

> The Father protects our members from diseases, sicknesses and all kinds of troubles on which they would normally spend their money. Now, since they don't experience all these situations, they consequently save the little money they have, which they would have spent had the Father not protected them from all these things. Secondly, since they do not drink or run after the lust of the flesh, they also save their money this way.[10]

But the reflexive effect of the increasing economic prosperity of some of these movements, sociologically speaking, is that some of them can no longer be labelled 'sects'. Religious sects typically come into existence with members who are generally poor and who tend to withdraw into their little 'spiritual enclaves' where no active economic or political activities take place. This means that, in some ways, the new entrepreneurial interest has been a great distraction for members of some of the movements from their hitherto purely religious or spiritual concerns. Such a distraction does serious damage to the early piety and religiosity of the movements. But where they thus lose spiritually, some of the movements gain economically. And for our purposes — speaking of Nigeria's economic development — the gain is a welcome experience, both for members of the religious movements as individuals and for the nation as a whole.

New religious movements and Nigerian social life

Perhaps the most observable impact of Nigeria's new religious movements is to be seen in the social functions that they perform for their votaries in particular and for Nigerian society in general. For their members, these movements generally provide certain compensations in the face of political and economic inequality and ethnic domination and oppression.

The Brotherhood of the Cross and Star, for instance, is actively involved in social welfare programmes. There is, for example, a huge canteen in Calabar built by their Women's Association. All over the country, the various fellowships and associations of the movement[11] visit orphanages and welfare centres and make huge donations in cash and kind — food, fruits and bedding. Leader Obu himself receives numerous invitations from groups and individuals performing ceremonies asking for financial donations. It is said that he honours all these invitations with generous donations.

The new religious movements also perform social functions in other areas of social life. For instance, where people had felt that they were 'nobodies' before becoming members of the movements, or where personal recognition and movement into the higher echelons of authority had been slow or even impossible (in the mission churches), members of the new religious movements now claim to achieve personal social recognition at almost all levels, thereby sharpening their capacities for large-scale organization and administration. These members now claim to *know* and *experience* love. One cannot but feel the warmth and affection vibrating from a member of the Brotherhood of the Cross and Star as he or she greets a fellow member: 'Peace, brother, or sister.' In this way, the new religious movements generally develop social solidarity among their adherents.

Furthermore, in these movements members claim to discover their identity and place in life because, they say, they love one another. In this process of discovering their self-identity and loving one another, enough of the traditional African spirit of community is recaptured, and members are consequently provided with dignity and integrity in the face of modern technological denigration and the depersonalization resulting from the growth of mass society. On this point James Fernandez correctly remarks:

> It may still be argued that these movements embody some of the cultural imperatives of autonomy which independence is still struggling to achieve; a fuller integration of the heritage of the past with the exigencies of the present and the future, a sense of purpose and unity providing meaning and motivation in the lives of the membership. (Fernandez, 1965: 73)

Moreover, many of the new religious movements offer stable points of reference amidst the uncertainties of transition — transition from African traditional religious experience to Christian religious expression. A good instance concerns the traditional practice of keeping menstruating women away from sacred objects or places in the belief that they would desecrate them. This article of African traditional faith has been brought wholesale into the Celestial Church of Christ, one of the largest new religious movements in Nigeria. Asked in an interview why menstruating women were not allowed in their places of worship, the founder and leader, Pastor S. B. J. Oschoffa, replied as follows:

> It is one of those things not yet clear to the world. The Lord is clean. There was no stain even when Moses was to be given the ten commandments. The Lord told him to cleanse himself for three days, wash his clothes without having any sexual intercourse, and said that it was then that he [God] would meet him. It is even in the book of Leviticus where the Lord forbade any woman on menstruation to enter any church whatsoever for seven days. It doesn't apply to the Celestial alone. (Nigerian Television Authority, 1981: 7)

188 Friday M. Mbon

And speaking approvingly of polygyny, another social and cultural practice of traditional Africa, Pastor Oschoffa said:

> It is better if you have many wives at home than many concubines outside — that is adultery. My church does not support the idea of one man, one wife . . . The idea of one man, one wife is un-African. (Nigerian Television Authority, 1981: 7)

Polygyny is also practised in the Aladura group (Omoyajowo, 1975: 95).

Moreover, almost all the new religious movements are syncretistic to one degree or another, in so far as their Christian religious expressions are integrated with such traditional religious elements as divination and spiritual help in the forms of fetishes, amulets, talismans, fortune telling, the use of holy water or 'green water' (Celestial Church of Christ), incantation, naming ceremonies and the use of drums and other musical instruments in worship. In the process of this syncretism, members experience some feeling of continuity and develop a sense of identity with the past (cf. Turner, 1979: 165–72). This feeling of continuity and identity with one's ancestors is seen as crucial in contemporary Nigeria where there is currently much talk about cultural revival as a significant factor in national development.

The new religious movements are very pragmatic and life-centred. They are more concerned with the existential problems of their members than are the older churches. These problems include anxiety about the future and one's lot in the here-and-now. Thus, people experiencing distress of any kind — unemployment, petty jealousies, sickness, financial or family difficulties or fear of both physical and spiritual enemies like witchcraft and sorcery — flock into these movements in search of allegedly sure and usually immediate solutions to these problems, for the movements are known to be able to handle all these problems in ways that members consider meaningful in their lives.

J. Akin Omoyajowo, speaking generally of the Aladura movements but specifically of the Cherubim and Seraphim version, describes the situation rather trenchantly in the following way:

> Africans generally fear the power of witches and the evil spirits, who beset them in their dreams; they worry about their future and want to know what it has in stock for them. In the traditional society, they consult the diviner. Orthodox Christianity repudiated this practice and substituted abstract faith for it. The Aladuras take the problems as genuine and offer solutions in the messages of the Holy Spirit given through the prophets and visioners. They give candles for prayers, incense to chase away evil powers and blessed-water for healing purposes. Consequently, the Christian suddenly finds himself at home in the new faith, and Christianity now has more meaning for him than ever before, for it takes special concern for his personal life, his existential problems and assures his security in an incomprehensively hostile

universe. This is what has endeared the Cherubim and Seraphim to the hearts of the cross-section of our society, irrespective of creed, status and class. (Omoyajowo, 1970: 134)

These remarks are applicable to most of the new religious movements to which Nigerians are drawn.

Albert Atcho, a preacher in one of the new religious movements on the coast of West Africa, the Harrist Church of Ivory Coast, once indicated in a sermon that it was proper for man to request from God those things which come from him, such as clothes, which many people in Ivory Coast did not have before being converted by Harris, whereas now they have schools, roads and modern buildings in the villages. The following statement by Atcho graphically captures the ethos of the Nigerian new religious movements:

> We worship God to have something, happiness, that is so that He will give life, to know how to make iron or lift up your country.
>
> What is the happiness that you desire to have? First, children, to be well paid in your job, to find a place of employment rapidly, to succeed in planting and to have a better life. (Bureau, 1975: 144)

Now, compare these motives with this piece of spiritual advertisement from the pen of one of the most prominent Apostles in the Brotherhood of the Cross and Star:

> . . . whoever wants power, must come into the Brotherhood of the Cross and Star . . . the centre for all wealth, peace, life, progress, health, freedom, wisdom, and youthfulness . . . Today it is a common belief and everywhere that if you want

Health	— You must come to the Brotherhood of the Cross and Star.
Money	— You must come to the Brotherhood of the Cross and Star.
Children	— You must come to the Brotherhood of the Cross and Star.
Popularity	— You must come to the Brotherhood of the Cross and Star.
Free[dom] from court cases	— Go to the Brotherhood of the Cross and Star.
Power	— You must come to the Brotherhood of the Cross and Star. [12]

Thousands have responded to this advertisement in more than 1,000 centres in Nigeria alone and also in the Camerouns, Ghana, the Ivory Coast, Liberia, Britain, the United States and elsewhere.

The ethos and sentiments articulated in the above advertisement are expressed by another member of the Brotherhood of the Cross and Star in the following poem entitled 'A Resting Place', in which he points to their leader, Olumba Olumba Obu, as the refuge and sole solver of human problems:

> Come unto Olumba,
> Ye who are weary and worn,
> Bring unto Him your burdens,
> And hearts with anguish torn.
>
> Come unto Him, ye toilers,
> Tired of stress and strife,
> Find in Him a resting place,
> And calm for that troubled life.
>
> Come unto OLUMBA,
> Ye restless, homeless and friendless,
> He will give you a resting place,
> A place in HIS HOLY Home.
>
> He knows what it is to be weary,
> With no place to lay the head,
> He shares the sorrows of many,
> And wept beside the dead.
>
> Come unto OLUMBA,
> Ye who are in distress,
> In HIM you will find
> A sweet and perfect rest. (Johnny, 1979: 7)

Since Nigerians from all walks of life do want one or the other of the blessings mentioned above at some time in their lives; that is, since many Nigerians often see themselves as 'deprived' of many of life's good things — health, wealth, friendship, power, security, children and so on — we consequently find people in these movements from all social strata — the poor, the lonely, lawyers, engineers, magistrates, medical officers, university lecturers, students, top civil servants, senior police and army officers and so forth (Hackett, 1981b: 55). Another prominent member of the Brotherhood of the Cross and Star has expressed the same point this way:

> The wisdom of God cannot be compared with the wisdom of men. He calls his children in various ways and in diverse manner. It may be during a severe illness incurable in all other places. May be during an [sic] impending judicial proceedings. When married couple had stayed for many years without a child, they are sometimes called into Brotherhood of the Cross and Star. The white sutan [sic] of members and the wonderful songs communicated by angelic Choir, these are but some of the ways God uses to call his children at the fullness of time.[13]

In a sense, Nigeria's new religious movements serve as enclaves not only for the disenchanted and alienated but also for the well-to-do. Indeed, one could say that the experience expressed by Christians of the

Middle Ages in the maxim, 'extra ecclesiam non est vita' ('there is no life outside the church'), is also the resounding maxim of members of Nigeria's new religious movements. Thus, as far as these movements are concerned, it is not altogether and necessarily true, as Susan Budd says, that religion's impact 'tends to be greatest among groups which are marginal to the obviously important political and economic aspects of modern society — women, the old, the very poor, the distressed and stigmatized' (Budd, 1973: 17–18). In Nigeria, however, one observes that well over 95 percent of the new religious movements are to be found in the urban areas. One possible reason for this is that in these areas they provide a sort of anchor and refuge for those whom the problems of city life bite hardest — the unemployed, the lonely, the alienated, the dehumanized, the socially displaced, drug and sex addicts and the like, regardless of their age or gender.

Another very important social function rendered by these movements is that they have created in Nigeria a situation of religious pluralism and tolerance. This function will certainly be appreciated by those who have not yet forgotten the *jihads* in Nigeria; the animosities that ensued as the various Christian missions of the colonial and early post-colonial period struggled for African land and converts; the hard feelings that existed among opposing converts as they argued about articles of faith; and, more recently, the Muslim uprisings in Northern Nigeria (1980–82) in which many lives were lost as factions of Muslims there argued and struggled over certain aspects of their beliefs and practices.[14] Moreover, the monopolistic spirit of the older historical churches has been pretty well broken down. And if it is true that the future of the human race largely depends upon the ability of men and women of different cultures, religious faiths and ethnicities to learn to live in accord, and if Nigerians can learn to appreciate and tolerate their religious differences, then there certainly will evolve among them a spirit of national unity — a kind of unity in diversity — which is pivotal for national development, understanding and good will in a country that is culturally and religiously pluralistic. For religious values are related to the concept of development, since they form the basis of ideologies which responsible statesmen must take seriously. These values can provide the most beneficial standards for a healthy, prosperous and progressive life at the national level; but they can also form a barrier to development.

Furthermore, the new religious movements provide a forum for national unity by bringing together people from different tribes under one umbrella of Christian fellowship. 'One of the striking features of the independent religious movements', remarks Turner, 'is the extent to which so many have succeeded in transcending the limitations of language, tribe and region, and have achieved a wider community'

(Turner, 1969: 46). As another observer has rightly noted, once a new religious movement has established itself in an ethnic group, 'the character of the whole movement changes from tribal to universal; tribal differentia recede in importance; membership is extended to other tribes . . . city congregations become multi-tribal; the appeal becomes universal' (quoted in Turner, 1969: 47; cf. Barrett, 1968: 156).

This state of affairs is socially significant because it develops in the minds of Nigerians new kinds of social bonds and brotherhoods in which the larger community of faith rapidly replaces the community of blood or tribe. Or, as Max Assimeng has said, these new religious movements have now taken over the functions of tribal groupings in moral regeneration (1978: 112). While this fact may be generally true, however, it may not always be true in every case, as is evident in the Aladura movement, where membership is largely and strongly Yoruba in language and cultural orientation (see Hackett, 1981a: 21). But the fact that most (if not all) of these movements encourage inter-ethnic or even international marriages, at least among their members, is a significant factor for social unity at both the national and international levels.

The new religious movements also claim, or attempt, to influence the social morality of their members by trying to 'preach them into' being honest, sincere and moral (especially sexually moral) in their interpersonal relationships. Sometimes their influence in the area of morality has been felt. For instance, in the early days of the Cherubim and Seraphim in the Lagos colony, the colonial administrator there spoke approvingly of the movement's impact on the social morality of its citizens, hoping that the influence of the leader of the movement would '[continue to] have a good effect on the thieving . . . ' (Omoyajowo, 1975: 112). In general, however, it is not always easy to determine the degree of the movements' success in this very sensitive matter of social morality and ethics; in Nigerian society today one cannot readily detect the influence of these believers on attitudes to work and on political decisions and business ethics (Ilogu, 1975: 516–17).

Another social impact of these movements is the confusion and sometimes open hostility that they bring into families where young people have been programmed or 'brainwashed' into membership against the wishes of their parents. Such parents are afraid that something terrible is going to happen to their children. Fears and objections are quite often due to the parents' uncertainty or complete ignorance about what really goes on in these movements and about the fact that, in reality, their children may be happier and may find more self-fulfilment in these movements than they ever experienced in their homes.

A final remark about the social impact of these movements may be noted. One group of young men and women in the Brotherhood of the Cross and Star, called 'Christ's Students', who number well over 300 at present, cannot get married because of their special calling in the service of 'the Father'. Sociologically speaking, this practice may be seen as having a negative and disruptive effect on the social institution of marriage. Alternatively, it may be seen positively as saving Nigeria from the pains of 300 broken homes.

Closing remarks
One of the reasons for the rise of new religious movements in Nigeria and elsewhere is that the country's former religions seemed to do nothing to relieve members of the Nigerian society of their various spiritual and secular anxieties. For instance, a report published in 1960 by the Christian Council of Nigeria on the theme 'Christian Responsibility in an Independent Nigeria' admitted that the Aladura groups have arisen 'out of dissatisfaction with the life of the Church (or its lack of life) and, as so often happens in such circumstances, there is over-compensation for the felt lack, so that what was missing was elevated to undue importance' (Christian Council of Nigeria, 1961: 103; quoted in Omoyajowo, 1978: 102).

In Yinger's words, 'a society that does not furnish its members with a system of beliefs and actions for handling the endemic anxieties of human existence and a system for modifying its inter-human conflicts will collapse from the load of personal anxiety and group tension' (Yinger, 1957: 38). This is tantamount to saying that religions that do not provide their members with the functions mentioned here will be rejected and that new religious movements will spring up to cater for the spiritual as well as the social and economic needs of the people. This seems to be exactly what Nigeria's new religious movements have done. Nigeria should, indeed, consider herself fortunate to have a Christianity that takes profound interest in its adherents' historical situation, providing them with answers, permanent and tentative, to their political, economic and social questions, thereby helping Nigerian Christians to recognize more fully the role that they can play in their urgent task of nation-building and national development.

It has been shown in the foregoing discussion that Nigeria's new religious movements in their small way are making their impact felt by thousands of Nigerians, and that as movements they have become an integral part of the religious culture of contemporary Nigeria. Their present achievements may not look too great or impressive, especially in the political and economic areas, but at least they are trying. Like the Apostle Paul, these new religious movements could declare in unison: '[we] do not consider that [we] have made it . . . but one thing [we] do, forgetting what lies behind and straining forward to what lies ahead . . .'[15] Such a declaration would be a statement of faith in the unlimited possibilities before them for greater accomplishments.

Notes

1. 'Aladura' is a Yoruba word meaning prayer. The Aladura group of movements therefore get their name from this word because of their emphasis on prayer and faith healing.
2. Daniel Ilega's personal correspondence with me, dated 9 April 1980.
3. In one of my interviews with him, Leader Olumba Olumba Obu, the Sole Spiritual Head of the Brotherhood of the Cross and Star, constantly and consistently repeated: 'We are neither a church nor an organization; we are a brotherhood. I don't know what church is.'
4. Interview with Apostle E. Ukpai, the Treasurer of the Brotherhood of the Cross and Star, 16 March 1982.
5. In the following discussion of the Aladura group of movements I am indebted to Omoyajowo (1975; 1978). The definitive works to date, however, on the Aladura movements are Peel (1968), Barrett (1977) and Omoyajowo (1982).
6. *Nigerian Chronicle*, 26 May 1981.
7. Unfortunately, the situation in Aiyetoro today has changed from what it used to be in the late-1940s and middle-1960s as a result of the secularization processes that have confronted the community. With the introduction of private enterprise in 1968, people began to demand wages for their labour, and, consequently, the spirit of the communal system began to disappear.
8. At the time of writing, one naira was worth approximately US$1.50.
9. Radio Nigeria national news, Monday, 7 December 1981.
10. Interview with Apostle E. K. Upkai, 16 March 1982.
11. Structurally, the Brotherhood of the Cross and Star is divided into about 30 fellowships and associations for the purposes of effective administration and co-ordination of its activities.
12. V. E. Ekpenyong, 'The Fate of Believers when their Leader is Wrapped', unpublished manuscript, n.d., pp. 5–6.
13. 'Brotherhood of the Cross and Star and the New Social Order', unpublished text of lecture delivered by Pastor S. Etuk during Brotherhood Academic Students' Week at the University of Calabar, 7 May 1983, p. 5.
14. On the Muslim uprisings in Northern Nigeria, see Hickey (1984).
15. Paraphrase of Philippians 3:14.

References

Assimeng, Max (1978) 'Crisis, Identity and Integration in African Religion', in Hans Mol (ed.), *Identity and Religion : International, Cross-cultural Approaches*. London: Sage, 97–118.

Barrett, David B. (1968) *Schism and Renewal in Africa. An Analysis of Six Thousand Contemporary Religious Movements*. Nairobi: Oxford University Press.

—— (ed.) (1971) *African Initiatives in Religion*. Nairobi: East African Publishing House.

Barrett, Stanley R. (1977) *The Rise and Fall of an African Utopia: A Wealthy Theocracy in Comparative Perspective*. Waterloo: Wilfrid Laurier University Press.

Budd, Susan (1973) *Sociologists and Religion*. London: Collier-Macmillan.

Bureau, R. (1975) 'La Religion du prophète', in Marc Auge (ed.), *Prophétisme et thérapeutique: Albert Atcho et la communauté de Bregbo*. Paris: Hermann.

Christian Council of Nigeria (1961) *Christian Responsibility in an Independent Nigeria*. Ibadan: CCN.

Fasholé-Luke, Edward et al. (eds) (1978) *Christianity in Independent Africa*. Bloomington: Indiana University Press.

Fernandez, James W. (1965) 'Politics and Prophecy: African Religious Movements', *Practical Anthropology*, 12(2), 71–5.

Hackett, Rosalind I. J. (1981a) 'Nigeria's Independent Churches: Gateways or Barriers to Social Development ?' *Africana Marburgensia*, 14(1), 9–25.

—— (1981b) 'An Aladura Healing Revival', *The Nigerian Field*, 46(1–2), 52–6.

—— (1985) 'From Ndem Cults to Rosicrucians: A Study of Religious Change, Pluralism and Interaction in the Town of Calabar, South-Eastern Nigeria'. PhD dissertation, University of Aberdeen.

Hickey, Raymond (1984) 'The 1982 Maitatsine Uprisings in Nigeria: A Note', *African Affairs*, 83(331), 251–6.

Ifeka-Moller, Caroline (1974) 'White Power: Social-structural Factors in Conversion to Christianity, Eastern Nigeria 1921–1966'. *Canadian Journal of African Studies*, 8(1), 55–72.

Ilogu, Edmund (1975) 'The Religious Situation in Nigeria Today: A Sociological Analysis', *Présence Africaine*, 96(4), 504–24.

Johnny, Alex (1979) 'A Resting Place', *The New World*, 1(3), 7.

Mol, Hans (ed.) (1978) *Identity and Religion: International, Cross-cultural Approaches*. London: Sage.

Nigerian Television Authority (1981) 'Meet the Founder of the Celestial Church of Christ', *Drum*, January, 6–7.

Offiong, Essien Akabom (1983) 'Schism and Religious Independency in Nigeria: A Case Study of Calabar', research project submitted to the Department of Religious Studies and Philosophy, University of Calabar.

Omoyajowo, J. Akin (1970) 'The Cherubim and Seraphim Movement: A Study in Interaction', *Orita*, 4(2), 124–39.

—— (1975) *The Cherubim and Seraphim Church in Relation to Church, Society and State*. Ibadan: Claverianum Press.

—— (1978) 'The Aladura Churches in Nigeria since Independence', pp. 96–110 in Fasholé-Luke et al. (1978).

—— (1982) *Cherubim and Seraphim: The History of an African Independent Church*. New York: NOK Publishers.

—— (1984) *Diversity in Unity: The Development and Expansion of the Cherubim and Seraphim Church in Nigeria*. Lanham, Md: University Press of America.

Peel, J. D. Y. (1968) *Aladura: A Religious Movement among the Yoruba*. London: Oxford University Press.

Turner, Harold W. (1969) 'The Place of Independent Religious Movements in the Modernization of Africa', *Journal of Religion in Africa*, 2, 43–63.

—— (1976) 'The Approach to Africa's Religious Movements', *African Perspectives*, 2, 13–23.

—— (1979) *Religious Innovation in Africa: Collected Essays on New Religious Movements*. Boston: G. K. Hall.

Walls, Andrew F. (1978) 'Religion and the Press in "The Enclave" in the Nigerian Civil War', pp. 207–15 in Fasholé-Luke et al. (1978).

Wilson, Bryan R. (ed.) (1981) *The Social Impact of New Religious Movements.* New York: Rose of Sharon Press.

Yinger, J. Milton (1957) *Religion, Society and the Individual.* New York: Macmillan.

8

The cult of Hūniyan:
a new religious movement in Sri Lanka

Gananath Obeyesekere

In this paper I shall deal with the rise and fall of deities in Sri Lanka as a consequence of rapid social and demographic change, focusing especially on the deity Hūniyan, who appears in urban religion. I shall also examine his apotheosis from demon to divinity. I shall show that, while changes in urban religious beliefs are sudden and dramatic from the objective standpoint of the investigator, they are not perceived in this manner by ordinary people. Quite the contrary: even drastic changes are articulated to very basic principles or cultural logics that give validation to the new cults. These principles are not deep structures noted by linguists and semiologists: they are philosophical principles basic to the dominant religion of Sri Lanka — Buddhism. These principles are not unconscious structures either, but are consciously recognized and exist on the level of content and give direction to religious beliefs.

Let me illustrate with a simple example. Demons are found in the pantheons of most cultures, but in Sri Lanka the Buddhist orientation of the culture defines demons as embodying the doctrinal notion of greed (*taṇhā*), a fundamental principle in Buddhism and of related Buddhist values such as *lobha* (lust), *krodha* (anger) and others. In countries like Sri Lanka, 'new religious movements' never become 'new religions', since the new movements are accommodated into a framework of old and continuing 'principles'. Thus change, even rapid change, is seen by the participants as a continuity of tradition. Though new religious movements are precipitates of external changes in the socio-economic domain, these external changes are articulated to an internal cultural logic intrinsic to the religion (Sinhala Buddhism). It is this dialectical process between external events (the changes are drastic) and internal logic (cultural principles are constant) that I shall discuss in this paper.

The cult of the god Hūniyan originated almost entirely in the culture of city dwellers in Colombo and its immediate environs. The shrines for this god are now scattered in various parts of the city and in small towns, and they are all of recent origin, most of them erected in the 1960s and after. The god's apotheosis and his cult were products of the city population of poorly paid proletarians and dispossessed people living in crowded slum or semi-slum conditions in Colombo. I shall show later that the rise of Hūniyan — the choice of the deity himself and the development of his cult — is causally related to conditions of urban living. Hūniyan is not a new deity in the religion of Sinhala-Buddhists. In the villages he is popularly known as the demon of sorcery; hence the word *hūniyan*, which literally means 'sorcery'. In village ritual he was known as Hūniyan Yakā ('the demon of sorcery'), and he was propitiated in rituals for curing people afflicted with the ill effects of sorcery. Let me consider myths of this deity in the repertoire of village exorcists (*kaṭṭaḍirāla*). In a perceptive account written in 1865, Gooneratne says:

> Oddy Cumara Hooniyan Dewatawa is the son of Susiri, queen of Sagalpura in Maduratta. He always rides on a horse. He has six different apparitions: in the first he is called Cala Oddisey, or demon of incurable diseases; in the second, Naga Oddisey, or demon of serpents; in the third, Cumara Oddisey, or demon prince; in the fourth, Demala Oddisey, or Tamil demon; in the fifth, Gopalu Oddisey, or demon of cattle; and in the sixth, Raja Oddisey, or royal demon. He is the principal demon that has much to do in that department of sorcery called Hooniyan. (Gooneratne, 1865: 26–7)

Gooneratne, further, tries to explain (not very satisfactorily) why Hūniyan is also addressed as *dēvatā* or godling, when he is in fact a *yakā* or demon: 'Though *dewatawa* is a term which is applied to the inferior classes of gods, and to the superior classes of demons, that do not inflict diseases on men, yet it is also sometimes used by Cattadiyas, as in the text, to inferior or malignant demons' (Gooneratne, 1865: 26, footnote). One might add that *dēvatā* is used as an honorific to flatter and cajole a demon, particularly if that demon is born of royalty. Thus Hūniyan Yakā, Sanni Yakā and Kalu Yakā are also addressed as *dēvatā* in traditional belief. In some myths and ritual dramas these demons appear in the guise of royalty or as godlings (*dēvatā*), two of their well-known apparitional forms. The term 'Oddisey' or 'Oddissi' strongly suggests that Orissa was the original homeland of this deity.

Paul Wirz, writing in the 1930s, recorded two well-known myths of Hūniyan from the Southern Province which I summarize as follows.

1. There was once a king in India called Paṇḍuvas. His queen Tuserin, while bathing in the eighth month of her pregnancy, picked a lotus flower and inhaled its fragrance. This meant that the child she bore would grow up to be a handsome prince. The queen also had extreme cravings during pregnancy: she longed to copulate with snakes and she took a huge cobra into her room. The king was troubled and consulted brahmins who told him that his son would grow up to be a very cruel person, would capture snakes and imbibe

their venom, would kill people and eventually would kill his own father.

As prophesied, the child grew up to be a handsome boy and the pride of his father. At the age of seven, however, he left home and went into the forest to live there. He captured many cobras and wound them around his body. He caught a viper, drank its venom, and was consequently endowed with supernatural powers. He then mounted a huge white horse and, with a sword in the right hand and a brazier in the left, resolved to come home to kill his father and devour humans. He was now a powerful demon. Sakra, the king of the gods, saw him coming and urged him to desist. He gave him permission to cause illness but said he must cure people who gave him offerings. He should also obey the word of the Buddha.

2. The second myth is very much like the first except that it adds Hūniyan's encounter with the Buddha Kāśyapa.

After Hūniyan became a demon swathed with venomous snakes all over his body, he came to the entrance of a temple where the Buddha was residing and demanded an audience. He wanted the power to make people ill so that they would placate him with offerings. Mugalan, the Buddha's disciple, shut the temple door in his face and the demon went back to the Himalayas. He returned for the second time roaring ferociously; this time the Buddha himself refused the demon audience. On the third occasion the demon came up and, pretending to be hungry, asked for food. But the Buddha ordered him to be clapped in irons and sent to *avici*, the lowest hell. However, while Mugalan went to execute the Buddha's order, the latter changed his mind, since as a Buddha he could not hurt anyone. He told the demon that his wish could be fulfilled if he agreed to go to the demon land of Tammannānuvara. There, when he is summoned by an exorcist and offered food, he must restore the health of the person. The demon agreed to follow the Buddha's orders.

External and socio-economic changes and the Skanda cult
The rise of Hūniyan must be seen in relation to contemporary religious conditions in Sri Lankan society. In a previous paper on 'Social Change and the Deities' (Obeyesekere, 1977), I dealt with the massive rise of the cult of Skanda or Kataragama in Sri Lanka. Skanda is one of the four guardian deities of Sri Lanka, protectors of the secular realm and the Buddhist order. In Sinhala-Buddhism, the Buddha is the head of the pantheon, but, in so far as he is no longer alive, he has no active intercessionary role in the affairs of human beings. It is the gods who can intercede on behalf of man and help him in his mundane affairs. Salvation and the achievement of other-worldly goals lie in the strictly Buddhist aspect of the religion — the

belief in the Buddha, the Dharma (doctrine) and the Sangha (the monk order). In my paper I pointed out that, while formally there are four guardian gods (and other gods of parallel status), the popularity of the deities is by no means uniform but varies with historical, socio-economic and political conditions. For example, the god Nātha was an important deity associated with the sovereignty of the Kandyan kings. When Kandy capitulated to the British in 1815, there was a precipitous decline in his cult.

So it is with Skanda. After the British conquest of Kandy there were several minor rebellions against them. The most serious one was by a pretender, Vilbāve, who launched his fight against the British at the central shrine for Skanda at Kataragama in 1817. But Skanda's help was not of much use, for the rebellion was quickly crushed and the pretender executed. Following the defeat of Vilbāve, there was a dramatic decline in the cult, and the shrine itself was in desolate and decrepit condition. For most of the nineteenth century only a small number of pilgrims visited the shrine for the annual festivities, so that in 1878 the assistant government agent responsible for co-ordinating the pilgrimage could say: 'I hope this may be regarded as a defunct institution.' In the early twentieth century the numbers picked up, but nowhere in relation to the population of the country. In 1948, however, Kataragama was connected by a main road, and in 1952 public buses were introduced along this route. The pilgrim traffic then rose exponentially, and in 1973 there were, according to official estimates, 800,000 visitors to the shrine. The population of the country at this time was about 13 million. Even if we reduce the official estimates by half, there is not the slightest doubt that Skanda has surpassed all the other deities in public popularity.

This popularity is also reflected in visits to Skanda shrines elsewhere in the nation. In 1968 I conducted a survey of the four major shrines in Kandy associated with the Palace of the Tooth Relic, these being the shrines of Nātha, Viṣṇu, Skanda (Kataragama) and Pattini (a goddess). During a ten-day period, it was found that, for every one person visiting the shrines for Viṣṇu and Pattini, there were five and six persons, respectively, visiting the Skanda shrine and no one visiting the shrine for Nātha.

The percentages of persons visiting the three shrines were also interesting and indicated a division of labour among deities (see Table 1). The female deity Pattini is associated very strongly with the cure of illnesses and childbirth, whereas the male deities are associated with instrumental tasks, including sex and marriage which in Sri Lanka involves complicated negotiations and is therefore within the purview of the male deity. However Viṣṇu, in contrast

TABLE 1
Percentages of persons visiting the Pattini, Viṣṇu and
Skanda shrines in Kandy for specified purposes

Purpose of visit		Name of deity		
		Pattini	Viṣṇu	Skanda
1. Exams, employment, business		6.6	18.7	25.3
2. Sex, marriage		—	8.4	7.5
3. Recovery of lost objects, runaway relations, court cases		3.0	8.6	9.4
4. Pilgrimages, trips abroad, other specific tasks		2.9	6.3	12.5
5. Punishment for wrongdoers		0.8	9.1	6.8
6. Childbirth		13.8	7.3	8.9
7. Non-specific blessings		21.7	22.8	13.0
8. Illness: infectious diseases	32.7 ⎫	51.4	18.7	16.7
other	18.7 ⎭			
Total		100	100	100

Skanda, is also strongly associated with non-specific blessings, which is consonant with his role today as an entirely benevolent deity.

This examination of the percentages of visits is misleading, since it does not indicate Skanda's popularity. If we shift our focus from each shrine, and look at the total number of clients visiting all three shrines for specific purposes or reasons, a startling picture emerges. In Table 2 I have shown the percentages of persons visiting all three shrines for specific purposes during a ten-day period. Assuming that the 576 persons interviewed out of a total of 1,958 visiting the Skanda shrine were truly random, I included in Table 2 the total numbers of persons visiting that shrine in a ten-day period.

The moment we focus on the total numbers visiting all three shrines for specific reasons, Skanda is seen to lead all the other deities in all respects. Thus, while it is true that 51.4 percent of persons visiting the Pattini shrine come there for problems of illness (Table 1), this number diminishes when we consider the total number of persons visiting all three shrines for purposes of illness. In Table 2 we note that 58.1 percent of the persons with illness problems visit the Skanda shrine, 28.6 percent visit the Pattini shrine and the rest go to Viṣṇu. With regard to every single purpose listed in Table 2, Skanda is well ahead of all other deities.

Table 2 implies that people have come to believe that Skanda is helpful for all types of problems, from getting jobs to curing illnesses.

TABLE 2

Stated purposes or reasons for persons visiting the shrines for Pattini, Viṣṇu
and Skanda during a ten-day period
(percentages)

Purpose of visit	Name of deity			
	Pattini	Viṣṇu	Skanda	Total
1. Exams, employment, business	3.5	12.5	83.9	100
2. Sex, marriage	—	18.4	81.6	100
3. Recovery of lost objects, runaway relations, court cases	3.9	14.9	81.1	100
4. Pilgrimages, trips abroad, other specific tasks	3.2	8.9	87.8	100
5. Punishment for wrongdoers	1.7	20.9	77.3	100
6. Childbirth	17.5	11.8	70.6	100
7. Non-specific blessings	16.4	21.7	61.7	100
8. Illness	28.6	13.1	58.1	100

Skanda has eroded the domain of the other deities; he has become the pre-eminent deity in the pantheon.

I interpreted the rise of the Skanda cult in sociological and personal terms as a consequence of socio-economic change, specifically of four features of the situation as it prevails in Sri Lanka.

1. As a result of universal education, political democratization of the state, the development of bureaucracy and many other factors, everywhere in Sri Lanka there is a new range of culturally desirable goals which are legitimate for persons to aspire to . These goals in general pertain to worldly success, specifically through jobs in the bureaucracy or professions and the political system. The goals are clearcut, well-defined and highly desired.

2. As a result particularly of universal education, the levels of aspiration have also increased dramatically, so that, for example, practically all educated sons of peasants want white-collar or professional jobs. While the levels of aspiration are high, however, the possibility of achieving the goals is limited for several reasons, particularly for the following one.

3. I refer to a phenomenon observable in many developing nations. 'Modernization' and 'development' have produced new goals, but the means or pathways for achieving these goals are ill-defined or fuzzy. There are several reasons for this. The pathways for the achievement of certain types of goals — generally pertaining to office in the bureaucracy or political system — are based on a rational blueprint imported from the West. Very often, the superimposition

of this blueprint on a traditional bureaucracy — such as feudalism — may produce a hybrid product in which neither the rules of the old order nor the rules of the new are truly operative. This may then account for the fuzziness of the means for achieving the new goals. Elsewhere in the developing nations, for historical reasons often unique to them, political power is vested in exclusive elites. Access to desired goals is dependent on the patronage of these elites, so that, even if in theory there may be a rational blueprint for the achievement of the new goals, this remains a 'fiction', and at best acts as a legitimation of the elitist patronage system. In fact, culturally desirable goals tend to be achieved by those who come from the elite ranks, or those who can establish political or social links with the governing elites. For most people this is an extremely difficult if not impossible task. When the goals are well-defined and highly desired but the means are ill-defined and problematical, the actor experiences considerable anxiety and frustration. This anxiety–frustration load increases with increasing attempts at (thwarted) goal achievement.

There are other reasons why the pathways must remain hazy for many actors in developing nations. In Sri Lanka many persons have been educated in village schools. These are the sons (or grandsons) of peasants; they have been socialized in the village and have lived most of their life there. Education is viewed rightly as a prerequisite for job achievement. But the formal education received by these villagers has not trained them to cope with the complexities of the political order centred in the metropolis. While some educational institutions — universities, technical institutes and training colleges — function latently in converting sons of villagers into 'middle-class' citizens or potential elites, for many the institutional apparatus of the political system and the bureaucracy are *terra incognita*. In so far as the means for achieving the new goals are located in these institutional apparatuses, the actor experiences uncertainty, anxiety and frustration.

4. Within the last ten years other changes have occurred. Not only are the means for achieving goals hazy and undefined, but the possibility of achieving these goals has become increasingly remote, largely owing to the fact that jobs have become scarcer in relation to the number of persons qualified to hold them.

Thus there are three interrelated problems: (1) the existence of new, culturally desirable goals, (2) the hazy pathways available for achieving them, and (3) high aspiration levels, coupled with an increasing awareness of the near-impossibility of achieving them. It is in relation to these problems that we have to see the ascendancy of Skanda, and particularly in relation to problem (2), the nature of the pathways available for goal achievement.

In the face of this situation the actor, it seems to me, can take several positions.

1. He can experience passivity–withdrawal, as a result of his failure to strike a pathway to achieve his goal. Alternatively, he may reduce his level of aspiration and seek less desirable goals commensurate with his situation. The latter is difficult, for even minor government jobs — office labourers — are controlled by the political patronage system.

2. He can seek political connections with the patronage network — which, as was pointed out, is a difficult task; hence this way out is available for only a few.

3. He can seek new or clearcut pathways to achieve the goal. One way is through political revolution, which is always a possibility in developing nations and was tried out (unsuccessfully) in Sri Lanka in 1971. For many people the lure of political revolution is the availability of the desired goals through clearly defined rational pathways.

4. He can adopt traditional pathways to achieve the new goals. This is where the deity comes into the picture. Traditionally, also, when people have been faced with tasks difficult to overcome they have resorted to the deity for aid. Of the deities of the pantheon, Skanda is eminently suited for the new situation. He is par excellence the resourceful deity, the vanquisher of the *asuras*, the deity who could overcome obstacles. Furthermore, the actor's psychological and social relationship to the deity is very important. Posed with accumulating frustrations, it is psychologically comforting to place oneself in a dependency situation where a strong authoritarian figure — be it natural or supernatural — can act on one's behalf. This Skanda is, and the ideology underlying his worship is based on filial piety; the son submits to the father, who then rewards him by granting his wishes, and acting on his behalf in a situation of general uncertainty. Moreover, in the kind of situation I have described there is no clearcut body of legitimate norms defining the means for goal achievement, and persons are willing to achieve the desired goals by normatively non-sanctioned, or even immoral, actions, as Merton (1957) pointed out in respect of US society. Here again, Skanda is most helpful. Unlike Viṣṇu, who is unequivocally a moral deity, Skanda is willing to do anything to help his devoted adherent. Hence he is par excellence the god of the politicians, the businessmen and the big-time crooks in the city of Colombo. I have known of professional people competing with their colleagues for promotion visiting the Skanda shrine at Kataragama and performing a well-known ritual of self-abnegation and submission to the deity, rolling bare-bodied

on the sandy floor round the Skanda temple premises. True faith implies total submission; by contrast, arrogance, criticism of the deity, scepticism and even inadvertent irreverence are strongly punished by Skanda. Stories of consequences that follow from these are numerous.

I believe that what I have said here accounts for the preoccupation, even of educated people belonging to the elite, with traditional forms of supernaturalism in order to achieve some of the newly emerged overvalued goals.

The logic of internal change: the *Karma* theory

The rise and fall of deities is not a new phenomenon, but a recurring one in the history of Sri Lanka. As noted earlier, the gods Viṣṇu and Nātha were very popular at one time: nowadays they have become less world-involved, more benevolent and progressively otiose. Two parallel processes of change seem to be occurring. The deity rises in popularity owing to external processes of change such as those I have analysed in the previous section. However, the very rise of the deity contains the seeds of his fall, owing to an internal logic of change in Sri Lankan society.

This internal logic is based on the *karma* principle underlying the Sinhala-Buddhist pantheon. Related to it is the notion that the major deities are Buddhist gods and aspirants to Buddhahood. The Buddha, as well as his disciples who have achieved *nirvāṇa* and are known as *arhats*, is totally benevolent and non-involved in the affairs of the world. These ideas, when translated in terms of the pantheon, mean that some of the gods are closer to salvation (*nirvāṇa*) than others. Thus Nātha, whose cult is practically disappearing, is the very next Buddha, Maitreya; and Viṣṇu, the current head of the pantheon, is already in the first stage of *nirvāṇa* known as *sōtapanna*. However, when a deity becomes elevated in status to Bodhisattva (Buddha-to-be), he becomes more and more benevolent; the more benevolent he becomes, the less involved he is in the affairs of the world. He becomes gradually otiose. From the point of view of the worshipper, the benevolent, *arhat*-type deity cannot help him to resolve his mundane problems and personal needs. In this type of religious system, then, the very popularity of the deity contains the seeds of this fall. To put it differently, when a god becomes popular as a result of external changes, several things happen, based on the fundamental logic of *karma* and merit transfer that Buddhists everywhere believe in.

1. People transfer merit or good *karma* to the god for the help he has rendered them. Since a god is a Bodhisattva, or an aspirant to Buddhahood, the transfer of merit by devotees accelerates the

Buddha quest of the deity. This means that he becomes less world-involved, more benevolent and consequently less able to help the world-involved devotee.

2. This can be stated differently. A deity is popular because he grants people their wishes. In Buddhist terms, he performs good deeds, thereby increasing his fund of good *karma* (merit), and also consequently promoting his quest for *nirvāṇa* and Buddhahood. Again, according to the *karmic* logic he must eventually become removed from the people and also become otiose. Take the case of Viṣṇu. In the sixteenth century he was a popular god with the masses. In the mythology of the period he has a wife; he was a warrior deity and vanquisher of titans (*asuras*), very much like the contemporary Skanda. Yet nowadays Viṣṇu is a saintly figure, totally unwarlike and benevolent; and like a good Buddhist *arhat*, he practises total sexual abstinence (*bramacārya*), so that he has no wife or consort in current iconography and myth.

3. When a god becomes otiose, inferior deities — demons and godlings (*dēvatā*) — from the lower reaches of the pantheon take his place. For example, Skanda is depicted in seventeenth-century accounts as an *asura* or titan, and a heretic deity. Now he is unequivocally a god and, given his popularity, he must in time end up as a benevolent bodhisattva-type deity, according to *karmic* logic. This is in fact happening now. More and more people are perceiving him as increasingly benevolent and less world-involved. Concomitantly dark and demonic figures from the lower reaches of the pantheon are striving to take his place. And Hūniyan is one of them.

The transformation of Hūniyan

But why Hūniyan, and not other demonic or semi-divine beings in the pantheon? Once again, the selection of Hūniyan must be related to personal and social problems of urban proletarians. These problems in turn make sense only in relation to the traditional status of Hūniyan as demon of sorcery, not just in Sri Lanka, but in neighbouring South India as well.

Hūniyan's strength is precisely that he is the deity of sorcery in village tradition. Before he became a popular god on the urban level, he had become, in the twentieth century, the personal guardian of exorcists and other ritual specialists. Exorcists who were engaged in cutting the effects of sorcery or *hūniyan* (*hūniyan käpilla*) were themselves vulnerable to ensorcelling by rival practitioners. In fact, one well-known explanation for the failure of *any* ritual is that rival sorcerers were doing evil magic to counter its success. Thus the dilemma: if the demon of sorcery can be enlisted to protect the individual, then evil sorcery directed against him is of no avail.

Indeed, such protection is more effective than the talismans generally worn by ritual specialists. Ergo, Hūniyan became the personal guardian of exorcists during this century. But a *yakā* or demon cannot, in Sinhala cultural logic and language use, be a personal guardian, since demons are unambiguously 'evil'. Hence Hūniyan in his guardian role must be converted into *dēvatā*, a deity whose status is intermediate between god and demon. We noted earlier that this is entirely possible, for several reasons. Some demons are in fact called *dēvatā* as an honorific. Thus the Sanni demon, because of his royal birth, is sometimes called *dēvatā*; so is Hūniyan for the same reasons. For identical reasons of royal birth, Sanni appears as a *dēvatā* and is known as Dēva Sanni, a (seemingly) benevolent form of the malevolent deity. Hūniyan also, in order to lure people, can take many apparitional forms, one of which is *dēvatā*. Thus, Hūniyan's form as *dēvatā* became important and part of a contrastive set: he was both *yakā* (as demon of sorcery) and *dēvatā* (as personal guardian, or *iṣṭa dēvatā*).

A similar process was occurring in respect of people living in and around the city. One of the impressive features of the current social situation is that, more than ever, people seem to be attributing personal misfortune to sorcery practised by jealous neighbours. This appears not only in interviews but also in the predictions and utterances of mediums and seers, for whom the most frequent interpretation of client illness and misfortune is sorcery. This pervasive fear of sorcery is endemic in crowded settlements in and around Colombo. Often informants say that neighbours are jealous of their well-being and practise sorcery to bring them down. At other times, family dissension is attributed to sorcery by others.

I interpret this kind of pervasive suspicion of neighbours to the actual absence of real neighbours and kinsmen in urban society and to the widespread urban anomie that prevails there. In addition, the family is cut off from its traditional moorings, and to compound the situation there is acute underemployment, unemployment and near-subsistence living. In this kind of situation it is easy to remove responsibility from the self to another — in some cases, to society itself, particularly the wealthy or capitalist class; alternatively, to one's neighbours or even jealous kinsmen where they exist. Furthermore, once the enemy is identified (often through divination), one can then justifiably hate him and if necessary practise counter-sorcery against him. This kind of situation is not entirely a product of fantasy, since these crowded areas do produce endemic theft, violence and abuse against neighbours and a general pattern of mutual distrust and suspicion. The widespread 'paranoid ethos' that is created is not true paranoia, resulting from personal pathology, but rather one resulting from the conditions of urban anomie, a sociological phenomenon. In this situation the individual seeks protection from the sorcery deity Hūniyan, who then, as among village exorcists, becomes converted to an *iṣṭa dēvatā*, or guardian. I have seen this process occur in several hamlets near Colombo. For example, Ihala Biyan-vila, ten miles from Colombo, is a 'village' that has lost much of its traditional homogeneous base. Many people living here work in Colombo in low-paid white- or blue-collar positions while others are labourers working in the Colombo port. Many houses in Biyanvila have a spirit shrine erected outside the main residence for Hūniyan. Several people I interviewed state explicitly that they do this because Hūniyan is their *iṣṭa dēvatā*, who can protect them from their enemies.

A protective deity is by definition benevolent as far as the individual is concerned, but he can be malevolent towards the individual's enemies. It is, of course, difficult to reconcile *any* kind of benevolence with the traditional Hūniyan Yakā (demon). Thus an ingenious theory was invented in the city that Hūniyan is both demon and *dēvatā* (godling): during the waxing (*pura*) of the moon he is *dēvatā*, and in the waning (*ava*), a demon (*yakā*). This ingenious myth can link Hūniyan, somewhat tenuously to be sure, with astrological thought, for the waxing and waning of the moon are related in astrology to the upward and downward flow of bodily energies (*bahina kalāva, nagina kalāva*). Furthermore, the needs of the devotee can also be resolved in this fashion: we can invoke Hūniyan in his good form to help us, and in his bad form to curse (*avalāda*), or practise sorcery against, our enemies.

One consequence of the elevation of Hūniyan to protector status is that individuals almost never refer to him as *yakā* (demon), even though he is demon at *ava*. His predominant status is that of 'personal guardian', and hence that part of the verbal set is stressed. But people are aware of his demon status: often individuals would say that you must light lamps daily for Hūniyan *dēvatā*; if you fail he may cause you some misfortune — the underlying threat from his demon status.

Several linguistic changes must occur when Hūniyan becomes *dēvatā*. The term *hūniyan* is associated with sorcery in common parlance: how can we call this protector 'a sorcery *dēvatā*', which is a contradiction in terms? One solution is to change the *h* in Hūniyan into *s*, since these two letters are often interchangeable in Sinhala. Thus the common *h* is used to refer to the deity as demon — Hūniyan Yakā — while the more elevated use of *s* is used to designate his *dēvatā* status — Sūniyan Dēvatā. Nevertheless, the *s* is substituted only in formal contexts (invocations, etc.): in everyday parlance he is referred to as Hūniyan.

In earlier publications I have shown that *dēvatā* is a category term for deities of intermediate status (e.g., the Twelve Gods) or deities moving from demonic to divine status. *Dēvatā* is a way-stage in the upward journey. Sometimes, of course, this may develop into a permanent position (Obeyesekere, 1982). Not so in the case of Hūniyan, who is addressed by his true devotees as Siddha Sūniyan Dēvatāvun Vahansē, 'The Perfect Lord — Dēvatā Sūniyan', or *nambukara mahēsākya deviyō*, 'honourable deity of the higher class'. With these kinds of epithets and honorifics, Sūniyan can be further removed from the pejorative connotations of Hūniyan. For the true devotee Sūniyan is really a god, as I shall soon show. For the devotee the obvious linguistic discrepancies can be resolved through the multiplication of honorifics and exalted modes of address. Nevertheless, for the hundreds of priests who are theoreticians of the cult, this is not possible. The resolution is to give the deity an alias, a classical solution in Sinhala mythology to a deity who is moving from demonic to divine status. Thus, Sūniyan is given an alias that has no prejorative connotation — Gambāra Deviyo, 'the god in charge of villages'. Gambāra Deviyo in all likelihood was simply a category term which refers to the *grāma dēvatā*, guardians of villages well known in Indian literature and ethnology. Such *grāma dēvatā* have become defunct in Sri Lanka. It is likely that this term was then given as an honorific to other deities. In any case, a defunct category term used to designate 'a god in charge of villages' is now used as an alias for the deity who is a personal guardian. It certainly helps resolve the language problem in relation to the term Hūniyan.

The attributes of the new Hūniyan

I noted earlier that when a deity becomes more benevolent, he also becomes more otiose. Demons are obvious candidates for promotion since they are entirely world-involved. Several informants could articulate this idea, at least indirectly. One *kapurāla* (priest) said:

> People increasingly offer *pūjas* [expressions of honour] to god Sūniyan because he generally associates (moves) with human beings. Gods like Viṣṇu and Saman have moved away from men, and they find it hard to help us. God Kataragama is also like that and that is why those who believe in Kataragama also light a lamp for god Sūniyan.

One Buddhist monk in a Colombo temple who professed a lack of interest in the gods explained the significance of the four shrines for the guardian gods constructed in 1949 and the Hūniyan *dēvāle* constructed in 1973 in the following manner: 'The Gods of the Four Shrines' are for *set sānti* (blessings), while Hūniyan is for problems like conflicts in the family, court cases, and conflicts in general.' A priest of the Hūniyan cult put it thus:

The god Sūniyan moves very closely with people. He observes their good
and their bad. Viṣṇu is a very benevolent being (sāntā kenek), one who
wants to acquire merit (piṅ). Gods like Viṣṇu and Kataragama are mahē
sākya (of the higher class). They are filled with compassion (maitri).
Therefore they have removed themselves somewhat from people. Beings
like God Sūniyan are servitors of Viṣṇu–Kataragama.

These are very widespread notions of Hūniyan and are held by
ordinary devotees of Hūniyan also. In addition, devotees see
Hūniyan as powerful, full of strength (sakti sampanna). He can
punish; therefore it is necessary to have him as your protector and
enlist his aid to curse or punish your enemies. A mechanic (age 50) in
the Railway Department said: 'Hūniyan is the one god among all the
gods of Lanka who can cause frightening punishments.'

If one looks at these statements critically, one sees that such sentiments were once expressed by devotees of Kataragama also.
Kataragama is powerful, a vanquisher of asuras; he moves with
people, he administers punishments. However, for these urban
people in Colombo, Skanda by and large has become more benevolent, very much like Viṣṇu. Indeed, the two terms are often
conjoined, and a seer will refer to them as 'Viṣṇu–Kataragama gods'.
Nevertheless, even if Kataragama is becoming otiose to some urban
peoples, why Hūniyan, and not other well-known deities in the
Sinhala pantheon who have similar — indeed, almost identical —
attributes? Take some of the demons who, along with Hūniyan, are
propitiated in village exorcisms: Riri Yakā, the blood-demon; Sanni,
sometimes taking the apparition of a god (dēva); Mahasōna, who
frightens people by his size and occasionally assaults people; Kalu
Kumāra, an attractive, black, erotic possessor of females. All these
are powerful beings and, like any demon, they are felt presences;
'they move among the people.' Yet none of them is even remotely a
candidate for apotheosis in urban society.

Even more surprising is the case of Dēvatā Baṇḍāra, the God of
Alutnuvara who has already moved from dēvatā to divine status
(Obeyesekere, 1982: 30–1). On the face of it, he seems an ideal
candidate since he is the tamer of demons, a powerful god who stood
by the Buddha during the Māra war when all other deities fled aghast.
He cures persons possessed with demons, and hundreds of possessed
patients go to his shrine in Alutnuvara — since at least the end of the
nineteenth century to the present day (Bell, 1892; Obeyesekere,
1984). Yet Dēvatā Baṇḍāra is losing his hold on urban folk, both
specialists and ordinary devotees. He is well known by name, but
clearly is not relevant to their needs.

The choice of Hūniyan from other demons of the same class, and in
preference to an already ascendant deity, Dēvatā Baṇḍāra, must be

seen in relation to the one distinguishing characteristic of Hūniyan in the traditional pantheon: that he is the demon of sorcery. This adds considerable plausibility to my view that the choice of Hūniyan is related to the massive preoccupation with sorcery among urban peoples, which in turn is related to the relative isolation of the nuclear family and the lack of external kinship support, the existence of lumpen neighbourhoods and the sense of distrust and mutual suspicion fostered by conditions of urban anomie.

There is yet another condition which helps Hūniyan's ascendancy, though it is not by itself the cause of his rise. I have described the phenomenal rise of Skanda after the 1940s. No deity, however, can supply the wants of such a mass of followers. While people rush to him for favours — jobs, promotions, success in business — many must suffer disappointment, for such things as jobs are strictly limited by the nature of an impoverished economy. The god must necessarily fail in meeting many of the instrumental needs of the devotee, though he may be more successful in meeting his expressive (spiritual or psychological) needs. Yet since many go to the god for the former reason, some expectations must inevitably be frustrated.

Moreover, gods like Skanda are feared and held in awe by most devotees — unlike some peasants in South India, who scoff at the deity when he does not deliver the goods (Srinivas, 1976: 327). Thus, if I fail to achieve my goal, I dare not attribute this failure to god Kataragama but must attribute it to some other cause, such as my unworthiness, my unfavourable horoscope or my *karma* (which nothing can avert), a taboo violation or whatever. But if another deity is moving up, the devotee can transfer his allegiance to the latter, in the hope that he, being more powerful and more world-involved, can help deliver the goods. This means that erstwhile devotees of Kataragama will switch their allegiance to Hūniyan (not, of course, in any deliberate or conscious manner). This action may then be justified by the classic rationalization that god Kataragama, by virtue of his increasing benevolence and *arhat*-like nature, can have no say in the affairs of the world. This must also be the reason for the fact that, while historically gods became otiose gradually and slowly, nowadays the pace has become accelerated, and Hūniyan himself may eventually suffer this fate.

We have isolated the Hūniyan cult at a certain stage in its evolution. The cult is still not formalized or fully brought in line with Sinhala-Buddhist culture. I shall now draw attention to some of the problems involved in the Hūniyan cult at this point in its development.

1. We noted that the most common theory about Hūniyan is his Janus-like nature: he is both god and demon, the two attributes fully

separated. Clearly, there are advantages to this dichotomy. It is possible for the deity as a god to help his devotee with material things. Such help, in Sinhala culture, cannot be solicited from demons, who are by definition malevolent and irrational. Since he is associated with sorcery, he is the individual's protector. Again, no demon can be a personal guardian in this sense. Yet the demonic visage of the deity during the waning of the moon has clear uses. For priests, the *demon* Hūniyan is indispensable for practising sorcery, *vas-kavi* ('poison-verses') and other kinds of magic for which there is a client demand and financial remuneration. Clients not only want to be protected, they also want to have revenge on those who do them ill. Furthermore, the public perception of the power of the deity is related to his demonic form.

2. Yet as long as Hūniyan has these two separate aspects, he must on the ideological level remain a *dēvatā* in spite of all the aliases or honorifics given to him. For him to be truly a god, he must divest himself of the demonic form or incorporate it within the divine (as in the case of Kataragama). To renounce the demonic form is no easy matter, owing to the known recent history of the god as a demon. Thus, at this point most priests view him as god in the waxing of the moon and demon at its waning. Yet this is clearly a stage in the continuing evolution of the god and his cult.

3. Irrespective of the cultural theory of Hūniyan as *dēvatā*, this is not how he is perceived by devotees. We noted in several previous quotations that priests refer to him as Hūniyan Deviyo, 'the god Hūniyan'. The impetus to full deification is there, though when questioned priests will affirm his dual nature. If priests refer to him both as *deviyo* and *dēvatā*, lay devotees most often simply call him Hūniyan Deviyo (god Hūniyan). This comes out clearly in a questionnaire we administered to 12 devotees, randomly picked at the Hūniyan shrine (*dēvāle*) at Baseline Road at a special service for the deity on 13 August 1975. We asked a simple, straightforward question: Is Hūniyan a god (*deviyek*), a *bhūta* (demon), or a *dēvatā*? All except one considered him a *deviyek* (god); the only exception thought of him as a *dēvatā*; none referred to him as a demon. In addition, during the more open-ended part of the interviews practically everyone referred to him as Hūniyan Deviyo, one informant saying 'deva hāmuduru vahansē' ('elevated-lord-god'). It seems inevitable that soon Hūniyan must shed his demonic guise, and that priests must evolve new myths to give Hūniyan the elevated status his devotees demand. Let us see whether there are any such trends among the priests of our sample.

A modern myth of Hūniyan

I summarize below a recent myth of Hūniyan from a young priest (*kapurāla*) (age 22) of Wellampitiya. The myth was communicated to devotees by the priest in a trance state.

The father of God Hūniyan (Hūniyan Deviyo) was a king who lived in India during the Buddha's time. He had seven sons, the youngest being the Lord Hūniyan Dēvatā. Brahmins predicted that the son would kill his father. The father decided to destroy the son but it was Hūniyan who killed his father and brothers. The citizens wanted to destroy Hūniyan but he fled into the forest. There he ate cobras and wrapped poisonous snakes around his neck. One day he came up to the Buddha to kill him, but people captured him, tied him to a post, and tried to molest him. The Buddha, however, knew that Hūniyan had a store of past merit and would eventually become a minor Buddha (*pacceka* Buddha). He asked the people not to harm Hūniyan and tried to tame the demon with his sermons. This did not succeed, so he sent Hūniyan to Sri Lanka. In Sri Lanka Hūniyan continued his depredations. He used to live in Kaballāva Rock and kill and eat humans. One day he met Viṣṇu (the guardian of Sri Lanka) at Devundara. Viṣṇu said: 'Do not take *bili* (sacrifices) but take *bali* (offerings) instead.' Hūniyan was made a commander of demons under the overlordship of God Daḍimuṇḍa of Alutnuvara. When he arrived in Sri Lanka, he was called Oḍḍissa; now he has the title Gambāra Deviyo ('the god in charge of villages').

After some time he went to meditate in the forest near Srī Pāda (Adam's Peak). He eventually became a god (*dēva*). It is then that the god Viṣṇu asked him to protect villages. After that, he obtained from Viṣṇu the power that, when he momentarily opens his eyes, he sees the 140,000 shrines and temples through his divine gaze. While he cast his protective gaze over these, he also began to watch over the good fortune and suffering of noble and decent folk. Thereafter, he was given the authority to make a report of the good and bad of all human beings and submit it to the assembly of gods. It is because he must submit details about humans to the divine assembly that the god Hūniyan comes close to people. The god Sūniyan appears at the waxing of the moon (*pura*) in the guise of a *dēva* and at waning (*ava*) as a *yakṣa* (demon). At the waning period he does *sānti karma* (good acts); at *ava* he practises woe.

Near the Buddha are four powerful persons. These four are saints (*rishis*). They are the lords of all the magical knowledge in the whole world. The Buddha has given god Sūniyan the charge of protecting magical knowledge. That is why, before one commences any magical act, one must light a lamp for god Sūniyan.

The myth advances Hūniyan further in his career towards deification and gives him legitimacy in the Sinhala-Buddhist pantheon. The latter is obtained initially through his relationship to the Buddha and then through warrant from Viṣṇu, the guardian of the Buddhist Church in Sri Lanka. According to this myth, he is a god who takes two forms, rather than a *dēvatā* composed of two forms — an important difference. He is, however, a special type of god, one who mediates between humans and the divine assembly. Finally, the interesting invention of the Four Rishis near the Buddha is simply an indication of the importance of magic in contemporary urban culture and the role of Hūniyan as the god of magic.

Hūniyan and urban anomie

In the previous section we related the rise of Hūniyan to urban anomie. 'Sorcery' is the symbolic idiom which expresses the conflicts endemic in urban society. Informants constantly state that enemies practised sorcery on them because of jealous neighbours envious of their good fortune. Appearances should be distrusted, since envious neighbours will often present a façade of friendliness. The effects of sorcery practised by envious neighbours are generally poverty, loss of income, and above all family conflict and dissension.

Family dissension caused by sorcery appears frequently in the statements of informants. In interviews with 12 priests in shrines in Colombo 9 and 10, all asserted categorically that the major reason for client visits to their shrines was family conflicts, generally conflicts between husband and wife and desertion by a spouse. One priest said: 'People come here to resolve conflicts in the family or fights in the home. Occasionally they come for children's illnesses.' Another said: 'Most people come here not so much for illnesses but for lies and dissension [bheda-binna] in the family. Women often come here and say that their husbands have deserted them, or left them in anger, or had forsaken them for another woman.'

It is interesting that, while all priests stated family dissension as the prime cause of client visits (followed by illness and obtaining of blessings), not one mentioned jobs or court cases so common in Kataragama shrines.

I tried to check whether the priests' assessments of the situation were correct in interviews with 40 out of 92 clients who visited the major Hūniyan shrine at Baseline Road on 13 August 1975 by simply asking them the purpose of their visit. The summary of the data is as follows: obtaining of general blessings (9); family conflict (8); jobs and business enterprises (7); illness (4); cursing enemies (4); redress in court cases or property thefts (3); success in marriage proposals (3); 'just came' (2). It is clear that, contrary to the priests' opinions, clients visit the Hūniyan shrine for a variety of reasons. This is predictable, since Hūniyan is an important god for most of these people, a deity who has taken the place of Skanda (Kataragama) in their allegiance. In the above sample the largest number came for no special purpose; they were special devotees of the god (the cult group) who came to seek the god's blessings. But after this were those who came to resolve family conflicts, an impressively large number. It is this unusual feature of urban society that impressed the priests whom we interviewed. It is clear therefore that the original choice of Hūniyan is due to his association with sorcery. But once apothesized, he can fulfil a variety of this-worldly needs of his devotees.

The legitimation of Hūniyan

In the contemporary myth of Hūniyan discussed earlier, the deity is given Buddhist legitimacy by his association with the Buddha and the god Viṣṇu who has charge of the Buddhist Church (*sāsana*) in Sri Lanka. However this myth, and similar ones circulating in urban Sri Lanka, are inventions of the priests of the Hūniyan cult, and not by the Buddhist Church. I shall now present data which indicate the acceptance of this cult by the Buddhist Church at least in the city of Colombo. I shall deal with Buddhist temples in Colombo 9 and 10 (Maradana–Dematagoda), where there is a large concentration of urban proletarians living in overcrowded ghetto-like areas. In addition, this area has other occupational groups — low-income white-collar and blue-collar workers, a few middle- and higher-income white-collar workers in government and business, and wealthy businessmen who run some of the business establishments in the area. The latter may not live here physically, but they have economic interests in the area and are patrons of some of the Buddhist temples.

Two of the country's great Buddhist monasteries are also located here — Vidyodaya Pirivena and Vidyalankara, founded in the late nineteenth century. In addition to these, there are several temples belonging to the reformist Buddhist fraternity, the Amarapura Nikāya. Above all, there are three temples which derive their ordination from the reformist and puritanical fraternities originating in lower Burma: Sulagandi and Sweggin. In Burma, the Sulagandi and Sweggin objected to the worldliness of the dominant fraternities, in particular the wearing of silk robes, sandals, handling of money and noisy functions in the temples (Mendelson, 1975). The major Buddhist fraternity, the Siyan Nikāya, is generally viewed as conservative, but in this area they were in the forefront of the Buddhist revival in the nineteenth century (Malagoda 1976). Their temples have spearheaded Buddhist modernism, and this tradition seems to have continued to the present day, since *some* of these temples and monasteries have resisted the intrusion of spirit cults and devotional (*bhakti*) religiosity into the temple complex. Yet the very fact that other temples, including some of the puritanical reformist ones, have succumbed to the recent changes indicates the power and strength of popular (mass) religions of urban peoples of this area. One would expect here the typical social changes referred to earlier — the family cut off from its larger kinship moorings, the absence of larger kin units, the levels of poverty of most people who live near or below subsistence levels.

In the 17 Buddhist temples surveyed in this area, 8 had subsidiary shrines (*dēvāle*) for gods, with resident priests or *kapurālas* (or more recently designated as *sāmis*); 3 had shrines for gods but no resident priests; while 6 had no shrines at all but only the standard Buddhist *vihāra* where strictly Buddhist rituals were practised. Let me deal with the eight Buddhist temples with shrines for gods.

1. In every case but two, the Buddhist temple complex or *vihāra* was built long before any of the shrines or *dēvāle*. Those who founded these temples viewed them as exclusively Buddhist places of worship. There are two exceptions: in one there was a Skanda shrine but the monk was unable to date it except to state it was old. In the other, a shrine for the four guardian gods was constructed in 1937 along with the temple (*vihāra*).

2. All but one of the temples had minimally the four guardian gods of this region installed in the premises: Viṣṇu, Saman, Vibhīṣana and Skanda. This indicates that, after the temples were built, the monks made concessions to lay needs but stuck to tradition in doing so.

3. Six temples had shrines for other gods also; in four these later deities were housed after the four gods had been installed. In all six cases, the later deities were installed during the period 1965–73.

4. Of the later deities, the most important is Hūniyan, since he appears in all six shrines noted above. Ganeś appears in three places, and a cluster of six other deities appear together in one temple compound.

Thus a reasonably clear stratigraphy of the structures can be observed:

Buddhist temples	(1800–1937)
The four traditional guardian gods	(1920–1967)
Hūniyan and others	(post–1965)

Several monks stated explicitly that they were yielding to public demand in constructing shrines for gods. Almost all monks affirmed the doctrinal position: they were indifferent to the gods but transferred merit to help them! Only one monk stated his firm belief in Hūniyan. By contrast, most monks dabbled in astrology, either helping laymen to interpret horoscopes or consulting their own in times of trouble — or both. This is because astrology can better be rationalized with *karma* theory than the belief in the gods (Obeyesekere, 1968). In general, the monks were traditionalist; nevertheless they yielded to popular demand. This included the two purist–ascetic fraternities founded in 1920 and 1922.

Note that, while the temples had installed the four gods in the post-1920 period, at least one of these gods, Vibhīṣana, was near moribund and Saman was almost otiose. Viṣṇu was viewed then and now as a benevolent deity at the head of the pantheon. It is very likely that the shrines for the four guardian gods were built as a result of the increasing importance of Skanda after the 1930s, but instead of having a separate shrine for him the monks followed tradition in installing the four gods collectively. In the post-1965 period one thing is clear: Hūniyan has risen conspicuously into prominence.

However, the fact that six temples refused to have any shrines for gods indicates the strength of the ascetic tradition in this area. Yet the data must be viewed with caution. Our information comes from head monks, who were continuing the ascetic traditions which received reinforcement in the late nineteenth century. We do not know about the views of the younger monks in these temples, nor can we use these data to indicate trends in areas other than Colombo 9 and 10.

One conclusion can however be drawn quite clearly: the importance of Hūniyan is such that monks were compelled to establish him in their temple premises after 1965, though Hūniyan's public popularity must have occurred somewhat earlier. He has found his way into the heart of the conservative Buddhist tradition.

The outward expansion of the Hūniyan cult
It was noted earlier that the god Hūniyan originated from the village cults of the demon Hūniyan as a response to the needs of urban proletarians. Once established in Colombo, the cult began to expand into other small towns in Sri Lanka. Thus there are shrines of Hūniyan emerging in many parts of Sri Lanka, especially those areas which have been subjected to increased demographic and societal change. I was especially struck by a very elaborate building put up for Hūniyan in Aluvihāra, a famous Buddhist temple on the outskirts of Matale, a large market town in the central province. According to tradition, Aluvihāra was the place where the Buddhist scriptures were put into writing in the first century BC. Thus once again, Hūniyan has moved into an old and traditional Buddhist temple. Furthermore, Aluvihāra, though located in the outskirts of a large town, also draws large numbers of pilgrims from all over the nation. Hence it is likely that it will serve as a conduit for the dissemination of the Hūniyan cult into village areas. Within a short radius of Aluvihāra are also a large number of old villages, rapidly becoming overcrowded and with increasing social differentiation, factionalism and conflict, and rapidly depleting economic resources. It is likely

that the Hūniyan cult will appeal to these villages and similar ones in the Western, Southern and Central Provinces which within the last 50 years have experienced drastic population increases, with social and psychological consequences paralleling those noted for the city of Colombo.

Urban middle-class people also have shown considerable interest in the Hūniyan cult, though for the most part they remain adherents of the Skanda cult. The elaborate shrine complex for Hūniyan in Baseline Road, Colombo, attracts businessmen, white-collar workers and professionals as well as the urban proletarians who live in the area. The cult, once established by the needs of the city proletariat, has begun to affect larger groups of Sinhala-Buddhists increasingly subject to the socio-economic frustrations brought about by drastic population growth, contracting economic opportunities and isolation from traditional kinship and familial supports.

Conclusion

In this chapter I have dealt with the rise of a new religious movement in Sri Lanka in recent decades. The Hūniyan cult is a response to massive socio-economic and demographic changes at the urban level. The cult itself seems to make a radical departure from tradition, in so far as it involves the transformation of a demonic figure in the traditional pantheon into a divine one on the urban level. Though this investigator has documented these changes, they are not perceived as such by the participants, since changes in the religious system are filtered through and interpreted in terms of basic principles that underlie Buddhism. In the present case the key principle is that of *karma*: the deity has moved up the pantheon owing to the merit transfer of devotees and also as a result of the merit acquired by him by helping people. The *karma* theory produces a logic of internal change, and the consequence of that logic is the eventual downfall of a popular deity who is elevated into a benevolent, *arhat*-type being. Such a being, in Buddhist cultural logic, is uninvolved in the affairs of the world, and this must render him eventually otiose.

The logic of internal change can also rationalize, justify or validate external change. Thus it is possible to blame the decline of a cult not on the failure of a deity to fulfil the demands of his devotees, but on his intrinsic goodness and Buddhist nature. The same cultural logic makes it possible for the priests of the cult to invent new myths that elevate the status of the deity. Thus, in the new myth of Hūniyan described here, he appears as a demon who becomes a god through the power of meditation. The Buddha himself predicts that Hūniyan will eventually become a Pacceka Buddha (minor Buddha). It is as though the priest who invented the myth was aware of the cultural logic himself and anticipated the eventual demise of Hūniyan! As a final triumph, Hūniyan gets incorporated into the Buddhist temple complex and begins to expand his sphere of influence.

References

Bell, H. L. P. (1892) *Report on the Kegalle District*. Colombo: Government Press.
Gooneratne, Dandris de Silva (1865) 'On Demonology and Witchcraft in Ceylon', *Journal of the Royal Asiatic Society, Ceylon Branch*, 4, 1–117.
Malagoda, Kitsiri (1976) *Buddhism in Sinhalese Society 1750–1900*. Berkeley and Los Angeles: University of California Press.
Mendelson, E. M. (1975) *Sangha and State in Burma*. Ithaca and London: Cornell University Press.
Merton, Robert K. (1957) 'Social Structure and Anomie', in *Social Theory and Social Structure*. Glencoe, Ill.: Free Press.
Obeyesekere, Gananath (1968) 'Theodicy, Sin and Salvation in a Sociology of Buddhism', in E. R. Leach (ed.), *Dialectic in Practical Religion*. Cambridge: Cambridge University Press.
—— (1977) 'Social Change and the Deities: Rise of the Kataragama Cult in Modern Sri Lanka', *Man* (n.s.), 12, 377–96.
—— (1982) 'The Principles of Religious Syncretism and the Buddhist Pantheon in Sri Lanka', in Fred W. Clothey (ed.), *Images of Man: Religion and Historical Process in South India*. Madras: New Era Publications.
—— (1984) *The Cult of the Goddess Pattini*. Chicago: University of Chicago Press.
Srinivas, M. N. (1976) *The Remembered Village*. Berkeley and Los Angeles: University of California Press.
Wirz, Paul (1954) *Exorcism and the Art of Healing in Ceylon*. Leiden: E. J. Brill.

9

New Hindu religious movements in India

Arvind Sharma

Introduction

A contemporary glance at the Hindu religious tradition discloses a proliferation of new religious movements since the advent of Indian independence in 1947. It should be noted at the very outset that the phenomenon of new religious movements is itself not new in the history of Hinduism. Many religious movements, new for the times, accompanied the rise of classical Hinduism (Majumdar, 1953: 360–1). Medieval Hinduism is similarly distinguished by the emergence of a wide variety of such 'new' religious movements (Sen, 1961: 11–17); the development of some of them is attributed to the presence of Islam on the Indian scene. Modern Hinduism in the pre-1947 period again found expression in a large number of 'new' religious movements (Sarma, 1944). This development is usually attributed, in the main, to the Western and Christian influences, which became strong in India in the wake of the establishment of British Raj. Thus, the phenomenon of new religious movements is quite old in Hinduism. One would not be surprised if this also turns out to be the case with other religious traditions as well.

This chapter will deal primarily with those new Hindu religious movements which either arose or achieved prominence after 1947. They have not received the attention they deserve (Srinivas, 1966: 132), and the present effort may go a small way towards rectifying the situation.

The new Hindu religious figures and movements which have appeared on the Indian scene since 1947 are numerous (see for example Singh, 1975; Brent, 1972; Balse, 1976). Some of them, however, have achieved more prominence than the rest; these include the Sai Baba movement, the Ananda Marg movement, the Siddha Yoga movement, the Chinmaya Mission, the Divine Life Society, Transcendental Meditation, the International Society for Krishna Consciousness (ISKCON), the Divine Light Mission and the neo-Sannyasa movement.

New Hindu religious movements: a typology

A preliminary reflection suggests that it is analytically helpful to treat these movements, which came into the limelight in the post-independence period, as logical expressions of patterns which had already emerged in the pre-independence period. The pre-independence period since 1800 was marked by the growth of several movements which were 'new' for the time (Farquhar, 1967). Among them the best known are the Brahmo Samaj, the Arya Samaj and the Ramakrishna Mission. Thus one could say that both 'the pre and post independent period of India witnessed the emergence of several religious movements' (Ambroise, 1982: 358).

An interesting question to raise at this point would be: Do these new religious movements display any basic similarity of patterns? Ambroise (1982) thinks that they do. These patterns may be labelled as orientations I, II and III. Orientation I is characterized by (a) emphasis on science and rationality; (b) willingness to assimilate from the West whatever is worthwhile; (c) a quiet confidence in one's tradition; combined with (d) absence of antagonism towards, and even appreciation of, other cultures and religions (Ambroise, 1982: 367). Orientation II is characterized by (a) emphasis on rationality combined with revelation; (b) willingness to assimilate from the West, but more markedly on one's own terms; (c) an exuberant confidence in one's tradition finding expression in missionary activity; and (d) a militant attitude towards other traditions (Ambroise, 1982: 371). Orientation III is characterized by (a) emphasis on rationality combined with mysticism; (b) willingness to help assimilate material techniques of the West, offering in return the spiritual techniques of the East; (c) self-confidence in one's tradition, expressed in an attitude of neither wishing to convert away from it nor wishing others to convert to it, combined with the propagation of Hindu ideas and ideals; and (d) emphasis on universality (Ambroise, 1982: 371). These orientations are seen by Ambroise as the hallmark of the following pre- and post-independence movements:

Orientation	Pre-independence	Post-independence
I	Brahmo Samaj	
II	Arya Samaj	Hindu Mahasabha
		Ananda Marg
		Rashtriya Swayamasevak Sangh
III	Ramakrishna	Hare Krishna movement
	Mission	Divine Light Mission
		Transcendental Meditation
		Sai Baba movement
		Rajneesh movement

This approach is useful but it suffers from two drawbacks: on the one hand it does not offer a broad enough spectrum to cover the various new Hindu religious movements, and on the other it does not do full justice to the combined impact of these various movements on Hindu society. K. M. Panikkar has referred to the phenomenon represented by the new religious movements of the pre-independence period collectively as the Hindu Reformation (1963: Ch. II). He includes four main movements under this title — the Brahmo Samaj, the Arya Samaj, the Theosophical Society and the Ramakrishna Mission — and notes both the combined contribution of these movements and the qualitative change in the Hindu context brought about by the achievement of Indian independence (Panikkar, 1963: 36).

It was remarked earlier that the canvas provided by Ambroise is not as broad as one might wish it to be. This remark may now be followed up with the help of some observations made by Ainslie T. Embree (1972: 273–6) while assessing the impact of the West on India. Embree identifies a four-fold pattern of reaction to the West (p. 275): (1) *indifference* to the West, inasmuch as British Raj marked merely a change of rulers; (2) *acceptance*, as when people converted to Christianity; (3) *critical–selective*, when some elements of Western culture were accepted and others rejected, and (4) *hostile rejection*, as represented by the Mutiny and later militant leaders like B. G. Tilak.

Interestingly, Embree places Ramakrishna under the reaction of 'indifference' and his disciple Vivekananda under the reaction he describes as 'critical–selective'. Moreover, he sees the Arya Samaj as representing a hostile rejection of the West, while Ambroise emphasizes the missionary as well as the militant character of that movement. Both of these cases suggest an unsuspected point: that the movement associated with the founder may move away from the *position* associated with the founder, may change category. Thus, Vivekananda developed the teachings of his master Ramakrishna in a more dynamic direction, and a wing of the Arya Samaj movement adopted a much more open attitude to Western learning than the views of its founder would lead us to believe (Jordens, 1979: 262). Incidentally, both these instances serve to illustrate how pervasive the influence of the West has been.

Both Ambroise and Embree leave out the Theosophical Society, the former deliberately (Ambroise, 1982: 369), the latter unintentionally (Embree, 1972: 322). The paradigmatic significance of the Society, however, in the context of neo-Hindu religious movements needs to be considered carefully. It was a society founded by Westerners for the propagation of Eastern wisdom, specifically Hinduism (Panikkar, 1963: 30). Although new Hindu religious movements do not exactly replicate this situation, such movements as

Transcendental Meditation and the Hare Krishna, which originate outside India and then make their presence felt in India largely though a Western following, suggest that this pattern still operates.

It is clear that variable responses to rapid social change are involved in all of these movements. The firm establishment of British rule in India was followed by a period of rapid social change. In the early stages of British rule in India the East India Company tried to accommodate itself to Indian society, but this policy changed after the first quarter of the nineteenth century when the British became firmly established and a series of actions followed which accelerated social change: for example, the abolition of suttee; introduction of the English language; abolition of slavery; and equality before the law (an innovation from the point of view of both Hindu and Muslim law) (Majumdar et al., 1951: 812). The Mutiny against the British (1857–58) is attributed, at least in part, to these changes. The Mutiny made the British more cautious in introducing social changes but it did not stop them; and the leaven in the form of Western education in particular and Western influences in general was at work. Indeed, after 1858, with the British even more securely established, the expansion of modern means of transport and communication and the spread of literacy helped maintain the pace of social change. The growth of the middle class was crucial in this respect (Nehru, 1960: 250–3). It is also an interesting point that the various reform movements in Hinduism, themselves the product of social change, often demanded and promoted it (Majumdar et al., 1951: Part III, Bk. II, Ch. IV).

These social changes and the attitudes towards them are closely connected with the three orientations (Ambroise) and the four responses (Embree) already discussed. Movements associated with Orientation I were most open to social change generated by the impact of the West; movements of Orientation II wanted change but under Hindu sponsorship; and movements of Orientation III also wanted social change with mixed sponsorship. Similarly, those most affected by Western social changes gravitated to movements of Orientation I, those least affected to movements of Orientation II and those falling midway to those of Orientation III. And if analysed carefully, Embree's responses are in fact the variable responses to rapid social change which was initiated by the advent of the West.

The same generalizations hold true of movements in the post-independence period. Fluency in and acceptance of English is a good indicator of social position in India, and the speed of the switchover from one's Indian mother-tongue to English is, similarly, a good indicator of the pace of social change. Most of the followers (not necessarily the leadership) of movements of orientations II and III divide along these linguistic lines. The other ways in which the post-independence religious movements intermesh with social change will be considered in the final section.

I shall now specify the movements which will be dealt with in this chapter. First, however, it might be useful to classify these movements. Two such possible sources of classification have been discussed. A reflection on the suggested categories in the light of the available data on the new religious movements in the post-independence period leads me to propose the following classification.

1. In this category belong those movements which are not new but represent the extension of tradition into the modern world, such as the Vallabhacharis and the Swaminarayans (Brent, 1972: 169–229), and the followers of Śaṅkarācārya (Brunton, 1951: Ch. VIII; Koestler, 1960: 54–63). People such as Ramana Maharshi and his followers may also be placed here, as they regard themselves as propagating the doctrines of the original Śaṅkarācārya (AD 788–820) as distinguished from his formal successors known by his name.

2. In this category belong those new movements which originated after 1800 but were concerned primarily with upholding the Hindu tradition, such as the Hindu Mahasabha, the Rashtriya Swayamasevak Sangh, the Rama Rajya Parishad and the Jana Sangh.

3. In this category belong those new Hindu religious movements which are predominantly traditionally Hindu in their orientation (as distinguished from those in category 2, who want to uphold the Hindu tradition). The Sai Baba movement and the Ananda Marg may be included among these, and also the Brahmakumaris and the followers of Anandamayee Ma (Koestler, 1960: 63–84). These new Hindu religious movements arose and made their influence felt in India before making an impact on the West. The Siddha Yoga movement, the Chimaya Mission and the Divine Light Mission of Bal Yogeshvar may also be included in this category; these movements have their base in India and their following is primarily Indian, also.

4. In this category belong those new Hindu religious movements which made an impact on the West before India and whose membership is conspicuously foreign. The Transcendental Meditation movement of Maharishi Mahesh Yogi and the Hare Krishna movement (ISKCON) belong here; the neo-Sannyasa movement of Rajneesh may also now be placed in this category.

The above classification is based on the nature and composition of the followers of the various movements. If different criteria were used, they would have to be classified differently. For instance, although the followers of the Hare Krishna movement are primarily Western, they observe orthodox practices more faithfully than those of many movements rooted in India. Similarly, if attitude to scriptural authority is regarded as an index of tradition, the Sai Baba movement does not accord it as much importance as the followers of the Chinmaya Mission or the Siddha Yoga movement.

Applications of the typology to the movements
In what now follows, Ramana Maharshi will be taken as representative of category 1; the Jana Sangh as representative of category 2; Sathya Sai Baba as representative of category 3 and the Hare Krishna movement as representative of category 4.

Ramana Maharshi
Ramana Maharshi (1879–1950) did not found any movement but lays claim on our attention as a religious or rather spiritual figure. He is representative of a certain strand of religiosity in India whose survival and persistence in modern times should not be overlooked.

Maharshi was born in 1879 in the town of Tiruchuzi in Tamil Nadu in South India (Osborne, 1971: 13). He had an uneventful childhood till he turned 17, but as a child was noted for his 'amazingly retentive memory' and 'abnormally deep sleep' (p. 16). In his seventeenth year, however, while he was living in Madurai, where his family had moved after the death of his father, he had an experience which changed the course of his life. He was suddenly seized by the fear of death (although in good health), and what followed was a profound mystical experience (Osborne, 1971: 18–19), which in Hindu thought is associated with the Realization of One's True Self, or Ātman, a realization which was subsequently located by him and others in the school of Hindu philosophy known as Advaita Vedānta (Mahadevan, 1971: 240–8). Soon after this experience Ramana left his home, settled down at Arunachala Hill and became a well-known religious figure. He died in 1950 from an inoperable tumour (Osborne, 1971: Ch. XVII). By the time of his death he was well-known in India and beyond as a spiritual master.

Although Ramana Maharshi founded no movement, a circle of devotees formed around him (Osborne, 1971: Ch. X), and as his fame spread so did his influence. He, however, belonged to the class of religious figures whose concern would seem to be primarily spiritual. He always sought to direct his disciples towards self-realization, and did not think much of social service in the usual sense of the word. A conversation with a Western disciple, for instance, went as follows: 'Master, can I help the world?' 'Help yourself and you will help the world.' 'I wish to help the world. Shall I not be helpful?' 'Yes, helping yourself you help the world. You are in the world, you are the world. You are not different from the world, nor is the world different from you.' The non-dualistic metaphysics implied in the concluding remark reflects Ramana Maharshi's philosophical stance (Mahadevan, 1971: 240).

In a sense, Ramana Maharshi represents a 'movement' that is not concerned with social change in a society undergoing rapid social change. Thus, when a member of the Arya Samaj movement, which emphasizes the removal of caste distinctions, met him for an interview, Ramana Maharshi kept deflecting the discussion away from the issue. He had the Vedas recited by Brahmins in the sanctuary, and believed in predestination and in the necessity of a guru for salvation (Osborne, 1962: 66, 95–110). Thus he was very traditional, and yet it cannot be said that he remained uninfluenced by the world around him. He took a marginal interest in political matters (Osborne, 1962: 88–9); did not insist on celibacy (pp. 79, 159) and believed that 'the realization of truth is the same for both Indians and Europeans' (Brunton, 1951: 115). Another way of looking at him would be to consider him as upholding the path of knowledge or *jñāna-yoga* above all others, just as Gandhi (whom incidentally he held in high regard) upheld the path of works, or *karma-yoga*.

Thus, Ramana Maharshi represents the typical, even archetypal, figure of the Master in the Hindu religious tradition who teaches a highly rarefied spirituality to a chosen set of disciples who seek him out and cluster around him, who instructs them on the basis of his own experience rather than through scriptural lore, and whose concern centres on the achievement of salvation by the individual. In a society departing rapidly from tradition, even an 'old' movement like this could appear novel!

The Bharatiya Jana Sangh

Jana Sangh is the name of a political party. It represents a new movement of a political nature with a Hindu complexion. Strictly speaking, it is not a new Hindu religious movement in the narrow sense; but, inasmuch as it draws its political strength from Hindu religious sentiment, it needs to be considered here.

The history of the Jana Sangh may be briefly recapitulated. It was formed in 1951 shortly before the first general elections and obtained 3 percent of the national vote in the elections (Weiner, 1957: 169). Its share rose to 9.37 percent in the 1967 elections (Lamb, 1968: 261). Mrs Gandhi triumphed in the elections of 1971, but in the 1977 elections, in which she was overthrown, the Jana Sangh won the largest number of seats out of all the members of the winning coalition. It then merged its identity into the Janata party. It has since been revived as Bharatiya Janata, but in this incarnation it has considerably reduced if not obliterated its Hindu element.

The political vicissitudes of the Jana Sangh are an interesting study in the context of the politico-religious aspect of a society undergoing rapid change. In the Indian context this change may be summed up in one word: Westernization (Srinivas, 1966: Ch. II). Ever since the advent of the British and even more vigorously since their departure, India has been undergoing Westernization. Now the Jana Sangh, as a Hindu communal party, (though it rejects this label — Baxter, 1969: 311–12), is anti-Western, where the word 'Westernization' carries the following four specific connotations (Weiner, 1957: 168–9): (1) Westernization in personal daily habits, such as eating Western rather than Indian food; (2) Westernization in social habits, such as preferring 'love marriages' to 'arranged marriages' or rejecting one's caste; (3) Westernization of political life, indicated by constitutionalism, secularism; and (4) Westernization of outlook, in terms of accepting scientific and rational criteria in one's attitudes. Essential to an understanding of the situation is the realization that 'Westernization . . . to many Indians has come to mean the antithesis of Hinduism' (Weiner, 1957: 168). Thus, when we call the Jana Sangh a Hindu party, it is implied that it is anti-Western in the above senses. What it was fundamentally opposed to was the reluctance that the Indian government felt about its 'identification with Hinduism', an identification it sought to promote.

The virtual abandonment of its original stance by the Bharatiya Jana Sangh after it had reconstituted itself as the Bharatiya Janata indicates that its original ideology has fallen by the wayside (a victim of rapid social change?). Attempts are being made, however, to revive it. One of the issues in the controversy surrounding the present state of the party is its association with the Rashtriya Swayamasevak Sangh (RSS), which is militantly Hindu in its orientation. The Jana Sangh has interacted, closely but not always amicably, with the 'communal' parties such as the Hindu Mahasabha, the RSS and, to a lesser extent, the Ram Rajya Parishad (Baxter, 1969: 27–8, 54, 103).

The main points which emerge from this quick survey are political, organizational and ideological. Politically, the original orientation of the Jana Sangh has not been sustained. It is clear, then, that rapid social change in India is not driving people to tradition as a way of denying it or coping with it — at least not politically; at least not yet. Organizationally, the problem the Jana Sangh faced in 1951 is one it still faces today with only slightly less force: the absence of supporting sectional organizations. There is hardly any women's front or labour front or a front among the depressed classes worth the name. Ideologically, its unresolved dilemma is thus articulated by Baxter:

The Jana Sangh tries to keep its roots deep in the soil of traditional Hinduism while idealistically looking forward to a modern and open society in India.

Yet it seems inevitable that the very modernization demanded by the Jana Sangh will go far to destroy, or at least undermine, the fabric of the traditional society. The Jana Sangh does not endorse the obscurantist program put forward by Swami Karpatri and the Ram Rajya Parishad, nor has it gone off on the tangent of Hindu Socialism espoused by the Hindu Mahasabha. It does, however, set up a block against Westernization, the very process which appears to this observer to be the necessary catalyst for India's development. The Jana Sangh would like to import Western technology and use Western capital while barring the entry of Western secularism and liberalism. It is doubtful that such a policy can succeed. (Baxter, 1969: 314)

The Sai Baba movement

The Sai Baba movement revolves around the figure of Sathya Sai Baba. Sathya Sai Baba was born in 1926 in the village of Puttaparthi in the Anantapur district of what is now Andhra Pradesh in South India in a Kṣatriya family (Swallow, 1982: 125). His rise to the present status may be seen as involving several stages.

The first of these occurred around 1940 when he was about 14 years of age. He suffered a fit. Subsequently this was explained as his having left his body to rescue a devotee. Upon recovering, the boy, then called Sathya Narayana Raju, claimed that he was an incarnation of Sai Baba of Shirdi (Sai Baba of Shirdi is a 'hot favourite' as an incarnatee and 'is being torn apart by at least three ascetics'! Balse, 1976: 58).

Thus, in order to find out more about Sathya Sai Baba, one is compelled to find out more about Sai Baba. Sai Baba was a religious figure associated with the place called Shirdi in Maharashtra, which he made famous. He appeared there in 1872 and died in 1918 (Swallow, 1982: 128, 131). The following aspects of his life and legend are of particular interest. (1) The ancestry of Sai Baba is shrouded in mystery, like that of the medieval poet–saint Kabir, so that it is not known for certain whether he was Hindu or Muslim by birth. (2) He combined elements of Hindu and Muslim worship in his ritual, of which an important part consisted of maintaining a fire in a hearth after the manner of Śaiva Yogis. (3) He was known for working miracles as well as for therapeutic thaumaturgy. 'He used the ash of his hearth as a sacramental substance' for these purposes. (4) One of his followers was Upasani Baba, who became a religious figure in his own right. The cult of Upasani Baba, who was a Brahmin, is prevailingly Hindu in its orientation. (5) Upasani Baba was succeeded by a lady ascetic called Godavari Mata. 'The female ascetics, trained in Sanskrit, perform Vedic rites and wear the brightly coloured ornaments and saris of married women.' The significance of these points will become clear in due course.

The second major stage in the life of Sathya Sai Baba came in 1963 when he made the claim that he was an incarnation of Śiva. This claim also followed upon seizures.

> He collapsed, became totally paralysed and went into a coma. For several days he remained in this state, once regaining consciousness to warn the devotees that he would have two more attacks. After this he once again regained consciousness. He insisted on giving his devotees *darshan* [*darsana*: Skt. 'a sight of him'] at the festival of *Gurupurnima*, and was carried in a state of semi-paralysis to the main hall of the ashram. There he performed a total cure on himself. Once again he explained that he had taken on a devotee's illness, but he also used the occasion to declare that he was the god Śiva in mortal form. (Swallow, 1982: 129–30)

In order to understand the full significance of this claim, it should be realized that Śiva is one of the two main gods of devotional Hinduism (Hiriyanna, 1978: 11) and that in Saivism the doctrine of incarnation (*avatāra*) does not play as important a role as it does in Vaiṣṇavism, of which it is a special feature. The fact that Sathya Sai Baba claimed to be an *incarnation* of Śiva is therefore important. He is really employing a device here which accounts in part for the popularity of Vaiṣṇavism (Gonda, 1970: 23) and also enhances his own. That he claimed to be an incarnation of Śiva and not Viṣṇu is also significant in view of the differences between the profiles of the two gods as their figures evolved. As Gonda concludes after comparing the two (1970: 13), 'In short, Viṣṇu is, generally speaking, a friend nearer to man; Śiva a lord and master, ambivalent and many-sided.'

Sathya Sai Baba thus made two primary associations, the first reincarnatory and the second incarnatory; the first with Sai Baba, the second with Śiva. This boosted his following. The question, therefore, arises: what prompted him to make these claims?

From the point of view of this study, the suggestions made by D. A. Swallow possess considerable explanatory power: 'I have argued that Sathya Sai Baba's demonstration of magical power is sufficient to attract devotees, and also places him in a well-established tradition. What, then, is the significance of his claim to be a reincarnation of Baba? (Swallow, 1982: 13). He suggests the following answer:

> Through his claim to be a reincarnation of Sai Baba, Sathya Sai Baba in the first instance has access to a heritage which derives from a number of saintly and ascetic religious traditions. Although the links are vague they are sufficient to connect him to a past, and give him respectability and authority. He does not, however, simply adopt Sai Baba's eclecticism wholesale. He has dropped the Islamic associations and instead places

greater stress on elements adopted from the Saivite tradition in a particular form used by Nathpanthis. In this way Sathya Sai Baba has made his connections with the god Śiva in preparation for the later claim he made to be the god himself. (Swallow, 1982: 135–6)

Swallow's answer may be supplemented with the observation that while, as against the obscure ancestry of Sai Baba, Sathya Sai Baba has developed a Brahmanical lineage connecting him with the Bharadvaja Gotra, he has also emphasized the Hindu element of the heritage (like Upasani Baba) without giving up the eclectic claims of Sai Baba entirely. Moreover, the upward ritual revaluation of women has been retained. The pattern fits in well with the demands of contemporary India in terms of both modernity and tradition. The rising status of women in modern times is given the stamp of approval, while the Hindu character of India (notwithstanding the secular status of the state) is recognized, as also is the fact that Hindu tolerance, while tolerant, is no doubt essentially Hindu.

Now that the possible reasons for association with Sai Baba have been discussed, a further question arises:

The claim to be an avatar is by no means uncommon among Hindu holy men. But why should Sathya Sai Baba seek a particular association with the god Śiva? His family were not strict Śaivites; Śiva is not their *istadevata*. What is there in that god's character that he seeks to adopt as part of his own personality, and what relation does the story explaining the claim have to the whole body of myth and belief about Śiva? (Swallow, 1982: 137)

In order to understand the nature of the association with Śiva, some prior understanding of the nature of god Śiva is necessary. This has been investigated and elaborated by students of Hinduism (for example, Gonda, 1970; O'Flaherty, 1973) and his chief characteristic has been mentioned earlier.

In this background, Swallow offers the explanation that Saiva mythology, to which Sathya Sai Baba attached himself, 'explores the paradox of conflicting aims' — ascetic and erotic — which are 'of universal concern'. This explanation needs to be supplemented, as there are other aspects of the Śiva story which take on a new relevance in the context of modern India. It has often been maintained that Śiva was an 'alien' god who was assimilated into the Hindu pantheon (Hiriyanna, 1978: 34 ff.). If such indeed was the case, then which god would be better qualified than Śiva to preside over the integration of the influences of an 'alien' West with Hinduism? Moreover, the fact that Śiva is a god more concerned with cosmic change, unlike Viṣṇu, who is more concerned with cosmic stability, makes him ideally suited for mediating transition in a society undergoing widespread and rapid social change.

How do we now translate the theology discussed hitherto into sociology? A crucial social fact comes to our aid here, the fact that 'Sathya Sai Baba's following comes almost exclusively from the urban middle classes' (Swallow, 1982: 152). If we place this alongside the other statistical fact that 'Sathya Sai Baba has a larger following than any of the contemporary Godmen of India' (Singh, 1975: x), then an interesting configuration emerges. India is undergoing rapid socio-economic change as the processes of industrialization, urbanization, modernization and Westernization gather pace. This has resulted in the expansion of the middle class, which finds itself caught in the tensions generated by the competing claims of tradition and modernity. The Sai Baba movement enables people to maintain contact with tradition as the country modernizes.

ISKCON or the Hare Krishna movement

ISKCON, the International Society for Krishna Consciousness, has achieved considerable visibility both in India and abroad.

The Hare Krishna movement was started in 1965 by Bhaktivedanta Swami in New York. 'He was seventy years old when he arrived in America. It was his first trip outside India, he had no money and no local means of support. But he did have a spiritually ripe Gauḍīya Vaiṣṇava tradition . . .' (Gelberg, 1983: 127). Although many are inclined to look upon the ISKCON, popularly known as the Hare Krishna movement, as a 'new' religious movement of the United States, it needs to be recognized that it is not new in the sense of having no roots in India, for its 'founder' belonged to an established line of disciplic succession which goes back to the fifteenth century. It *is* new in the sense that it represents the appearance of that tradition for the first time in the West. It is also 'new' from the Indian point of view in the sense that, after having been founded in the United States, it is now interacting with the original tradition in India. This process started in earnest when the founder visited India in 1970.

When the ISKCON is thus viewed as a 'new' religious movement in India, several aspects of this movement deserve attention. One is the light it sheds on the nature of the interaction between India and the West. It has been suggested, for instance, that, as the West is imbibing the spiritualism (one hesitates to use the word 'spirituality') of India, India is in turn absorbing the materialism of the West through the various neo-Hindu religious movements (Mehta, 1980). Thus the life-style of Maharishi Mahesh Yogi, the founder of Trans-cendental Meditation (Petersen, 1975: 189), and that of Guru Maharaj Ji of the Divine Light Mission, has aroused adverse comment in India and abroad. The ISKCON, however, draws upon the prosperity, but not necessarily the materialism, of the West. Thus it has built US-financed temples in Bombay and Vṛndāvana. Hindu leaders often criticized Christian missions for receiving money from beyond India, but with movements such as the ISKCON 'certain leaders who accuse other religions of receiving money from abroad for their support, themselves witness today the same phenomenon in Hinduism' (Ambroise, 1982: 373).

More important than the financial aspect, perhaps, is the social aspect. The presence of local people at the ISKCON temple and the use of the ISKCON greeting over the local one are indications of the movement's acceptance at the local level (Gelberg, 1983: 24, 25). But there are limits to such acceptance. The Hare Krishna movement raises some of its members to the status of a Brahmin, but the attitude of the Hindus towards them is ambivalent.

> On the one hand, many caste Hindus seem to feel that brahmanhood is determined by birth in a brahman family, and therefore one not born into a brahman family — let alone one born not even into a Hindu/Indian family — can never actually become a brahman. Such people resent the Western devotees being awarded brahminical status. On the other hand, many other Hindus in India respect the western Vaiṣṇavas as *bona fide* brahmans and find support for their position in Vaiṣṇava texts which indicate that brahmanhood is a matter not of birth but of personal quality. (Gelberg, 1983: 249)

Moreover, even those who accept Hare Krishnas as Brahmins may not marry their daughter to such a Brahmin. In other words, in India, Hinduism continues to remain strongly ethnic socially, though it has become universalistic spiritually.

Historically, the appearance of the Hare Krishna movement in the West is of great importance for Hinduism in many ways. First, it boosts Hindu self-esteem, both in India and abroad, and replaces a closet Hinduism with something practised openly (Gelberg, 1983: 112). It is also a very significant fact that for ISKCON there is a distinction to be drawn between being in the West (or of the West) and being Westernized. It is in this context that the next point becomes important: of all the various neo-Hindu movements in the West, ISKCON is the one which has compromised least in the matter of Hindu ritual and life-style. Finally, its existence underscores the growth of the missionary spirit in Hinduism. The interesting point here is that the parent tradition of ISKCON in India had always been known for its evangelical zeal but was relatively late in responding internationally to the missionary spirit with which Hinduism in general is becoming imbued. But although it has been late in coming, it has arrived in style. Moreover, its arrival is all the more significant because, whereas the other neo-Hindu movements usually centre on meditational techniques and thus do not directly compete with Christianity, the Hare Krishna movement is devotion-oriented, like Christianity. This makes its success more puzzling and the Christian response to it more ambiguous (Gelberg, 1983: 195).

In the course of the discussion of the Sai Baba movement, it was indicated that, in identifying himself with Śiva rather than Viṣṇu, Sathya Sai Baba may have tuned himself finely to the psychological needs of the members of a society undergoing rapid change. The point is suggestive — but its limits need to be recognized. Muslim India witnessed considerable social change, and political, economic and religious changes as well. These changes, however, were mediated religiously by the emergence of new movements centred primarily on Viṣṇu. The orientation of most of the major new Hindu religious movements under British rule was also Vaiṣṇava, with the Arya Samaj being the main exception. Even here, although its founder was born in a Saiva family (Jordens, 1979: 5), the movement he founded can hardly be regarded as Saiva. The fact that the Hare Krishna movement is a Vaiṣṇava movement (Gelberg, 1983: 173) which seems to meet the religious needs of some Americans living in a plural, protean and permissive society induces one to reflect further on the point. At this time, perhaps both Western and Indian societies seek stability, but Western societies seek what may be called normative stability while Indian society seeks structural stability.

Concluding remarks
In the first section of this chapter the fact of new religious movements being an old phenomenon was mentioned. In the second section the relationship between the new religious movements within Hinduism and older religious traditions and organizations of Hinduism was discussed; and an attempt was made to set up four paradigms for classifying the new religious movements. In the the third section a movement representative of each paradigm was presented and analysed. In this final section some comments of a general nature suggested by the foregoing survey will be attempted.

To begin with, there are certain spheres of life in which the influence of the new religious movements in Hinduism is not very marked. For instance, these movements have not affected the composition and function of the Hindu household, nor have they played a major role in evolving new Hindu modes of sociation, co-operation and conflict to any significant extent. (One possible explanation of this phenomenon could be what has been called 'compartmentalization' — (Singer, 1972: 323)). Also, on the basis of existing evidence, the new religious movements do not seem particularly connected with a specific community, such as that of migrants (Bharati, 1978: 255). It is true that at one time the RSS was gaining rapidly in popularity among the Hindu refugees as they poured into India after the division of the subcontinent into India and Pakistan — and through it they were drawn to the Jana Sangh, which could be considered as a political arm of the RSS. This state of affairs, however, did not last long (Baxter, 1969: 41, 68–9). In the sphere of the development of political and legal theory, the new movements in India have made little impact, compared with neo-Hindu movements overseas, which are involved in legal battles, one even involving the definition of religion (Baird, 1982). One could expect some movement in this area from the Jana Sangh, especially around the issue of a secular state v. Hindu state; but not much is forthcoming, though there is some sign of renewed activity (Madhok, 1982a). The effect of the new movements has hardly been felt on the modes of production, or on the relationship between capital and labour and, within labour, on the dealings of trade unions and employers' organizations, though the Jana Sangh has given the issue some consideration (Ashby, 1974: 111–12). It may be added, however, that, as a result of interaction with the West, the many other new movements themselves seem to respond to and transmit what is called 'demonstration effect' by economists, namely, the imitation of the West in matters of both consumption and production (Kindleberger, 1965: 140–2). But the effect on the economy as a whole is negligible, as also is their contribution to the production or productivity of the economy.

In other areas, however, the new religious movements have made a greater impact. Almost all of them have established contact beyond India in some way; and some have done so in a major way. Such internationalization has had a profound effect on the Hindu *Weltanschauungen*, in the sense that it has speeded up the process of the transformation of Hinduism from an ethnic into a universalistic religion. Similarly, most of the new movements have a major social service component which finds expression in the setting up of schools and colleges (Tripathi, 1978: xiii, 206–15). The Sai Baba movement is very strong in this respect.

In a few other areas, not only have the new religious movements made a mark, but one can be more definite about the impact. There is little doubt that these movements are patronized essentially by the urban middle classes, both lower and upper. Although their membership is not restricted to this class, the bulk of followers do belong to it. The following is also, in most cases, pan-Indian and cuts across regional lines. This phenomenon has historical roots (Desai, 1982: 214–17). The mass media take an avid interest in the activities of these movements (Tripathi, 1978: 231), and the movements in turn cannot be held guilty of neglecting publicity.

On another front, these movements in general have induced an upward revision of the status of women: first, by de-emphasizing ritual, and thereby considerations of ritual purity; second, by being open to both sexes; and third, by giving women positions of control and management within the movements. This said, the exact situation differs with each movement. The Hare Krishna tends to be more conservative in this respect, for instance, and the neo-Sannyasa movement very liberal; and in the sect of Brahmakumaris women are considered spiritually superior to men (Tripathi, 1978: 193).

What the new religious movements are in effect achieving, if one might for a moment throw scholarly caution to the wind and indulge in a sweeping generalization, is the modernization of Hinduism. Most have tended to emphasize conduct or experience over scriptural authority, and to de-emphasize caste and the ritual inferiority of the female. All of them have had the effect of making Hinduism a missionary religion in effect if not in intention, and most have shown increasing social concern. A contrast with the pre-independence new movements reveals an interesting point: almost all of these aspects have precedents in the pre-independence movements except that the evangelistic aspect of Hinduism was less marked then. Now it seems to have become the trademark. Whereas the pre-independence new religious movements were concerned with preventing conversions *from* Hinduism, many of the post-independence movements are concerned with promoting conversions *to* it, especially in the West (Kinsley, 1982: 23). But Hindu public opinion as a whole has still not come round to accepting this position wholeheartedly (Ashby, 1974: 67; Tripathi, 1978: 174–8).

If the literature in the area is closely examined, one discovers that at least five models of explanations have been presented to account for the phenomenon of the new religious movements discussed above. The first of these may be called the *evangelical model*. This is a trifle dated now, but on this view the upsurge in new religious movements could be seen as an indication of the impending demise of Hinduism, just as the collapse of the Roman religion and its replacement by Christianity was heralded by an increase of various cultic movements within the Roman Empire. The main representatives of this view were Christian missionaries who thought this to be the case with the 'new' religious movements of pre-independence India. Serious advocates of this view in the present context will be hard to find. Even those who foresee an end of traditional Hinduism may feel that new movements from within Hinduism might replace the old Hinduism.

A *psychological model* may also be proposed. According to this view, the gurus act, in effect, as psychiatrists and enable their followers to handle psychological pressures. At a more sophisticated level, it is argued that, in view of the repressed nature of relationships in the Hindu home, the unique relationship between a guru and a disciple outside the home, while perpetuating emotional dependency, helps preserve the mental equilibrium of Indians in an extended patriarchal family. But anyone familiar with the Hindu way of life knows that the joint family itself provides avenues of escape from such pressures. Such a view also seems to take an unduly pathological view of Hindu society.

A *Marxist model* can also be proposed. This would see in the proliferation of new Hindu movements signs of a heightened neurosis, especially in the bourgeoisie — a sign of the impending intensification of the class struggle. It is easy to hold such a view among the Marxist circles in India, but it seems to involve elements of wishful revolutionary thinking.

Much more relevant to the case may be the *Westernization model*, which would see in the new Hindu movements the last gasp of traditional Hinduism before it finally disintegrates and collapses in the face of the forces of Westernization. This model has greater plausibility than the others, but it should not be overlooked that Hinduism could as well be seen as adjusting to these new forces, and not always as a 'pleader, but also as a leader' in the process.

The most viable model seems to be the *sociological* one. This model contains such elements of the previous models as seem to correspond to reality. Thus, there is no doubt that some forms of Hinduism are perishing, that psychological factors are involved in the emergence of the new religious movements, that the various classes in both the social and economic senses may be seeking upward mobility through these movements, and that the leaven of Westernization is indeed at work in India. But the net and overall effect of these trends is to call for readjustments within the Hindu value system and Hindu society as a whole, and this is what the new religious movements seem to be all about.

Finally, some remarks seem to be in order on the Gandhian heritage in the context of the new religious movements in India. It is true that standard discussions on the subject do not include Mahatma Gandhi and his movement in the discussion of new religious movements, but observers of the Hindu scene will realize the danger of not noticing something because it is everywhere. This statement no doubt exaggerates Gandhi's influence, but it is clear that he has profoundly influenced the political and moral culture of contemporary India, from its rhetoric down to the techniques employed for seeking redress. It is in the vast backdrop of the Gandhian movement for liberation from social and economic as much as political shackles that the 'new' religious movements need to be viewed. Vinoba Bhave tried to maintain the vitality of the Gandhian movement in our own times, but its future is uncertain. It is a sobering reflection that the new religious movements of both pre- and post-independence are dwarfed by the Gandhian movement in terms of both the scope of the enterprise and the magnitude of the impact. However, as has been aptly said, India alone could perhaps have produced a Gandhi, but India alone cannot explain him. This is a characteristic that his movement shares with many of the new religious movements of India.

References

Ambroise, Yvon (1982) 'Hindu Religious Movements: A Sociological Perspective', *Journal of Dharma*, 7(4), 358–73.

Ashby, Philip H. (1974) *Modern Trends in Hinduism*. New York: Columbia University Press.

Baird, Robert D. (1982) 'Religious or Non-religious: TM in American Courts', *Journal of Dharma*, 7(4), 391–407.

Balse, Maya (1976) *Mystics and Men of Miracles in India*. New Delhi: Heritage Publishers.

Bancroft, Anne (1978) *Modern Mystics and Sages*. London: Granada.

Baxter, Craig (1966) 'The Jana Sangh, A Brief History', pp. 74–101 in Donald E. Smith (ed.), *South Asian Politics and Religion*. Princeton: Princeton University Press.

—— (1969) *The Jana Sangh: A Biography of an Indian Political Party*. Philadelphia: University of Pennsylvania Press.

Bharati, Swami Agehananda (1978) *Great Tradition and Little Traditions: Indological Investigations in Cultural Anthropology*. Varanasi: Chowkhamba Sanskrit Series Office.

Brent, Peter (1972) *Godmen of India*. London: Allen Lane.

Brunton, Richard (1951) *A Search in Secret India*. New York: Rider and Company (first published 1934).

Croy, Dick (ed.) (1975) *Sai Baba: The Holy Man and the Psychiatrist*. San Diego: Birth Day Publishing Company.

Curran, Jean A., Jr (1951) *Militant Hinduism in Indian Politics: A Study of the RSS*. New York: Institute of Pacific Relations.

Daner, Francine (1976) *The American Children of Krisna*. New York: Holt, Rinehart & Winston.

Desai, A. R. (1982) *Social Background of Indian Nationalism*. Bombay: Popular Prakashan.

Ellwood, Robert S., Jr (1973) *Religious and Spiritual Groups in Modern America*. Englewood Cliffs, NJ: Prentice Hall.

Embree, Ainslie T. (ed.) (1972) *The Hindu Tradition*. New York: Modern Library.

Farquhar, John Nicol (1967) *Modern Religious Movements in India*. Delhi: Munshiram Manoharlal (first published 1920).

Gelberg, Steven J. (1983) *Hare Krishna, Hare Krishna*. New York: Grove Press.

Glock, Charles Y. and Robert N. Bellah (eds) (1976) *The New Religious Consciousness*. Berkeley: University of California Press.

Gonda, J. (1970)   *Visnuism and Sivaism: A Comparison*. London: Athlone Press.
Hiriyanna, M. (1978)   *Essentials of Indian Philosophy*. London: Unwin Paperbacks (first published 1948).
Hopkins, Thomas J. (1971)   *The Hindu Religious Tradition*. Belmont, California: Dickenson.
Jordens, J. T. F. (1979)   *Dayananda Sarasvati: His Life and Ideas*. Delhi: Oxford University Press.
Judah, J. Stillson (1974)   *Hare Krishna and the Counterculture*. New York: John Wiley.
Keer, Dhananjay (1930)   *Savarkar and His Times*. Bombay: A. V. Keer.
Kindleberger, Charles P. (1965)   *Economic Development*. New York: McGraw-Hill.
Kinsley, David R. (1982)   *Hinduism: A Cultural Perspective*. Englewood Cliffs, NJ: Prentice-Hall.
Koestler, Arthur (1960)   *The Lotus and the Robot*. London: Hutchinson.
Lamb, Beatrice Pitney (1968)   *India: A World in Transition*. New York: Frederick A. Praeger.
Madhok, Balraj (1982a)   *Rationale of Hindu State*. Delhi: Indian Book Gallery.
—— (1982b)   *The Stormy Decade*. Delhi: Indian Book Library.
Mahadevan, T. M. P. (1967)   *Ramana Maharshi and His Philosophy of Existence*. Tiruvannamalai: Sri Ramanasramam.
—— (1971)   *Outlines of Hinduism*. Bombay: Chetana.
Majumdar, R. C. (ed.) (1953)   *The Age of Imperial Unity*. Bombay: Bharatiya Vidya Bhavan.
——, H. C. Raychaudhuri and Kalikinkar Datta (1951)   *An Advanced History of India*. London: Macmillan.
Mehta, Gita (1980)   *Karma Cola*. London: Jonathan Cape.
Needleman, Jacob (1977)   *The New Religions*. New York: E. P. Dutton.
——, A. K. Bierman and James A. Gould (eds) (1977)   *Religion for a New Generation*. New York: Macmillan.
Nehru, Jawaharlal (1960)   *The Discovery of India*, ed. Robert I. Crane. New York: Doubleday.
O'Flaherty, Wendy Doniger (1973)   *Asceticism and Eroticism in the Mythology of Siva*. London: Oxford University Press.
Osborne, Arthur (ed.) (1962)   *The Teachings of Bhagavan Sri Ramana Maharshi in His Own Words*. London: Rider.
—— (1971)   *Ramana Maharshi and the Path of Self-Knowledge*. New York: Samuel Weiser.
—— (ed.) (1972)   *The Collected Works of Ramana Maharshi*. London: Rider.
Panikkar, K. M. (1963)   *The Foundations of New India*. London: George Allen & Unwin.
Patterson, Maureen L. P. (1981)   *South Asian Civilizations: A Bibliographic Synthesis*. Chicago: University of Chicago Press.
Petersen, William J. (1975)   *Those Curious New Cults*. New Canaan, Conn.: Keats.
Pratt, S. (1966)   *Hindu Culture and Personality: A Psycho-Analytic Study*. Bombay: Manaktalas.
Sarma, D. S. (1944)   *Studies in the Renaissance of Hinduism in the Nineteenth and Twentieth Centuries*. Benares: Benares Hindu University.
Sen, K. M. (1961)   *Hinduism*. Harmondsworth: Penguin.
Sharma, Arvind (1974)   'The Hare Krishna Movement: A Study', *Visvabharati Quarterly* 40(2), 154–78.

Singer, Milton (1972)   *When a Great Tradition Modernizes: An Anthropological Approach to Indian Civilization*. New York: Praeger.

Singh, Khuswant (ed.) (1975)   *Gurus, Godmen and Good People*. New Delhi: Orient Longman.

Smith, Donald Eugene (1963)   *India as a Secular State*. Princeton: Princeton University Press.

Srinivas, M. N. (1966)   *Social Change in Modern India*. Berkeley and Los Angeles: University of California Press.

Swallow, D. A. (1982)   'Ashes and Powers: Myth, Rite and Miracle in an Indian God-Man's Cult', *Modern Asian Studies*, 16(1), 123–58.

Tinker, Hugh (1962)   *India and Pakistan*. London: Pall Mall.

Tripathi, B. D. (1978)   *Sadhus of India: The Sociological View*. Bombay: Popular Prakashan.

Weiner, Myron (1957)   *Party Politics in India*. Princeton: Princeton University Press.

White, C. S. J. (1972)   'The Sai Baba Movement: Approaches to the Study of Indian Saints', *Journal of Asian Studies*, 31(4), 863–78.

Index

Notes on contributors

SAÏD AMIR ARJOMAND is Associate Professor of Sociology at the State University of New York (SUNY) at Stony Brook. He is author of *The Shadow of God and the Hidden Imam* (1984) and the editor of *From Nationalism to Revolutionary Islam* (1984). He edits the State University of New York series on Near Eastern Studies, and his book on the Islamic Revolution in Iran was published by Oxford University Press in 1986.

JAMES A. BECKFORD is Senior Lecturer in Sociology at the University of Durham. He is President of the International Sociological Association's Research Committee for the Sociology of Religion and Editor of the ISA's journal *Current Sociology*. His publications include *The Trumpet of Prophecy* (1975), *Religious Organization* (1975), *Cult Controversies* (1985) and numerous scholarly articles.

SYN-DUK CHOI is Professor of Sociology at Ewha Women's University, Seoul. She earned her MA from the University of Chicago and her PhD from Ewha Women's University. Her publications include *A Comparative Study of New Religions in Korea* (1965), *Anthropology* (1972), *Marriage and the Family* (1978), and *Social Anthropological Study of the Rural Villages of Korea* and *Ageing and Society* (ed., trans.) (1983). She is an ex-President of the Korean Sociological Association.

LAËNNEC HURBON is a researcher with the Centre national de la recherche scientifique, France. Most of his work relates to the study of religion in the Caribbean region. His publications include *Dieu dans le vaudou haitien* (1972), *Cultures et pouvoirs dans la Caraïbe: langue créole, vaudou, sectes religieuses en Guadeloupe et en Haïti* (1975) and *Culture et dictature en Haiti: l'imaginaire sous contrôle* (1979).

MARTINE LEVASSEUR is a sociologist who holds the Diploma of Social and Cultural Anthropology from the Sorbonne. Her publications include *Sociologie d'une secte* and (with Eliseo Veron) *L'Espace, le corps, le sens.*

FRIDAY MBON is Lecturer in Religious Studies at the University of Calabar, Nigeria. He was born in Nigeria and educated there to the undergraduate level. He studied English Literature and Religious

Studies as a graduate student in Canada and the USA. He has taught both subjects in universities and is currently teaching the Sociology of Religion. His present research interests are in the new religious movements in Nigeria, especially the Brotherhood of the Cross and Star, although he has also written about African traditional religions and Islam.

GANANATH OBEYESEKERE is Professor of Anthropology at Princeton University. He has previously taught at the University of California, San Diego, the University of Washington, Seattle, and the University of Sri Lanka, Pendeniya. He has done extensive field-work in Sri Lanka and is the author of *Land Tenure in Village Ceylon* (1967), *Medusa's Hair: An Essay on Personal Symbols and Religious Experience* (1981), *The Cult of the Goddess Pattini* (1984) and numerous scholarly articles.

ARVIND SHARMA received his BA in 1958 from Allahabad, his MA in 1971 from Syracuse, his MTS in 1974 from Harvard Divinity School and his PhD in 1978 from Harvard University. Formerly of the Indian Administrative Service (1962–68), he now lectures in the Department of Religious Studies at the University of Sydney, Australia. He has also taught in the USA (Temple University, Philadelphia; Northeastern University, Boston) and Canada (McGill University, Montreal) in visiting positions.

SUSUMU SHIMAZONO received his MA from the Department of Religious Studies, University of Tokyo. Following research at the University of Tsukuba, he became a Lecturer at Tokyo University of Foreign Studies. He has written extensively on Japanese religiosity and particularly on the new religions. His publications include *A Handbook for the Study and Research of the New Religions* and numerous articles. A new study of Tenrikyō and Konkokyō is forth-coming.

ROBERT WUTHNOW teaches sociology at Princeton University. His publications include *The Consciousness Reformation* (1976), *The Religious Dimension* (1979), *The New Christian Right* (1983) and *Cultural Analysis* (1984). He is currently working on a comparative study of the social production of ideology since the sixteenth century.